Storming the Wheatfield

John Caldwell's Union Division in the Gettysburg Campaign

James M. Smith II

Battlefield maps by Phil Laino

GETTYSBURG
PUBLISHING

Storming the Wheatfield
John Caldwell's Union Division in the Gettysburg Campaign
James M. Smith II

Library of Congress Control Number: 2017957006
ISBN 9780999304938

Printed and bound in the United States of America

Front Cover—"Pride of Erin" by *Dale Gallon*   www.gallon.com
              "Wheat Image from Wheatfield" by *Chris Bagley*

Back Cover—Colonel Edward Cross & General Samuel Zook
              Library of Congress
           Colonel Patrick Kelly
              Gettysburg National Military Park Library
           Colonel John Brooke
              Gettysburg National Military Park Library

Maps—Phil Laino

Please visit our website www.Gettysburgpublishing.com

*To my beloved Uncle Eddie
and Aunt Lorraine.
Always in our memories.*

Table of Contents

Key to Maps

Hancock	**Union Personnel**
Pettigrew	**Confederate Personnel** (Note different font for Union and Confederate troops)
Hood	**Names in a gray font indicates that person has been killed or wounded**
14CT	**Union regiments**
38VA	**Confederate regiments**
	Union Corps designation
	Union infantry **Confederate infantry**
	Union cavalry **Confederate cavalry**
	Previous position of a unit
	Skirmish line or disorganized advance or retreat
	Routed troops
	Marshy area
	Orchard
	Woodlot
	Worm fence
	Rail fence
	Stone wall
	Cannons (Six-gun battery, four-gun battery, two-gun section, and single gun)

Reprinted with permission from *Gettysburg Campaign Atlas* by Philip Laino.

Foreword

GETTYSBURG PENNSYLVANIA, JULY 1863. Perhaps no other battle fought on the North American continent has earned a place in American Civil War history as this sleepy town of 2,400 citizens. Over 160,000 men, North and South, congregated here using a vast system of roads and would spend three days in bloody combat that resulted in a turning point in the war and the destiny of a country.

The battlefield is imposing, encompassing an entire town and the fields, hills, and ridges surrounding it. All in all, about 26 square miles. Many visitors today will find exploring the field a daunting task. Many come here expecting to find a much smaller area to explore, only to realize how complicated visiting and studying this battle can be.

Perhaps no other area on the field can be more intimidating than the Wheatfield. Approximately 20 acres in size, it would play host to over 20,000 soldiers blue and grey in the late afternoon and evening of July 2. Owned by George Rose whose farm was nearby, his Wheatfield was almost ready for harvest. By the end of July 2, his crops would be ruined, trampled and bloody. Thousands of men would lie dead and wounded trapped in a no man's land. Many of these men would lie until the close of the battle before receiving care or burial. Rose's Run, a small stream like Plum Run, would run red with the blood of soldiers who were killed and wounded along its banks.

The "Bloody Wheatfield" exchanged hands nearly six times in the span of about two hours. Confederates of Lieutenant General James Longstreet's Corps and his brigadiers, Generals George Anderson, Paul Semmes, Joseph Kershaw and William Wofford would face their Union counterparts. One such command was that of Brigadier General John C. Caldwell. Caldwell commanded the First Division of the Second Army Corps in the Army of the Potomac. His brigadiers, Edward Cross, Samuel Zook, Patrick Kelly and John Brooke would play an instrumental role in this melee. It would cost Cross and Zook their lives. The blood that would be shed by Caldwell's men came from all walks of life. Many of those lives would end abruptly, many would linger crying out in pain for relief, even a drink of water from the now murky blood red streams. Men attempting to carry their wounded comrades to the safety of the rear lines would be themselves, wounded or killed. The wounded waiting hours, if not days, for medical care in woefully undermanned makeshift hospitals, added to the misery. It is at times like these that the words of General Robert E. Lee resonate the ugly truth of armed conflict: "It is well that war is so terrible, otherwise we would grow too fond of it." Let us not forget that when things are at their worst, even in war, soldiers of both armies can put aside hostilities to aid their fellow man. Ordinary citizens render aid when and where able, and aid will come from afar as well as volunteers to treat the wounded.

The town is now transformed, forever ingrained into our history. The stories of the men who fought here should also be ingrained into our memories as well. Abraham Lincoln would attend the dedication of the Soldiers' National Cemetery on November 19, 1863, to give a few appropriate remarks. He simply asked of those in attendance and of us, do not forget that which was done by the men who fought here. The men of John Caldwell's Division, the men of James Longstreet's Corps and the countless others who gave their last full measure of devotion.

Today the Wheatfield is a peaceful place. Marked with tablets and monuments of stone and bronze, one is reminded of the words of Joshua Chamberlain: "In great deeds something abides, on great fields something stays. Forms change and pass, but spirits linger to consecrate ground for the vision place of souls." Perhaps the ground can still speak to us today, all one must do is listen and read the stories from a time not so long ago.

Chris Bagley
Licensed Battlefield Guide
Gettysburg National Military Park

Acknowledgments

THIS BOOK HONORS THE BRAVE MEN of Brigadier General John C. Caldwell's Union infantry division in the Gettysburg Campaign in the summer of 1863. They were a valiant group of soldiers, and it has been an honor writing and studying about their lives and actions.

I am forever grateful for several people who have assisted me along the way in this work:

Chris Dean, my humble co-worker. I don't believe that I would ever have accomplished such a feat without your motivation and assurance. Every time I missed a step or felt the breath of failure breathing down my neck, you were there to help control my doubts and calm my nerves. Our friendship is one of a kind, and I'll never forget all that you have done for me and my writing career.

Kevin Drake, I am forever in debt to you for all that you have done. When I had any question about which direction I should go, you were always there to step in and guide my steps. It has been one of the greatest privileges, of my young career, to learn from you as you continually teach me all that I know. I'm thankful for this friendship that we have established and hope that it continues on in the future.

Jim Miller, without your continued guidance through this task, I don't know where this book would have ended up. He helped me in a way that not a lot of people would have given me advice and pointers all the way. I'm eternally grateful to be able to call him my friend.

To the National Park Service and John Heiser, without your aid this book would have never become what it is. I'm forever grateful to you.

In addition, I'm in great debt to my father and mother. These two people were always there for me from the start and provided more much needed motivation. I'm extremely thankful to be able to call these people family. In that category, I need to also thank several battlefield guides for their help. Ray Hinchey and Paul Bailey, to name a few, have helped when I was out of answers and information on several sources.

I'm grateful to have been able to study at the Gettysburg National Military Park's Library. There, I met John Heiser. His knowledge and endless effort in helping me gather information have been nothing short of remarkable. Any time I had a question, you were just a short e-mail away with an answer in a very timely response.

To Scott Mingus Sr., for his insight and help with the edits that made this book what it has become. I could never quite thank you enough and am fortunate to be able to call you a true friend!

I would also like to acknowledge the Adams County Historical Society. The tireless efforts that have been put into the research that was conducted there have been nothing short of awesome. I'm thankful to have the opportunity and to meet some wonderful people.

I would like to thank Rich Kurtz, Cindy McWreath, and Valerie Testa. First, Rich. I took you to Gettysburg several years ago and you fell in love with it as much as I did. Since then, you have been a key component to these writings that I have been conducting in an effort to learn to write better and teach better. Cindy and Valerie. I'm forever in gratitude that you first brought me to Gettysburg. I was 12 at the time, but you knew that once I was there, I'd fall in love with the history of the place and the beauty of the landscape. Since then, I have conducted countless hours of studying on this particular battle, furthering my educations, until I was able to obtain the knowledge to write this book. I'll never forget all that you two have done, and I will never forget you, Cindy.

I would also like to acknowledge Mr. Ken Rich, who helped steer me in the direction that I should take. Before I began this book, I was determined to focus only on the Irish Brigade only. You spoke to me and convinced me to change my mind and cover the division as a whole. I have not regretted that decision. I'm blessed to be able to call you a "friend."

Throughout the rigors of writing this book, I have come into contact with some of the most knowledgeable people someone can get to know. People like Charles Joyce, whose personal collection of various images of soldiers that fought with the division is second to none. I'm entirely grateful to you, as you brought an entire new life to this story.

To Michael Snyder and his personal collection: Whenever I was at my breaking point in finding the correct image, you always came through. It is with a grateful heart that I'm able to acknowledge you and your personality within this book.

Various organizations also helped contribute stories to this manuscript as well as images. Places like The Horse Soldier, who allowed me to bring a huge sense of uniqueness to this work by allowing me to publish a picture of the boots General Zook was wearing at the time of his mortal wound. Other organizations such as the Carlisle Barracks, I'd like to acknowledge for allowing me to use some of their fine pictures to add to the quality of this work. Also, Washington and Jefferson College. Their help with Captain David Acheson and the image of him was a totally awesome find.

To the Pottstown Historical Society. The dedicated work that the staff helped in bringing me images of John Brooke was unbelievable.

I would also like to recognize the Library of Congress. Without their images, this book would nearly be an impossible feat. To the personal collections of Ira

Dennis, Jack Mord, Frank Walker, and the Thanatos Archives. You all helped me bring this book to life. Thank you all so much!

I would, finally, like to acknowledge Philip Laino. His maps are one of a kind, and his book "The Gettysburg Campaign Atlas" served as more of a help to me while doing this study than I ever imagined. Thank you so much for your generosity and your guidance through your work.

There have been plenty of others along the way that have contributed in some form or fashion into the making of this book in some small way. Several guides and park rangers that conducted talks or wrote about such events. If I have forgotten to mention anyone, I hope that you can forgive me.

James M. Smith II

–

Introduction

THE DIVISION OF JOHN CURTIS CALDWELL was roughly handled throughout the entire war to the point of Gettysburg. Battles such as the Seven Days, Antietam, Fredericksburg, and Chancellorsville had diminished the ranks to a shell of their former size by the time of the Gettysburg Campaign.

The design of this narrative is to give the reader a broader understanding of the horrors that took place within this particular division at Gettysburg. It is imperative that we, as students of the battle and campaign, must familiarize ourselves with the adversities that soldiers, such as the men in Caldwell's Division, endured to make a nation whole again. The division contained some of the finest soldiers this nation has ever produced. Commanders like Patrick Kelly, Edward E. Cross, Samuel Zook, and John R. Brooke would bring about a more defined explanation

John Caldwell and staff (*Library of Congress LC-usz62-116218*)

and characterization as to what it meant to lead your men selflessly into battle against a far superior foe. Even the Irish Brigade's familiar motto of "Faugh A Ballagh"—the Gaelic battle cry for "Clear the way"—gave a representation of what this division stood for as a whole. It is now forever embedded on the top of the 28th Massachusetts monument at the Gettysburg National Military Park.

During the Battle of Gettysburg, the division witnessed acts such as Sickles's Third Corps' movement forward, and a religious ceremony before being ordered into the fight, and it took part in some of the heaviest fighting that America ever had seen on her soil on those three hot July days. When the smoke cleared, scores of men from both sides lay on the ground and became part of the casualty totals that reached nearly 51,000 by the end of the conflict.

I encourage the reader, if they find it convenient, to take this book along when you visit the battlegrounds that these men fought over. Remember the sacrifices that they made that consecrated this as ground hallowed and visit the various locations this book strives to pinpoint where such heroic deeds that occurred.

The division is held in high regard to amateur and armchair historians alike. To me, it gives a sense of pride as the 140th Pennsylvania's Company K was recruited primarily in my hometown. They fought on those fields of valor and many paid for it with their lives. On their own homeland. Against an unjust cause that so many were opposed. A captain, David Acheson, in Company C of the same regiment, would be felled by an enemy bullet on this field and gain a notoriety that will be preserved forever.

Caldwell's Division at the Battle of Gettysburg made a desperate stand against a tough and determined Confederate force. It is the author's opinion that in order to better understand what the men fully endured during the battle, what they were thinking, and how they reacted, we must first understand their lives before this tragic event that was bestowed upon them.

CHAPTER 1

Caldwell's Commanders and Brigade Histories

*"The heroes of the north
Who swelled that grand array.
And rushed like mountain eagle forth
From happy homes away."*[1]

CALDWELL'S BRIGADE

John C. Caldwell (*Library of Congress Photograph Division Civil War Photographs, LC-D.G.-cpb-04997*)

JOHN CURTIS CALDWELL was born April 17, 1833, in Lowell, Vermont. An educator by profession, for five years before the Civil War he was the principal of Washington Academy in the state of Maine. In 1857, he married Martha H. Foster and later fathered three children: Harriet, Charles, and Calais. Soon after Confederate artillery bombarded Fort Sumter in April 1861, the 28-year-old Caldwell joined the Federal Army in response to President Abraham Lincoln's initial call for 75,000 troops.[2]

Caldwell lacked previous military experience. However, he was well liked among his troops and he displayed leadership qualities. That led to his appointment as colonel of the 11th Maine Infantry in November 1861. He received a promotion on April 28, 1862, to brigadier general during the Peninsula Campaign and took command of the First Brigade, First Division, Second Army Corps. At the time, he was one of the youngest generals in the Union Army.

The soldiers of Caldwell's Brigade (then consisting of the 5th New Hampshire; 7th, 61st, and 64th New York; and 81st Pennsylvania) fought at the Battle of Seven

1

Pines/Fair Oaks in late May and early June 1862. They aided Brig. Gen. Philip Kearny's embattled Third Corps division in repulsing repeated enemy attacks. Caldwell's divisional commander, Brig. Gen. Israel B. Richardson, noted in his official report, "My division, which had been reduced to a skeleton… cannot too much commend the admirable manner in which my three brigadier generals— French, Meagher, and Caldwell—have done their duty with their brigades."[3]

At the Battle of Antietam on September 17, Caldwell's Brigade arrived on the field about 9:45 in the morning. Elements of the Confederate Army of Northern Virginia occupied a sunken farm lane well in front of Caldwell's position, out of their sight. Caldwell formed his men in line of battle on the left flank of the famed Irish Brigade under its charismatic leader, Brig. Gen. Thomas F. Meagher. Finding no hostile troops in his immediate front, Caldwell pivoted his brigade by the right flank and "commenced to wheel the brigade cautiously."[4]

General Richardson soon sent orders for Caldwell to relieve the Irish Brigade, which had, in the meantime, attacked the Confederate position in the sunken road (soon to gain fame as "Bloody Lane"). Caldwell later wrote that his soldiers moved "to the front in the most perfect order, under a severe fire of musketry." His line briefly wavered under intense enemy fire from Confederate Col. John B. Gordon's 6th Alabama ensconced in the steep-banked lane. However, many of the Rebels soon climbed out of the road and withdrew because of a mistaken order issued by Gordon's second in command, Lt. Col. James N. Lightfoot. Stepping inside the abandoned "natural rifle pit," Caldwell's men stumbled over dead or wounded Confederates who lay in droves in the sunken road. Scrambling out of the trench, the Union boys pushed into farmer Henry Piper's cornfield. "Here the enemy opened upon us a terrific fire from a fresh line of infantry, and also poured upon us a fire of grape and canister," Caldwell reported. "My regiments bore this fire with steadiness."

Soon, the Rebels counterattacked. Colonel Francis Barlow, realizing an opportunity, shifted the 61st and 64th New York to the left and repulsed the enemy, which soon attempted a second assault. During the fighting, Barlow received a severe wound in the groin that put him out of commission for several months. Eventually, the rest of Caldwell's Brigade moved forward as the Rebels finally pulled back. General Richardson suffered a mortal wound when an enemy artillery shell exploded near him while he directed the fire of a nearby cannon. As a result, John Caldwell found himself in temporary command of the division. He ascertained the status of each of the brigades and awaited further orders while he prepared for a possible enemy attack. Soon, the Army of the Potomac's commanding officer, Maj. Gen. George B. McClellan, dispatched highly regarded Brig. Gen. Winfield S. Hancock to take over the division. Caldwell resumed command of his brigade.

After the battle, Caldwell reported, "I cannot contemplate the action of my brigade in this battle without emotions of pride and satisfaction. It drove the enemy in its first attack, foiled two successive efforts by a superior force to turn its flank… captured six stands of colors, 300 prisoners, and 8 officers." He lost 43 men killed and 280 wounded in the conflict.

However, after the battle, some observers claimed that Caldwell cowardly hid in the rear of the line, a charge the general denied. Nevertheless, the actions of his men that day under his leadership were of true metal. In the face of heavy Confederate musketry and artillery fire, they maintained good order and discipline as they moved forward. They successfully drove the enemy and gained the ground they had been ordered to take. Caldwell's men left plenty of dead, dying, or wounded Rebels in their wake. Private David L. Thompson of the 9th New York mentioned, "As I looked down on the poor, pinched faces, worn with marching… all enmity died out. There was no 'secession' in those rigid forms, nor in those fixed eyes staring blankly at the sky. Clearly it was not 'their war.'"[5]

Fredericksburg

In mid-December at Fredericksburg, new army commander Maj. Gen. Ambrose Burnside (who had replaced McClellan at President Lincoln's orders) with his army of 122,000 men attacked Robert E. Lee's 79,000 well-entrenched Confederates.[6] Caldwell's Brigade, along with the rest of Hancock's Division, was ordered forward to support attacks on Rebels behind a stone wall on Marye's Heights. The soldiers wound their way through the streets amongst a stiff enemy artillery fire "by which several of my men were killed," Caldwell recalled. Once in position, his soldiers formed as the third brigade in the tiered divisional line, lining up behind their comrades of the Irish Brigade.

General Hancock rode up to Caldwell and ordered his men forward. They soon came under a constant fire from Confederate batteries posted in their front until they reached a line of men in the forward brigade "lying down and occasionally firing." The men of the left of Caldwell's brigade halted in the face of heavy Rebel musketry in their front and began returning fire. Caldwell, unsheathed sword in hand, calmly walked along the rear of his line urging his brigade to stay steady. Caldwell noted in his official report, "The brigade was now exposed to a terrific and well-directed fire of musketry and artillery, by which its ranks were rapidly thinned."[7] Scores of Federal infantrymen fell on the cold Virginia ground. Soon, groups of men began to break for the rear. Finally, the 145th Pennsylvania, which had just joined Caldwell's Brigade, broke and fell back after its colonel, Hiram L. Brown, fell severely wounded. Most of the men in the ranks saw the popular Brown fall, which greatly demoralized them.[8]

Meanwhile, the rest of the brigade continued to advance toward the Confederate battle line, finally halting near a road junction. "The fire here was terrific," Caldwell reported, deeming the spot to be "the hottest I have ever seen. The men fell by the hundreds." Colonel Nelson A. Miles of the 61st New York sought out Caldwell during the fray and requested permission to charge up one of the roads, from where enemy fire was causing havoc within his ranks. Caldwell later noted, "Had there been any support, I should not have hesitated to give him the order to do so; but, with the small force at my disposal, it seemed to me a wanton loss of brave men," so he rejected Miles' proposal.[9]

Instead, Caldwell instructed Miles to form his men to the right of the road to support his main body. However, about the time of this movement, a Confederate

Minié ball struck Miles in the throat, incapacitating him after he had advanced within 40 yards of the Rebel-held stone wall on Marye's Heights. For a while, few of the men knew who was now in charge of the regiment. Caldwell, during this pivotal time, also soon fell, receiving a painful wound in his left side. He refused several entreaties that he be taken to the rear. However, when a second lead missile struck him, this time in the shoulder, the wounded brigadier agreed to be escorted to a nearby temporary field hospital.[10]

His brigade, meanwhile, fought on until they were relieved as darkness fell. The hillside was covered with nearly half of the brigade. Caldwell lamented, "All my regiments… fought with desperate courage under great disadvantages. The enemy fought behind rifle-pits and stone walls, while our troops were entirely uncovered, and exposed to a murderous fire of artillery and musketry combined. They advanced bravely to within a few yards of the enemy's line, when their ranks were so thinned and their numbers so reduced that it was impossible to go farther… Of the noble dead I may truly say that braver or better officers or firmer patriots never fought on a battle-field."[11] While he gave much of the credit to his men for their success and their bravery, Caldwell's reputation suffered again because of the early retreat of the 145th Pennsylvania and his perceived inability to hold them in position.

Chancellorsville

John Caldwell, after recovering from his injuries, next saw combat at Chancellorsville in Spotsylvania County, Virginia. Part of the brigade was briefly engaged during the fighting on May 1, 1863, while the rest of the regiments were elsewhere deployed. General Hancock rode up to Caldwell and ordered his command to the rear. The men traversed a narrow road but soon arrived at the designated spot. Once in position, "the enemy followed up very rapidly," Caldwell remembered, and soon he heard the roar of battle near the position of Brig. Gen. George Sykes' brigade. Quickly, Caldwell faced his men about and established a line of battle in an open field supporting Sykes.[12]

The two regiments of his right flank, the 148th Pennsylvania (which had just joined the brigade) and 61st New York, were forced to lie down to allow the Federal artillery to fire over top of them, resulting in one man killed. Eventually, the Confederate line was repulsed. Caldwell's Brigade then formed on the left flank of Col. John R. Brooke's Brigade. The men "worked all the evening cutting an abatis," Caldwell reported. "About dark the enemy shelled our line, but without doing any harm."

About 3 a.m. the next morning, May 2, Caldwell received orders to have his brigade fall back from its advanced position to the area of the Chancellorsville Manor. There, again, some of his regiments were detached and sent elsewhere. Caldwell and the remainder of the brigade were ordered to dig entrenchments to withstand a possible Rebel attack. Soon, enemy artillery shells fell among Caldwell's men as the assault commenced. Colonel Edward E. Cross took command of three regiments, while Colonel Miles, who had recovered from his Fredericksburg wound, ordered the 61st New York to deploy as pickets for the division. It was with this force that Miles "skirmished all day long with the enemy… repulsed… a determined attack of the enemy," as Caldwell reported. "I do not doubt that this repulse of the enemy, which kept them from our main lines, was due principally to the skill and gallantry of Colonel Miles."

On the morning of May 3, his troops hunkered low in their entrenchments while Confederate batteries again shelled their position. One of Caldwell's soldiers claimed, "The men [were] behaving with the greatest coolness." About 10 a.m., Caldwell was instructed to report to the army's commanding general, Maj. Gen. Joseph Hooker. He ordered Caldwell to take "between 500 and 600 men, and march by the right flank down the road toward the United States Ford." The men executed the maneuver splendidly. Eventually, they reached an open field facing an area of thick woods. There, according to Lt. Col. K. O. Broady, they were ordered to "halt and throw up breastworks." However, in about twenty minutes, Hooker ordered Caldwell's Brigade "into the open field and through the woods from a point designated."[13]

The brigade moved forward under a tremendous enemy fire of grape and canister until they "encountered the rebels, in rifle-pits" on their right flank. This exercise, according to Caldwell, "killed and wounded many of the officers and men."[14] After a few minutes of intense fighting, the Confederates broke and retired to the rear. Caldwell, sensing the enemy was demoralized, ordered a charge in an attempt to sweep them from the field. However, after being pushed nearly 300 yards, the Rebels rallied, formed into line, and fired into the oncoming Federals. Dozens of blue-clad men fell, yet Caldwell's men recovered, opened fire, and eventually drove the enemy back again.

Caldwell ordered his men forward as the Rebels halted near the edge of the woods as reinforcements arrived. Caldwell witnessed "a battery coming into position and… a line of at least 1,500 of the enemy moving at double-quick around our left flank." He quickly sent back a request for reinforcements to Maj. Gen. George G. Meade, commanding the Fifth Corps, which was in reserve. Meade sent word that he had no orders to advance into the woods and "that if the force of the enemy was too strong for us we must fall back."

Caldwell realized that he could not advance any farther nor hold the position against such superior numbers. He decided to retire, "facing about in line every 100 yards" to ensure that the enemy did not pursue his men. Finally, they regained their former line and re-formed. By then, Caldwell had lost 278 men killed, missing, and wounded.[15] After twice having his reputation tarnished for alleged on-field misconduct, he redeemed himself by protecting the retreat from the Chancellor House. He finally received the praise he so desperately wanted.

A frustrated Maj. Gen. Darius N. Couch resigned on May 22 from command of the Second Corps because of his abject lack of confidence in General Hooker. This opened the door for Winfield Hancock to step into the corps commanders' slot, while John Caldwell assumed permanent command of the division, with the veteran brigades of Patrick Kelly, Samuel Zook, and John Brooke. Colonel Edward E. Cross of the 5th New Hampshire took over Caldwell's former brigade.[16]

CROSS'S BRIGADE

Edward E. Cross (*Library of Congress LC-usz62-57879*)

EDWARD EPHRAIM CROSS was born April 22, 1832, in Lancaster, New Hampshire. His father, Ephraim Cross, served as a United States senator and his mother, Abigail Everett, was the daughter of Richard Everett who had served as an associate justice of the Court of Common Pleas.[17]

At an early age, Cross began to write for a local newspaper, the *Coos Democrat*. He filled that position for two years until he traveled to Canada to assist his father in the trade of steamboat-building. At the age of twenty, he traveled to Cincinnati, Ohio, and became employed as a reporter for the *Atlas* office, and eventually became the editor of the Cincinnati *Daily Times*.[18]

Later, Cross traveled to Washington, D. C., where he wrote and edited articles for a local paper and took up his pen as a correspondent for the New York *Herald*. However, military service was in his blood. Cross's grandfather was a veteran of the Revolutionary War. While a teen, Cross watched as his father recruited young men to fight during the Mexican War. While in Washington, Cross was appointed as the adjutant of an Ohio regiment being formed for duty in the Utah Territory. However, the regiment was never fully mustered into service.[19]

In 1858, Cross traveled to Arizona to establish a mining company in the newly founded territory. During the 1,700-mile trek, a tired and irritable Cross quarreled with "a Lieut. Mowry." The latter challenged Cross to a duel with "rifles at thirty paces." Mowry's first shot grazed Cross's cheek. Cross then fired his round, which passed through the lieutenant's coat. Cross's rifle misfired on the second shot, giving Mowry a golden opportunity to finish off his adversary. However, according to an observer, "The affair now assumed a most serious character, but Col. Cross, nothing daunted, threw down his weapon and coolly folding his arms stood up to receive the fire of his opponent." Mowry, astonished and impressed at his foe's noble conduct, dropped his rifle and exclaimed, "I can't fire at such a man as that."[20]

When the Confederates bombarded Fort Sumter on April 12, 1861, Cross commanded a garrison at El Fuerte, Mexico. Shortly thereafter, he resigned to travel home. He received a commission as colonel of the 5ᵗʰ New Hampshire on September 27.²¹

On June 1, 1862, at the Battle of Seven Pines/Fair Oaks during the Peninsula Campaign, Cross's regiment was positioned in line of battle ready to assault an enemy position. Suddenly, a lone Rebel officer rode up asking for "General Anderson." When he realized that he had inadvertently ridden into the Federal lines, the Confederate wheeled his horse to escape. However, Colonel Cross quickly snatched him by his collar and brought him "down on the run." With an arrogant, "You're just the chap I was looking for," Cross sent his chagrined prisoner to the rear.²²

Cross's brigade commander, Brig. Gen. Oliver Otis Howard, soon was ordered to move forward. He later stated, "As usual, the 5ᵗʰ is always first." He sent Cross and the 5ᵗʰ New Hampshire to clear a section of woods the Rebels were using as a sharpshooter's nest. They encountered strong enemy resistance. This being most of the boys' first battle, the line staggered. Undeterred, Cross halted the wavering line. He soon gave to order to fix bayonets and began making preparations to charge whenever Howard so ordered. However, a Minié ball struck Cross in the left leg and he fell heavily upon the ground. According to one of his men, the colonel "raged like a lion through battle, and they say that when his long body fell he went down like a pine tree."

Cross attempted to get to his feet but found his effort to no avail. He crawled slowly toward a large tree in the rear of his line and propped his head against it. Soon, another round grazed his head, covering his face with blood. He shouted, "Charge 'em like Hell, boys; show 'em that you are Yankees, damned sorry I can't go with you."²³ After his men drove off the Rebels, some of them placed the fallen colonel on a stretcher and took him to an aid station. He was eventually taken home to Lancaster, New Hampshire, to recover from his grievous wounds.²⁴

Cross returned in time to lead the 5ᵗʰ New Hampshire at Antietam. After his men crossed the creek and prepared to enter the battle, he stood on the stream bank and addressed his regiment: "Soldiers, the rebel army is in front; the Potomac is in their rear. We must whip the enemy this day or we shall all be disgraced and ruined. I expect every officer and soldier to do this duty like a man… If I fall, leave me on the field until the fight is over. Stand firm and fire low."

Before the men deployed into battle line, division commander General Richardson rode up and demanded, "Where's General Caldwell?" Cross answered "in the rear," and soon someone else from the regiment yelled out, "He's behind the hay stacks." Agitated at his brigade commander, Richardson yelled out, "General Caldwell, come up here, sir & take command of your Brigade." Turning to Cross, he pointed to the Sunken Road and ordered, "Go on Colonel & do all you can— relieve that regiment." How promptly Caldwell obeyed is a matter of conjecture. Lieutenant Thomas Livermore claimed that Caldwell still had not taken command until well after the fighting had ceased. The men moved forward under their own direction, without his command influence.²⁵

Immediately after Richardson left, the New Hampshire boys and the rest of the brigade began to advance. A shell exploded near Cross and his subordinates. A small fragment struck him over his right eye, while another hit "on the left cheek, and his hat was knocked off, but with his wounds bleeding and a red silk hand-kerchief around his head he pushed forward." Cross later penned in his journal that, despite being under heavy fire, "My Reg't marched bravely up to the line of battle under a heavy fire without faltering in the least."[26]

As Cross urged his men forward, enemy artillery roared across the battlefield. "One discharge of canister killed and wounded eight men in one company & tore the state colors of my Reg't in two pieces," Cross recounted. A piece of shrapnel struck his right arm. Not long after Cross gave the command to halt and open fire, Lt. George A. Gay came up, caught him by the arm, and exclaimed, "Colonel, the enemy are outflanking us." From his position, Cross could not see the Rebel movement and stated that that notion was "impossible." The desperate lieutenant pleaded his case until Cross finally decided to go to the left side of the regiment to see for himself. To his surprise, Cross found that "sure enough the enemy were coming—a whole Brigade." He counted at least five battle flags.

Cross quickly changed his line's front to meet the new threat. His men unleashed a volley that staggered the Rebels. At the same time, he sent a courier back to obtain reinforcements. Again, General Caldwell could not be located and the responsibility fell upon the commanders of the 81st Pennsylvania and 7th New York to come to Cross's aid. Together, the three regiments broke the Rebels' momentum and forced them back.

Later that day, the Confederates again assaulted Cross's position. He deployed skirmishers to meet them but much of this effort was in vain. Cross noted that most of his men's muskets were so dirty that "in some cases the rammers could scarcely be forced home." No relief arrived, so his beleaguered men held on for the next three hours until dark. "Shells were flying & bursting all around us," Cross wrote, "while every now & then rifle balls came whistling over our heads or striking close at hand." Night spelled relief for the crippled regiment. The next morning, they were ordered out of their position.

Colonel Cross proudly noted after the battle, "My brave boys, knowing that all depended upon promptly checking the rebels, raised the wild Indian yell and poured an awful volley into their ranks… I had been in seven battles before, but they were nothing in comparison with Antietam. We shot down the rebel color-bearers as fast as they could get up, killed their officers, broke their ranks and piled them in heaps among the tall corn… As for myself I was hit five times but not seriously injured."

Cross walked over to the stricken Lieutenant Gay. He had been struck in the head by a shell fragment toward the end of the conflict and was "instantly paralyzed—though his body continued the vital principle for some hours." Cross recollected, "I sat for a long time & held the hand of my young friend—hoping that he might yet evince some consciousness. But in vain. The night waned, & he still lay in the stupor of death… All his young hopes & the bright dreams of his youth had been scattered by the ruthless hand of the Angel of Death. Long shall his memory be cherished."

At the Battle of Fredericksburg in December, Cross was sick but he entered the battle with his men. Before he did so, however, he had the inclination that he would be severely wounded, if not killed, in the upcoming fight. Therefore, he made his will before the fight commenced. On December 12, he received orders to move the 5th New Hampshire to a designated spot near Maj. Gen. Edwin V. Sumner's headquarters. There, they witnessed the beginning of an intense cannonade. This fire quieted several annoying Southern sharpshooters and allowed the Federal pioneers to lay a pontoon bridge across the Rappahannock River. Cross admitted that the army "expended tons of ammunition to no purpose, while we lost several brave officers and not less than 40 or 50 men."

The following day "dawned bright and warm," according to Cross. His regiment crossed the pontoon early in the morning and formed a line on the opposite bank. There, the boys "fished out tobacco which had been thrown into the river in boxes by the rebels." The act lightened the mood of most of the men in the ranks, as they began to puff their new treat. They camped that night in a street, while Cross and two other officers slept in a nearby house.

On the morning of the December 13, Cross, though still unwell, remained with his regiment. Shortly after noon, General Hancock rode to the Irish Brigade commander, General Meagher, and ordered the "Sons of Erin" to take Marye's Heights at all hazards. Meagher responded by addressing "his troops one of those frothy, meaningless speeches" and ordered them forward. Cross later opined in his journal, "There is not in the United States, certainly not in the Army of the Potomac, another such a consummate humbug, charlatan, imposter, pretending to be a soldier as Thos. Francis Meagher! Nor do I believe him to be a brave man, since in every field he has been drunk and not with his Brigade."

Cross knew what would soon be expected of him and his regiment, which then had 249 men in the ranks. Cross told them that "it was to be a bloody strife-to stand firm & fire low—to close on their colors—be steady." He went to the front of the 5th and prepared his men to march forward, placing them in the best position possible to follow the Irish Brigade up the heights.

Cross and his anxious men witnessed the Irishmen suffer heavily as they clambered to the top and lay down under a hail of enemy lead. Upon finally receiving the order to advance, Cross noted that "the Reg't rose up as one man and started forward." However, not far into the advance, another shell exploded about eye level near him. A piece tore into his chest and lodged near his heart, which a smaller chunk knocked two of his teeth out, filling his mouth with clay and blood. A fragment grazed his forehead. Another opened a cut above his eye and still another skipped across the back of a hand. Cross remembered, "I was knocked clean off my feet, & lay insensible until roused by a violent blow on the left leg-made by a piece of shell."

After much effort, he finally got to his hands and knees to spit the sediment out of his mouth. He quickly looked about and realized that his men "were in the van!" He attempted to get to his feet but, in vain, could not stand. He then tried to crawl "but the balls came so thick & tore up the ground so spitefully that I could not go it," he recalled. After another ball struck his scabbard and knocked him over, he decided to lie still.

At one point, the rear brigade, coming in to support Caldwell's men, stopped short of its target. A long-range battle ensued which left the stricken Cross laying in the middle of the field between the two lines. "Thus I lay," he remembered, "while the awful battle raged." Well ahead of the wounded officer, his men fought on until nearly destroyed and the colors were shot down six times. Cross lay on the ground for nearly three hours until a few men from his regiment, on their way to the rear, gathered their fallen commander up and took him to see a surgeon. He would start his road to recovery on December 17 in Washington, until he was able to travel home on the 31st.

At Chancellorsville, on May 3, 1863, General Hancock ordered Cross to hold the line of reserves. As the tide of battle shifted, the 5th New Hampshire became engrossed in the heavy fighting. The enemy, pressing to within 200 yards of Cross's position (near the Bullock house), slugged it out with the 5th New Hampshire for nearly an hour. Each man expended about 120 rounds apiece, and all were spent in due time. The colonel recollected, "for about 40 minutes my command was under the heaviest fire it ever experienced. Every instant someone in each Regt was hit. The air seemed full of bursting shell. From our rear from the left from the front came a storm of missiles."[27]

Unlike his previous battles, Cross came out of Chancellorsville unscathed. Upon Hancock's elevation to corps commander, Caldwell was elevated to division command. Cross was assigned to lead Caldwell's former brigade but was not promoted to brigadier general.[28]

KELLY'S IRISH BRIGADE

Patrick Kelly (*New York State Military Museum*)

PATRICK KELLY commanded Caldwell's Second Brigade during the Gettysburg Campaign. Kelly was born in 1822 near Tuam in the Irish midlands. Early in his life, young Patrick and his sister lost their father to an untimely death so their mother had to raise them. The family survived the Great Famine of 1846-48 and later sailed to America in search of a new beginning. As he grew older, Kelly made New York City his home and opened a successful mercantile business.[29] A contemporary described him as a "grave man, a man of few words, gentle, kind, unassuming, feeling his responsibilities in fullest measure, and with a disciplined bravery that would send his men, himself at the head, to storm the very gates of hell, if ordered, and stay there till ordered back."[30]

Kelly answered President Lincoln's call to arms in April 1861 and enlisted as a private in Company E of the 69th New York. He was soon elected as its captain and then took part in the Battle of Bull Run where his fine performance attracted the attention of several higher-ranking officers. He was promoted to lieutenant colonel of the 88th New York on September 12, 1861.[31]

Kelly's next action came at Fair Oaks during the Peninsula Campaign. There, he, along with two companies of infantrymen, were placed in great danger when General Richardson ordered them forward alone, having halted the other eight companies of the 88th New York. Kelly led the detachment through a woodlot toward a field teeming with Confederates. The subsequent fighting was intense before Capt. James P. McMahon ordered the other eight companies forward to aid Kelly.[32]

On September 17, Kelly's men crossed Antietam Creek and "advanced in column until within sight almost of the enemy." He then formed his men into line of battle while his pioneers tore down a fence directly in his front so as to not impede his impending assault. Once the fencing was gone, the 88th New York "got into action at once," moving toward the Sunken Road.[33] Shortly after they began their advance, General Meagher "rode up along the line, encouraging the men… until his horse was killed and he himself got a severe fall," as Kelly later reported. Following the battle, rumors spread about the cause. A chaplain, the Rev. John Stuckenberg, was among those who later claimed "at one of the battles they say (at Antietam I believe) he was so drunk that he fell from his horse."

Whatever the case may have been, one thing remains true: Patrick Kelly led his men onward against a well-fortified enemy and he led them well. Soon, a staff officer rode up and ordered the 88th and 63rd New York forward to "charge and take the enemy's colors if possible." Quickly, Kelly ordered the troops into position to comply with its new order. However, his men did not advance more than thirty paces when he ordered his regiment to halt after seeing that no other regiment had supported his own. He quickly tried to find Col. John Burke of the 63rd New York and inquire why they too had not heeded the order. Captain Joseph O'Neill responded that the colonel could not be located and "he would advance… if he had anyone to command the regiment." After the battle, Burke would be court-martialed for cowardice.

The men remained in line of battle until their supports, Cross's 5th New Hampshire, came up to their relief. Upon withdrawing to the rear, Kelly approached General Richardson. "Bravo," the division commander greeted him, "Eighty-eighth; I shall never forget you." Praise be praise, but time was of the essence. Richardson placed Colonel Kelly in command of the 108th New York and ordered him to support a nearby battery.[34]

Of the 302 riflemen that Kelly brought with him to the field that day, 104 lay dead. He reported after the battle, "With regard to the conduct of the officers of the Eighty-eighth on that occasion, I must say that they acted to my entire satisfaction—so much so that I cannot say one is braver than another. I have the same to say of the rank and file."[35]

Patrick Kelly and his Irishmen next saw action at Fredericksburg. They advanced upon the pontoon bridge on December 11 and halted at General Sumner's headquarters to await further orders. General Meagher came up late in the day, about 4 p.m., with orders for the Irish Brigade to "advance about 1 mile" before they camped for the night in some woods.[36]

On Friday morning, December 12, the brigade continued its advance toward the pontoon bridge, which the men crossed later that day. Just on the other side, they remained all day and received orders to make camp for the night. Second Corps commander Maj. Gen. Darius N. Couch ordered that "no fires should be lighted, which order was willingly and uncomplainingly complied with by my men." There, the brigade slept, in the cool, crisp, night air. The men gazed up at the stars pondering what fate had in store for them the next day.

They were awakened the next morning and ordered to file to the right to their campsite of the previous night, nearly half a mile away. There, they deployed into a line of battle "in connection with the other regiments of the brigade." Eventually, General Meagher ordered his Irishmen forward to begin their assault up Marye's Heights. They came under intense fire almost immediately. Lieutenant Colonel Kelly remembered that they did this "under a terrific enfilading artillery fire from the enemy." Men were being knocked to the ground, tossed in the air, and covered with dust and blood from the exploding shells. "We then advanced in line of battle under a most galling and destructive infantry fire," Kelly reported, "crossed two fences, and proceeded as far as the third fence, where my men maintained their position until their ammunition was exhausted."

At this third fence, Kelly realized that the charge was ill-fated and that his regiment was being dropped in detail. He made his way over to Col. Richard Byrnes of the 28th Massachusetts. The two officers came to the agreement they should "go over the field and collect the remnants of our regiment."[37] After rounding up the survivors, Kelly, Byrnes, and the infantrymen retired to the rear. Once there, Kelly and his regiment received orders to cover the retreat of the Federal forces off the battlefield. General Hancock ordered his men in two lines of battle and determined to make his stand near the Chancellor Manor. There, the Irishmen kept the enemy at bay with a heavy dose of fire and ultimately kept the parts of the Army of the Potomac from being completely routed.[38]

The next day, Hancock ordered his men to cross the Rappahannock River again and resume their former position. After the battle, Kelly summed up the results, "The gallantry and bravery of the men is too plainly visible in their now shattered and broken ranks, having lost on that day about 111 killed and wounded."[39]

In May, just before the fighting at Chancellorsville, General Meagher resigned from the Army of the Potomac, paving the way for Patrick Kelly to become the next commander of the Irish Brigade.

ZOOK'S BRIGADE

Samuel Zook (*Library of Congress
LC-DIG-cwpb-07289*)

SAMUEL KOSCIUSZKO ZOOK led the Third Brigade, Second Division, Second Corps during the Gettysburg Campaign. Zook was born on March 27, 1821, at Tredyffrin, in Chester County, Pennsylvania. His parents, David and Eleanor (Stephens) Zook, were of the Mennonite faith, which contributed to Zook's cleanliness and well-mannered demeanor. At an early age, Zook's parents took him to Valley Forge to the home of his grandparents. There, he grew and learned to respect the American heritage and love for the country. Early in his adulthood, he traveled to New York City where he maintained a strong interest in the military. Zook was elected as the lieutenant colonel of the 6th New York State Militia.[40]

Zook worked for the Magnetic Telegraph Company before the Civil War. After the telegraph line first opened, an early morning dawn revealed that a wire had broken not far down the line. With no repairman on duty, Zook was elected to find the break and repair it. James Reid, his supervisor, recalled, "I therefore directed him to go to Norristown by cars and walk back till the break was found. He was then to send me a message by planting a piece of wire in the ground and tapping on it with the line wire. That done, he was to find a puddle of water, in which he was to stand, and, putting the line wire to his tongue, receive my acknowledgment." All went according to plan as Zook located the wire and followed Reid's instructions. However, after Zook planted his tongue to the wire there was, what Reid described as, "an ominous silence, and soon after… the hugest of Pennsylvania profanity." Zook came back to the office "covered in mud, and madness in his eye." Reid went on to explain, "What most grieved Zook was, that he had performed his electrical gymnastics in the presence of a large crowd, who had rather enjoyed his very original entertainment."[41]

During the Battle of Bull Run, Zook served as military governor of nearby Centreville and saw no combat action. When his three-month term of enlistment expired on July 31, he returned to New York. He soon began to recruit the 57th New York, which led to him being commissioned as its colonel on October 19, 1861.[42]

Zook had his first taste of combat on June 27, 1862, during the Seven Days battles of the Peninsula Campaign. There, after falling in line of battle twice and remaining in that position nearly an hour, "a general fusillade opened all along the line," Lt. Josiah M. Favill of his staff noted, "and the troops were kept under arms till seven o'clock [a.m.]." A lull then commenced over the battlefield and the men were permitted to have their breakfast. The lull lasted until about 2 p.m. when the Rebels renewed their attack. "This time no skirmish line commenced the fight, but immense lines of infantry," Favill continued, "under cover of scores of guns, marched directly to the attack, followed by several other lines in succession."[43]

Zook and his regiment, then part of the brigade of Brig. Gen. William H. French, nervously watched as part of Maj. Gen. Fitz John Porter's Fifth Corps broke in the distance before an enemy assault. They "wondered whether we were to stand by and see them thrashed." Zook crept beyond his picket line to ascertain the situation. He witnessed many slaves "parading, beating drums, and making a great noise," and realized that many of the Rebels in his immediate front had departed to reinforce the attack on Porter.[44] He immediately rode his horse to General Sumner and requested his blessing for him to lead a counterattack against the weakened enemy position. Sumner refused to give permission without consulting Maj. Gen. George B. McClellan, in command of the Federal army. Sumner quickly dispatched an aide to seek out McClellan and request orders. However, the orders were never given, and Zook became "amazed at the want of activity on Sumner's part, feeling certain we could have got into Richmond or into the rear of Lee's army."[45]

Eventually, the Federals began to break under the weight of the Confederate attack. Zook's men fell back "slowly and reluctantly, fighting every inch of the ground," his aide, Lieutenant Favill, later wrote. "The hills soon became entirely enveloped in thick smoke, the flashes only visible from the big guns, so we could only judge of the result by the sound of the musketry; this sufficiently indicated the gradual advance of the rebels and increased our anxiety." Finally, the Irish Brigade arrived to relieve them.

Colonel Zook missed Antietam because of a severe bout with rheumatism. The brigade, temporarily under Col. John R. Brooke, fell in at daylight on the morning of September 16, 1862. Soon, an artillery duel began and the Empire Staters lay on their "backs and speculated as to where certain shells would burst as they went rushing over our heads," a soldier noted.[46] Some of the men crawled up the slope to look over the field and "watched the flight of the twenty pounders shell and marked where they struck or exploded."

The next day, the brigade took part in the assault on the Sunken Road. Throughout the day, General McClellan ordered his men forward "one corps at a time." The process, though it always kept men in reserve, never fully allowed his forces to entirely overwhelm an enemy position. Richardson's Division and the other attackers faced intense fire. "The fight was murderous," Favill remembered, "the musketry terrific and the number of guns in action almost incredible." About 9 a.m., orders came for the brigade, along with Caldwell's and Meagher's brigades, to fall in behind French's Division.[47]

Zook's men, resting in the damp grass as they awaited their turn to attack, watched in horror as the other brigades made their piecemeal attacks. Some of the soldiers noted the Irish Brigade's beloved General Meagher fall from his horse and saw him carried to the rear. However, his soldiers "remained… in line of battle, loading and firing as fast as they could, their men falling in the ranks every second, and we could see them gradually melting away," Favill observed. Just then, a captain from General Richardson's staff rode up and ordered the brigade forward to relieve Caldwell's and Meagher's battered commands. An officer recalled, "The order to fall in was given and with nervous force, teeth firmly set and without a word spoken, we marched steadily forward."

The men came under a terrific fire as they passed through the beleaguered ranks that were previously in their front. Caldwell deviated from his position to the left and gained ground in that direction, while the rest of Richardson's Division pressed on. The 57th and 66th New York forced the Confederates in their front out of the Sunken Road and up onto the other side of the field. Richardson's men pursued them toward the Piper house with such aggression that those Rebels who did not surrender were bayoneted.[48]

The Federals only held the position for a few moments when incoming Confederate artillery fire became too much for the exhausted men. They were compelled to fall back, taking position near the Cornfield. There, the men hunkered low to the ground as the artillery shells screamed across the open fields. Colonel Brooke rode up to Lieutenant Favill and ordered him to take over and move the men to plug a gaping hole in the line next to Caldwell's Brigade. Favill recalled, "I walked across the field right on the edge of the cornfield, my ears fairly burning with the singing of the deadly Minnie, I could see nothing, but the tips of the cornstalks were constantly toppling over, cut by the rebel infantry fire."

Immediately, Favill sought out the 61st New York, led by future Eleventh Corps division commander Francis Barlow, and ordered the regiment to advance on the Confederates. Barlow, who reported to Caldwell's Brigade, surprised Favill by refusing the order because he "did not recognize Colonel Brooke's authority." The argument became heated before Brooke personally intervened and ordered Barlow forward. Barlow reluctantly rose and moved forward with his men, taking a severe wound along the way. Favill admitted that he always "thought [it] served him right." The brigade held its ground for several minutes until ordered to the rear where it re-established the line. The order again came to move forward. This time they "drove these fellows back and so far as we were concerned, the battle was over," a soldier recalled.[49]

Colonel Zook returned to his brigade in time for the fighting at Fredericksburg. On December 10, he ordered the 57th and 66th New York to assist in constructing pontoon bridges then being strung across the Rappahannock River. Lieutenant Favill penned in his diary, "There was a heavy fog over the river, which seemed at first to be greatly in our favor, but as soon as the men began to lay the bridge and ply their axes and hammers, the enemy opened a sharp musketry fire, aiming in the direction of the sound." Eventually, the workers had to fall back until the fog cleared enough to carry out the operation. About this time, Rebel artillery began to shell the Federal-occupied town. One of Zook's soldiers recalled, "It was a magnificent sight to see the bombardment of the sleepy old town, and we expected to see it quickly reduced to ashes, but the effect was ridiculously out of proportion to the noise and weight of metal thrown into the place."

By the time their relief arrived, two hours later, the 57th New York had lost two men killed and twenty-three wounded, while the 66th also suffered minor losses. On December 12, the brigade crossed the Rappahannock near the Lacy House Bridge and took position near the southern sector of Fredericksburg. Zook deployed the 53rd Pennsylvania as skirmishers near the rear of the town and drove several enemy skirmishers from the outskirts, losing one man in the process.[50]

The next day, about noon, French's Division filed toward the rear of Fredericksburg, with orders assault Rebels on Marye's Heights. Hancock's Division was to be in support. Zook formed his brigade, with his flank next to a railroad, and awaited further orders.[51] At 2 p.m., French advanced on the enemy position. A soldier noted that "pandemonium at once broke loose." Soon, General Hancock sent orders for Zook to move his men forward. "The whizzing, bursting shells made one's hair stand on end;" Lieutenant Favill recalled, "our guns added to the confusion as they fired over our heads." The point of attack could not have been worse. They were advancing on the strongest part of the enemy line, until they were within 300 yards of the solid line of Rebels behind the stone wall. A loud cheer went up and the troops pressed forward, but so great were their losses, the charge failed. The soldiers stumbled back, dropped to their bellies, and watched as "line after line of fresh troops, like ocean waves, followed each other in rapid succession."[52]

Zook's men remained huddled on the ground. The colonel "was very wretched, quite sick and thoroughly disgusted" at what his men had endured. He and many of his soldiers worried that the enemy would charge down the hill and capture them. Fortunately, there would be no counterattack. Hancock was able to extricate his division under the cover of darkness. Zook reported, "7 commissioned officers killed and 31 wounded; 52 enlisted men killed, 395 wounded, and 42 missing. Total, 527." Despite having failed to break the enemy's line at Fredericksburg, Zook received a general's star in recognition for his abilities.

Five months later, during the Battle of Chancellorsville, much of Zook's Brigade was on picket duty on the flank of the Army of the Potomac. Most of the hardest fighting occurred well south of their position. Some of Zook's men did participate in the battle, however. Private Robert L. Stewart of the 140th Pennsylvania remembered, "As the Confederates advanced from right to left all along the line with their blood-curdling yells, some of the troops who had nothing but the bayonet to resist them, fell back." He added, "A beautiful young woman had fled from the Chancellor House, now the very center of the concentrated fire of the enemy. There was a dash of crimson on one side of her pallid face which indicated a slight hurt. Her strength and courage seemed to be equal to the occasion, however, and she was soon beyond the range of our vision as well as the destructive fire of her friends—the enemy."[53]

Francis A. Walker, the acting adjutant general, reported, "The field was lost… The Chancellorsville plateau was now a hell of fire—shot screaming over it from every direction but the northeast; the house itself in flames; yet Hancock's division, alone where seven divisions had been, stood in two lines of battle."

Eventually, intense Rebel fire compelled the entire division to fall back. During the retreat, General Zook ordered the 140th Pennsylvania to advance to cover the withdrawal of the 5th Maine Battery, which had unlimbered off to the brigade's front. The men tossed their knapsacks over the edge of their makeshift rifle pits and advanced "at such a pace that General Zook, who superintended our part of the advance in person, could hardly keep his place ahead of the line." Once in position, Zook ordered his men to lie flat. They remained in that position for nearly a half-hour "amid a tempest of iron hail which might well have appalled the stoutest veteran," until the battery had successfully fallen back.

During this stand, General Hancock rode past and noticed that the Chancellor Manor was ablaze. He quickly ordered William Shallenberger of the 140th Pennsylvania to "make a detail to assist in the rescue." His quick action led to Company F saving many of the people trapped inside the fiery building. Zook's men eventually were ordered back from their advanced position. The soldiers suffered heavily, and the brigade was a mere shadow of its former self. After Chancellorsville, Samuel Zook went on leave to Washington. He would not return until after the army began its advance north toward Pennsylvania.[54]

BROOKE'S BRIGADE

John Rutter Brooke (*G.N.M.P.*)

JOHN RUTTER BROOKE was born in Pottstown, Pennsylvania, on July 21, 1838. He was the son of William Brooke, a captain in the War of 1812, and Martha Rutter. At an early age, John received his education at Bolmar's Seminary in West Chester, where he did particularly well in his classes. When war broke out, he was among the first to join the army when President Lincoln called for 75,000 volunteers in April 1861.[55]

Initially, Brooke was a captain in the 4th Pennsylvania until his three-month term expired on July 27, 1861. Upon his return home, Brooke immediately began recruiting a three-year regiment. On August 17, 1861, he was appointed as colonel of the 53rd Pennsylvania. Brooke and his men were mustered into the Union army on November 7.

Colonel Brooke and his regiment participated in their first engagement at the Battle of Seven Pines/Fair Oaks during the 1862 Peninsula Campaign. On May 31, the brigade received orders to move forward across the Chickahominy River and get into position before dark.[56] The next morning, the men engaged the enemy and withstood their fire for more than four hours. Brooke had a horse shot out from under him. Though shaken, the young officer never wavered despite the stress of being under fire for the first time. General French noted, "After a few moments' pause the heads of several columns of the enemy threw themselves upon the intervals of the regiment... For some time, the most desperate efforts were made to break our line. The left of the Fifty-third Pennsylvania, consisting of seven companies, led on by the gallant Colonel Brooke, repulsed them again and again."[57]

John Brooke, temporarily in command of the third brigade in Zook's absence, took part in the Battle of Antietam. He and his men splashed across Antietam Creek and "marched rapidly to the support of French, who was being pressed, and formed line of battle in a small valley in the rear of Meagher's Irish Brigade." Brooke's soldiers came under immediate fire once they began to show themselves. Shot and shell rained down upon the men, yet they pressed onward toward the Sunken Road. Upon reaching their assigned position, they found that Caldwell's Brigade had already relieved the Irish Brigade. Brooke, not wanting to take needless casualties, ordered his regiment to lie down on the field. The Confederates left their line and charged the brigade. The right flank of the brigade came under heavy enemy fire, leaving Col. Paul Frank of the 2nd Delaware no other option but to change his front to face this new threat.[58]

Colonel Brooke, meanwhile, ordered the 57th and 66th New York, along with the 53rd Pennsylvania, to wheel to the right to "check any attempt the enemy might make to reach our rear." Eventually, the fire slackened and the Confederates took possession of farmer Roulette's trampled cornfield. Brooke sent his former regiment, the 53rd Pennsylvania, forward in an attempt to dislodge the dug-in foe, which ended with success. The 57th and 66th New York then advanced to relieve Caldwell's Brigade. Brooke remembered his line "passing... with steadiness and regularity, the two gallant regiments... drove the enemy from the field in great confusion, capturing two colors and covering the ground with dead and wounded."[59]

Shortly afterward, the field fell silent. General Hancock rode up and took personal command of the scene and nothing more occurred other than a few sharp cracks of a skirmisher's rifle. The Army of the Potomac celebrated stopping the Confederates in what later was considered a tactical draw.

John Brooke's next battle was at Fredericksburg. He and his comrades crossed the river and arrived in town on the morning of December 12. Brooke again assumed command of the 53rd Pennsylvania after Colonel Zook returned to duty from ill health. In the morning, the 53rd was sent out to drive the enemy skirmishers that were firing from within the town. Having done so, they were relieved about two o'clock in the afternoon and rejoined the rest of the brigade.[60]

On the morning of the 13th, the brigade formed in line of battle on Main Street, which ran next to a set of railroad tracks. At 12:30 p.m., Brooke received orders, via Colonel Zook, to "march up the railroad, and upon reaching the outskirts of town to bear to the right and form rear of General French's last line." The 53rd Pennsylvania, in position less than 60 yards from the Confederate rifle pits, obeyed the order. Brooke reported, "the whole advance (was) being made under a deadly shower of canister and musket balls."

As the men were under continual heavy enemy fire during their advance, Brooke found it nearly impossible to advance farther, so he threw the right wing of his line "into and behind the houses." He then began to withdraw his left flank under a galling fire. His men fired repeatedly until all their rounds were exhausted. It was during this stand by Brooke's right flank that he realized the Rebels were beginning to envelop his line. Instead of panicking, the colonel sought a way out. He soon found it when he witnessed Col. Nelson Miles' 61st New York of Caldwell's Brigade moving forward in support. Brooke immediately directed the regiment to fill the gap that the withdrawal had created. This was filled "not a moment too soon," Brooke reported, "as the enemy were evidently trying to turn our right."[61]

Brooke sent several requests for additional relief to Colonel Zook, but none came. Brooke later said, "I did not retire, but, when all the ammunition of living, dead, and wounded, was exhausted, fixed bayonets, and stood fast, determined to hold the point to the last. After a time, I went to Colonel [Joshua] Owen, commanding a brigade in General Howard's division, and asked for men, to return the fire of the enemy, which was harassing us greatly. The men were sent, and did good service." The support finally allowed Brooke to retire from the field. He later reported his losses at 155 men.[62]

Colonel Brooke was formally promoted to command the Fourth Brigade of Hancock's Division. On May 1, 1863, he received orders to move forward his regiments (the 27th Connecticut, 2nd Delaware, 64th New York, and 53rd and 145th Pennsylvania) to strengthen Caldwell's First Brigade. After a few hours, Brooke received orders to withdraw from the line and redeploy near where he started.[63]

The next day, orders came for Brooke to retire farther to the rear. Caldwell's Brigade was then about 150 yards to the left of the Chancellor Manor and was beginning to take heavy Confederate fire. Brooke subsequently received fresh orders to move his brigade up and support Caldwell. Once in position, he "threw up a rifle pit, and with skirmishers well to the front, awaited the attack. The enemy was engaged feeling our lines all day, but could make no impression."[64]

The anticipated assault did not begin in Brooke's front but instead commenced farther to the right near the Eleventh Corps' position. The respite allowed Brooke to organize and refit his men for another fight. On the morning of May 3, the Eleventh Corps again came under heavy enemy fire as the attack resumed. All signs indicated that Lee would again work his way down the Federal line and Brooke's men would soon be engaged.

About this time, General Hooker sent orders for the 145th and 53rd Pennsylvania, along with the 2nd Delaware, to break off from the brigade to reinforce the picket line. As time passed, the 27th Connecticut was also ordered forward to support the same line. Colonel Brooke, in a short time span, lost immediate tactical command of four of the five regiments in his brigade.

About 9 a.m., Brooke reported, "Our right was evidently beaten back. I received the order of the general commanding to move directly to my rear and meet the enemy." After he arrived in position, he found that Caldwell's Brigade had nearly all vacated the area. He was then "ordered to occupy his old place in the rifle-pits." He remained in that position until compelled to move up near the Chancellor Manor and take a strong position there. "Here," the colonel remembered, "we experienced a most destructive fire of artillery, many officers being killed and wounded." Yet, none of his men wavered from their position until compelled to do so when the manor caught fire and the ranks broke to help tame the blaze.

The Battle of Chancellorsville was over for John Brooke and his new brigade. Ordered to the rear about 11 a.m., he subsequently deployed his men near the position they had held on the night of April 30. Brooke took time to reflect on what he and his men had accomplished. After the battle, he reported, "Of my staff I can say that officers could not behave better; cool and efficient, they deserve the honorable notice of the general commanding."[65]

CHAPTER 2

The Long March to Gettysburg

"On, on they came, nor faltered in their tread,
Each man a hero—giants at their head.
We stood amazed at courage so sublime,
No braver record on the page of time."[1]

Robert E. Lee (*Library of Congress LC-DIG-cwpbh-03116*)

In early June 1863, **CONFEDERATE GENERAL ROBERT E. LEE** began to push his Army of Northern Virginia toward the North for the second time in nine months. His first attempt had led to the Battle of Antietam at Sharpsburg, Maryland, in 1862, which ended in his withdrawal and Abraham Lincoln's issuance of the Emancipation Proclamation, which had taken effect on January 1, 1863.[2] Lee, now short on supplies and fearing that the longer the war went, the more powerful his opponent would become, knew he had to force Lincoln's hand. He wrote to President Jefferson Davis describing the conditions within his army:

Conceding to our enemies the superiority claimed by them in numbers, resources, and all the means and appliances for carrying on the war… We should not, therefore, conceal from ourselves that our resources in men are constantly diminishing, and the disproportion in this respect between us and our enemies, if they continue united in their efforts to subjugate us, is steadily augmenting. The decrease of the aggregate of this army, as disclosed by the returns, affords an illustration of this fact. Its effective strength varies from time to time, but the falling off in its aggregate shows that its ranks are growing weaker and that its losses are not supplied by recruits.[3]

PURSUING THE REBELS NORTHWARD THROUGH VIRGINIA

Following his recent victory at Chancellorsville, Lee became determined to take the war to the North. He needed to resupply his army, which entering central Maryland and southern Pennsylvania would allow. His main goal, however, was to destroy the Federal Army of the Potomac, hopefully decisively this time, on Northern soil and try to force the Lincoln administration to the negotiating table.

For the men in Hooker's army, still struggling to find success in Northern Virginia, morale was nearly at an all-time low. They had suffered through most of the war up to this point under incompetent commanders. On May 22, a change occurred, as mentioned in the previous chapter, when Maj. Gen. Darius Couch, the Second Corps commander, requested a new assignment. His resignation allowed for the very capable Maj. Gen. Winfield Hancock to fill the void.[4] Father William Corby, a Catholic chaplain in the Irish Brigade, described Hancock as being a "polished gentleman and had a keen sense of propriety. Addicted merely through force of habit to the use of profane language, when excited, he would invariably stop short when he discovered the presence of a clergyman."[5]

The War Department promoted John C. Caldwell to the command of Hancock's First Division, while Col. Edward Cross took over Caldwell's former brigade. Cross's First Brigade consisted of the 5th New Hampshire, 61st New York, and the 81st and 148th Pennsylvania. Colonel Patrick Kelly led the Second Brigade (Irish Brigade) with the 28th Massachusetts; 63rd, 69th, and 88th New York; and 116th Pennsylvania. Brigadier General Samuel K. Zook retained command of the Third Brigade, made up of the 140th Pennsylvania and the 52nd, 57th, and 66th New York. Colonel John R. Brooke led Caldwell's Fourth Brigade, with the 27th Connecticut, 2nd Delaware, 64th New York, and the 53rd and 145th Pennsylvania.[6]

On June 3, Lee began moving the first of his troops away from Fredericksburg toward the Shenandoah Valley in preparation for the planned subsequent movement toward Pennsylvania. Confederate Maj. Gen. Lafayette M. McLaws withdrew his division from Fredericksburg, marched northwesterly, crossed the Rapidan River, and finally halted two days later near Culpeper Court House. During this time, Caldwell's Division, along with the rest of Hancock's Second Corps, was stationed across the Rappahannock River near Falmouth, Virginia. On June 4, Maj. Gen. Daniel Butterfield, Hooker's chief of staff, sent a dispatch to General Hancock, "A bridge is now being laid at Franklin's old crossing. Keep your communications good for sending in information of what is seen… in your front."[7]

A day later, Hancock gazed across the Rappahannock and noted fresh Rebel movements. He informed Brig. Gen. Seth Williams, the army's assistant adjutant general, "The enemy threw a regiment or two of infantry into the rifle-pits, first and second lines, about the mill… They have three guns in the grove behind the rifle-pits… I suppose the arrangement was entirely a defensive one." He did not know that these Rebels, of A. P. Hill's Third Corps, had moved to disguise the fact that several Confederate divisions of the First and Second Corps had departed.[8]

Lieutenant Alexander Sweeney of the 140th Pennsylvania wrote, "The recollections of the closing days of May and early days of June, too, to us are very vivid: the rigid drilling, the rumors of movements, and of Lee's army heading northward, the breaking up of camp, the stewing of our beans, rice, etc."[9] Lieutenant Thomas Livermore, who served in the 5th New Hampshire and also as chief of the Second Corps' ambulance corps, wrote in early June that "the weather had got warm, the roads were dry, the army seemed to be in good condition, and various surmises were entertained as to when we should move again, and at last the time came when unexpected."[10]

On June 7, Colonel Cross informed his brigade that "an order had been issued from Army Headquarters for the selection of 5,000 of the best marching and fighting men in the army." These men were to be able to endure a full-blown cavalry attack if necessary and were to prepare to march "in light order." General Hooker planned to probe Lee's line to ascertain the particulars of his northward movement. Major Robert H. Forster of the 148th Pennsylvania recollected, "No daylight hours were wasted in idleness. Life, activity, and industry were present in every camp."[11]

While Livermore insisted that 5,000 men were to be designated for the assignment, the official dispatch from Hooker to General Halleck, the general-in-chief of the Union armies, read, "As the accumulation of the heavy rebel force of cavalry about Culpeper may mean mischief. I am determined, if practicable, to break it up in its incipiency. I shall send all my cavalry against them, stiffened by about three thousand infantry."[12] Of the 3,000 men requested, 125 men were selected from the 5th New Hampshire to join the detachment. Lieutenant Livermore commanded one of the companies and the 5th's Captain James Larkin led the other one.

The next day, the special detachment began pursuing the Army of Northern Virginia. Livermore remembered, "Leaving everything but blankets and arms and equipment in camp, we marched away to the north with lively curiosity and pleasure excited by the entirely unknown undertaking we were destined for."

The soldiers marched until they reached Stafford Court House at nightfall. Here, they made camp and rested. The next day, they marched more than twenty miles until they halted near the Rappahannock River. There, Colonel Cross addressed the men: "Gentlemen, I have called you up to tell you that we are now at Kelly's Ford. Upon the other side of the river the rebels have a strong battery; the cavalry who are with us are to cross the river tomorrow morning, and we are to clear the way for them. We have been selected as a forlorn hope to storm that battery... You will cross the river in boats, and will storm the battery without firing a shot, and your uncle (meaning myself) will be there to lead you."

At 4 a.m. on June 9, the infantrymen silently filed into ranks, marched to the riverbank, and commenced to cross in groups of eighteen to twenty men. During the first crossing, one of the men who attempted to push off the first boats tried to keep his feet dry because there was nothing worse for a foot soldier than to have wet feet on the march. That situation almost always led to blisters and foot sores. However, one of the officers kicked the young soldier into the water. The splashing alerted the Confederates on the other side.

Almost immediately, the New Hampshire boys heard several shots ring out, along with the dreaded hisses from the passing rounds. The men, already in the boats, hunkered low until they reached the other side. There, they found the riverbanks to be ten feet high in some locations, which forced them to make a steep climb to engage the enemy. Once over the top, the men crouched down in thick vegetation as they tried to locate the Confederates. By now, it was steadily becoming brighter as morning approached, and a quick investigation of the area revealed several discarded articles. It was apparent the Rebels had hastily withdrawn from the area after firing a few desultory shots.

The only sign of the enemy was a small cavalry force that could be seen in the distance retiring from the banks of the river. The Federal force, once concentrated, shifted ranks and moved northward, up the river, until reaching a meadow. Once there, the soldiers deployed into line of battle and awaited an enemy attack. Two hours later, no assault had come forth.[13]

To investigate, the detachment entered the meadow and cautiously moved forward. They soon spotted a Confederate cavalry regiment, which "bravely rode along in front and near our skirmishers with a flag flying." The Rebels made their presence known but did not attack, other than lobbing a few artillery rounds. The Southerners soon retired off the field.[14]

Shortly after this incident, the men heard a long, continuous roar of musketry off of their left flank, not far from Brandy Station on the Orange and Alexandria Railroad. Brigadier General David Russell ordered the Federal line forward to try to sniff out the enemy. "We marched down from the elevation we had attained," recollected Livermore, "and pursued our way through a country diversified with woods and clearings." The Federals eventually contacted the Confederate front and began to take fire. One Union officer remembered that "shells began sailing over the trees and exploding so near us as to spur us ahead to meet the worst."

The line finally emerged from the woods near the railroad depot. The men noticed that Union cavalry had engaged the enemy. Livermore remembered Stuart's Confederate cavalry "galloping, wheeling, and charging, and the horse artillery hotly engaged." The Federal line immediately shifted to the left, and the men awaited orders to advance. Those orders never came, however, and instead the men were instructed to face about and reform in the rear. This action ended the Battle of Brandy Station for Caldwell's special infantry detachment. The fighting that day marked the largest mounted cavalry battle during the entire war. At the end of the day, the results proved to be inconclusive.

After being ordered to reform to the rear, Lieutenant Livermore and the rest of the detachment encamped from June 10 through the 12th. On June 13, orders came to rejoin the main body of the Second Corps.[15]

Meanwhile, at Falmouth, for the past few days, the rest of the Second Corps and the men of the Sixth Corps had watched anxiously for Hill's Corps to make a move. None had been forthcoming. "For several days the vast encampment of the Army was in great commotion;" Sergeant Thomas P. Meyer of the 148th

Pennsylvania said, "the pioneers drilled with their respective companies in hourly anticipation of a general move."[16]

Captain David Acheson of the 140th Pennsylvania's Company C had written to his mother on June 9:

> Things begin to assume a warlike appearance again… Two divisions of Sedgwick's Corps now lie upon the plain… I came off picket today. The crossing is just at the lower end of our line and I expected to witness the battle if it should have come off. There was some firing between the sharpshooters on the other side… It is much more pleasant to stand off and observe such skirmishing than to be engaged in it. The reb batteries have not replied to ours at any time I believe. They are perfectly confident of their ability to thrash us if we go over there and are quietly awaiting us…. Alex Sweeny brought a Washington Review into my quarters yesterday evening and read the editorial. It is no wonder you have treason among you while such papers are published. I sometimes almost feel ashamed of our country when I hear persons from other parts of the state speaking of her as they would of South Carolina. Much as I love my country I have often thought if our family and friends were out of it, I could wish to see it swept with the besom of destruction—wiped out of existence and all the black-hearted copperheads sent to keep company with those who once rebelled against Heaven's high rule. What can they mean? Has the last spark of patriotism died out in their breasts? I hope a day of reckoning will soon come—when loyalty will be truly appreciated and open-mouthed treason compelled to be silent.[17]

On June 14, Sergeant Meyer's anticipated movement became fact when Hooker ordered two Union corps northward in pursuit of the Confederate army. Major General John Sedgwick's Sixth Corps was the first to cross the river, followed by Hancock's Second Corps. Caldwell's Division, the rear guard of the army that day, was the last to cross.[18]

The 140th Pennsylvania's Private R. L. Stewart mentioned, "Enveloped in clouds of finely powdered dust, which had been pulverized and stirred up by passing trains and troops, we took our place in the line and moved out." Along their way, the men encountered the Occoquan River. Alexander Sweeney of the 140th Pennsylvania wrote, "It rested on our knapsacks a quarter of an inch deep! Blistered feet! The waters of the Occoquan soothed them." Soon, the men had tramped fourteen miles on their first day's march before camping near Manassas Junction.[19]

Early the next morning, June 15, orders were received about 4 a.m. for the Second Corps to continue its advance northward. Stewart remembered, "The 15th of June was one of the hottest days in that unusually torrid summer, and the march over the dusty roads under the burning sun, was the most trying and fatiguing we had yet experienced. Hundreds of strong men fell out by the wayside and were left under the protection of the rear guard."[20] Moving along the Alexandria Road, the men reached Wolf Run Shoals and camped for the evening after covering nearly twelve miles.[21]

On June 16, Caldwell's Division remained in camp until nearly 5 p.m. when the general finally received orders to proceed to Fairfax Station, only four miles away.[22] Though short in distance, the march was hot and exhausting, so much so that the men made haste to the river to soak in its cool waters. Private Stewart penned, "How refreshing it was to plunge into this clear flood of running water after the long day's march under a burning sun and amid the ever present clouds of dust." Up to this point in the campaign, the men had to suffer through their exhaustive thirst with empty canteens. Many soldiers broke from their ranks at the first opportunity to venture to nearby streams to refill their canteens. They had to hurry back to "avoid the imputation of straggling." Stewart went on to proclaim, "Sometimes there was not a drop of water in sight for miles and too often the only supply we did find by the way was in muddy streams or stagnant pools, along whose borders dead horses or mules were lying."[23]

St. Clair Mulholland (*Library of Congress LC-USZ62-61455*)

ST. CLAIR MULHOLLAND, the popular Irish-born major of the 116th Pennsylvania, remembered the heat as being "oppressive." He noted that "the dust rising in clouds stifled the men. Water was not to be had. Hundreds of men fell by the way to be picked up by the ambulances, which were soon filled with very sick, and in many cases, dying, men."[24]

Father William Corby of the Irish Brigade agreed, penning in his memoirs, "The poor soldiers who had to carry about sixty pounds daily under the burning sun of a more southern climate that they were accustomed to, found the continued marching from sixteen to eighteen miles per day very severe. Many of them dropped dead from sunstroke."[25]

Despite the long days of tiresome marching, the soldiers tried to maintain their contact with loved ones at home. They took the time, as they settled in, to write letters, read newspapers, and sew their names into clothing for identification purposes. Time would tell, for Caldwell's veterans, what may lie ahead. The only thing they knew for sure was that they were steadily moving northward, in pursuit of the Army of Northern Virginia, and the next fight would, seemingly, be fought on Northern soil.

When the division moved out on the night of June 16, Sergeant Thomas Meyer of the 148th Pennsylvania and a group of pioneers were left behind for a special mission. He recollected, "I was ordered… to destroy all abandoned property, such as commissary and ordnance stores, wagons, ammunition, etc.…. The telegraph poles were cut down, and the men with blunt edge axes, cut the wire in pieces. This work detained us and fatigued the men so much, that, when night came on we were miles in rear of the Army; we marched as rapidly as the men in their fatigued condition were able, till late in the night in our effort to overtake our Division."[26]

The next day, June 17, Lieutenant Livermore and the soldiers that had been detached on special duty filed back into camp. Dr. William Child, the regimental surgeon of the 5th New Hampshire, noted, "Colonel Cross was now in command of the brigade… The detail [that] had been absent ten days, had been constantly on active duty and was much exhausted, the men being foot-sore, lame and destitute of supplies." Meanwhile, the men stayed in camp until nearly 2 p.m. when orders came to move the division forward two miles to a point between Fairfax and Union Mills.[27]

On June 18, Caldwell's Division remained in camp. A detail of men was instructed to construct breastworks and to support a battery in the division's front. This order was promptly followed, but no enemy arrived and the men remained in their positions. That same day, Zook's trusted aide, Lt. Josiah Favill, arrived in Washington at the general's request. He "received a hospitable greeting," as the duo discussed the upcoming conflict and Robert E. Lee's possible intentions with his northwardly movement. The men stayed in the city until the 21st and then moved back to their command.[28]

On June 19, the division marched from Fairfax to Centreville, a distance of only five miles. The next day about noon, the men began their march toward Thoroughfare Gap. After arriving there, Capt. David Acheson again took up his pen to send a note to his mother, "The weather has been very warm during the march and consequently the boys have suffered a great deal. On Monday and Tuesday, we had the hardest marching—the men drank gallons of water. The first evening our corps numbering 8,000 came into camp with 3,000. I can hardly bear the heat… I threw away everything but my haversack and canteen, and would have dropped them if I could not have kept up with the regt… We are drawing near the old Bull Run battle ground and it may be that it may witness another conflict. God grant the issue may be better than formerly."[28]

As Caldwell's Division continued its pursuit of A. P. Hill's rear guard, the road-weary soldiers passed through the former Bull Run battlefield. They could only gaze with sadness at the countless graves as they passed by. Sergeant Winthrop Sheldon of the 27th Connecticut remembered, "Time had not effaced the evidences of those disastrous days. Silently the troops moved over the field, and the thoughts of many a one among the older regiments, and of some in our own, hurried back to those scenes with impressive distinctness, as the bleached bones of the fallen, or the rubbish of battle, lay scattered along the roadside."[30]

Years later, the 61st New York's Lt. Charles A. Fuller recalled the devastation, writing, "I should say the bodies had been laid close together, and a thin coat of earth thrown over them. As the bodies decayed, the crust fell in exposing in part the skeletons. Some of our men extracted teeth from the grinning skulls as they lay thus exposed to view. On the field of 1862 from one mound a hand stuck out. The flesh instead of rotting off had dried down, and there it was like a piece of dirty marble. Such sights are not refreshing to men going forward in search of a new battlefield."[31]

The gruesome scenes haunted the passing troops. Surgeon Alfred T. Hamilton of the 148th Pennsylvania mentioned, "An occasional skull protruded from a small heap of earth indicating the burial place of friend and foe." Sergeant Thomas Meyer, of the same regiment, recollected, "The unburied remains of men and horses lay scattered all over the field… skulls in great numbers. These we took up and wiggled out some teeth preferring those with gold fillings for mementoes."

As the men passed the scene, Meyer and his pioneers picked up some skulls from the ground and began examining them. He judged that most of the dead men were "very young… many having every tooth and all sound. In some…the third molars were still absent, showing that the soldiers were still under eighteen years."[32]

The men continued their trek toward Thoroughfare Gap with the recent sights still fresh in their minds. The march became very weary as rain began to fall, soaking the troops and covering them in mud as they trudged along. Late in the day, about 6 p.m., Capt. John Teed of the 116th Pennsylvania began to gather sticks from alongside the road. He planned to use them to prop up his shelter tent, assuming the march would soon be halted. The order to stop failed to arrive, however, and the men continued onward, hour after hour, mile after mile. Captain Teed's sticks became heavier with each step he took, but he "was not going to be fooled by casting them away." As they passed into a valley, he again anticipated the welcome order to halt for the night, but, again, no such respite came. The soldiers grumbled among themselves as the rain continued to fall. Teed exclaimed, "Well, no use talking, gentlemen, we are going to march all night!" Finally, after having enough of his heavy burden, the captain threw the sticks to the side of the road and continued his march, now free from their weight. Unfortunately for him, after another half-hour of marching, the order to halt was finally given. His "sticks were a mile away" and he had to sleep "in the mud and without his shelter tent." Second Lieutenant John B. Noyes of the 28th Massachusetts agreed, writing, "Weary and worn we threw ourselves… on the ground and slept till sunrise of the 21st."[33]

The division remained stationary in this position for several days. On June 21, Caldwell's men could hear artillery fire to their front, and they began preparing themselves for what they believed to be an oncoming fight. No conflict was destined this day for the men of Hancock's First Division, however, and they slumbered in that position that night. On the 22nd, Captain Acheson took advantage of the temporary break in marching to write his mother again. He told her, "There was some artillery firing ahead of us yesterday… Three cavalry brigades passed us last evening. I saw a good many of the Washington county boys among them."[34]

June 23 proved to be another welcome day of rest for the men of the division. Many again took the time to write letters home and describe their condition to their loved ones. However, not all was quiet for Sergeant Meyer and his pioneers. In the early morning, they were sent up into Thoroughfare Gap to cut down "every tree in reach into and across the road." The goal was to block the roadway to hinder enemy movement. "It was wonderful to see how these expert choppers kept the trees crashing," Meyer wrote, "and how cheerfully they worked, in the heat of summer weather completely soaked with perspiration."[35]

While thus busily engaged, some soldiers took the opportunity to attack a grove of cherry trees "loaded with ripe fruit." A few hungry individuals climbed up the long limbs to knock down the cherries. The feast was short-lived, however, when a provost officer rode up and sternly shouted, "Come down, or I will shoot you down!" Sergeant Meyer, who was up in one of the trees, feared for his life when he noticed that the officer had leveled his pistol directly at him. Meyer accordingly climbed down and approached him, stating, "Captain, we are your prisoners; no doubt you outrank General Hancock, by whose orders we were detailed to do some work out here." Turning to his men, the sergeant called out, "Fall in, boys!" Each man, with axe in hand, fell in line. The provost looked at the soldiers in a bewildered fashion and said, "I took you for stragglers, the devil take you," and rode away. The cheerful men gave the captain the "rebel yell" as he disappeared into the distance and they quickly went back to work, chopping down tree limbs and eating cherries.[36]

Just outside the gap at Gainesville, Virginia, General Zook, who resumed command of his brigade a few days earlier, arrived from Washington. He was ordered to relieve General French, who had been sent to Harper's Ferry, and take immediate command of the town. "Zook promptly made himself acquainted with the position," Lieutenant Favill observed, "He established a picket line personally, completely surrounding the camp with detachments of cavalry, pushed well out on every road converging on the place."[37]

The following morning, a stir was in the air as "every man of the staff was in the saddle and all the troops under arms," Favill recalled. Zook mounted his horse and rode out to an advanced position. He spent the morning there gathering information and "inspecting the position of the advanced guard." Meanwhile, at Zook's headquarters, several messages arrived from General Hancock informing his staff, "Stuart skirmish(ed) all around his position, that his pickets were frequently driven in, and cautioned us time and again to be on the alert." The matter seemed "superfluous" to the men of the brigade, however. As Favill stated, they "sleep with one eye open and never more than half of us at a time."[38]

On June 25, the sun rose over the camps of the opposing armies. It promised to be another hot day on the road for John Caldwell's soldiers. "The regiment fell in at an early hour," remembered Winthrop Sheldon of the 27th Connecticut, "ready to fight or march... for the rebels were approaching with malicious intent." Rumors of an impending attack forced the division to deploy into line of battle several times in anticipation. The attack, again, never came and orders were for Hancock to retreat at 9 a.m. Major General J.E.B. Stuart's Confederate cavalry followed closely. Near the village of Haymarket, just after General Hancock shifted his corps to the north, Stuart's horse artillery opened fire, "killing or wounding several men" in the Second Division, serving as the rear guard. Lieutenant Charles Fuller of the 61st New York stated, "When we moved, the enemy followed us up quite sharply with artillery."[39]

Stuart's demonstration posed a problem for Caldwell's First Division. Zook's Brigade remained back at Gainesville and had yet been relieved. General Hancock finally issued orders at 10:30 in the morning for Zook to withdraw his troops from the area and rejoin the division. Within the hour, "The telegraph operator cut the wires, removed his instruments, and rode with us." Zook's men did not make it very far before they realized that the Confederate cavalry had them "completely surrounded... keeping at a respectful distance, but in full view all the time." Hancock would be without an entire brigade during this brief stand. No matter, however, as Stuart's fire slackened after a short time and the Federal infantrymen were finally able to resume their march.[40]

In Zook's Brigade, the 140th Pennsylvania's Private Stewart remembered "From early morning until far into the night there were almost continuous showers of rain... the red Virginia clay clogged our feet and seriously impeded our progress." They too, eventually, found themselves near Bull Run at about two o'clock in the afternoon. They began crossing at the ford. Arnold's Battery went first and then deployed on high ground on the opposite bank. General Zook personally placed each command that filed across the river, while Lieutenant Favill remained on the bank of the opposite side supervising the crossing. Favill remembered that there were "eighty wagons and ambulances, and it was a considerable undertaking to keep them all in motion."[41]

Within a half-hour, an orderly notified Favill that "the enemy [was] pressing the rear guard, and a rebel battery [was] coming up." Quickly, Favill sent the orderly to notify Zook, while he and other officers searched the river for another ford. Finding one in close proximity, Favill began to utilize it to augment the original crossing site. Only a few moments passed before the Confederate artillery opened on the troops. Arnold's Battery replied and "soon drove them away."[42]

When all of his men were safely across Bull Run, Zook allowed them to rest for nearly an hour. Their respite ended after one of Hancock's orderlies rode up and directed Zook to take his brigade to Gum Springs to join the rest of the Second Corps. The men took up the march "at once" but soon found themselves on the wrong road. This significantly delayed their schedule. Zook's men eventually located the same roads that the rest of the corps had taken several days earlier. They, too, passed the former Bull Run battlefield. According to Favill, they "saw hundreds of human skeletons bleached white as snow, a ghastly monument of those who had fallen in the great cause. We were considerably depressed by this horrible side of war, and I noticed the soldiers were anxious to hurry away." Private Stewart of the 140th Pennsylvania recalled, "Many mounds were passed where the dead had been hastily buried by heaping skeletons of arms, hands, feet, skulls, and other parts of the body more or less exposed... Every tree and house in sight was riddled with Minié balls or torn and gashed with shot and shell. It was a sad, gruesome, and never-to-be-forgotten sight." The brigade rejoined the corps at Gum Springs about 9 p.m.[43]

They were in for a miserable evening. "It rained during the whole night in torrents," Surgeon William Child of the 5th New Hampshire recalled. Private Stewart remembered halting next to a pine grove where they "were wet to the skin and too weary and indifferent to make fires, much as we longed for a steaming cup of coffee." The men of Company K of the 140th Pennsylvania found themselves in a little better situation than their comrades. They encamped next to a stream that ran by their temporary bunks. Alexander Sweeney, of that company, recalled the men "wrapped with his scant remnant of hard-tack and coffee, gun and ammunition, in a gum blanket or piece of tent, and the cap drawn down over the face. Never were sleep and rest sweeter." The men had marched nearly twenty miles this day.[44]

Early on June 26, the men of the 61st New York found themselves near a small pasture. They gazed through the morning mist at a small calf, grazing in the meadow. Lieutenant Fuller admitted, "Some of our wickedest men ended the life of that calf skinned it, and gave me a chunk." They looked forward to what would have been their best meal in several months. However, it was not to be. Within a few minutes, shortly before 6 a.m., they received orders to fall in.[45]

After raining all night, the roads were now nothing more that miry swamps. Sergeant Meyer said that "the mud was something appalling." Nevertheless, the men broke camp and continued their march toward Maryland and, subsequently, the Army of Northern Virginia.[46]

Lieutenant Favill admitted in his diary that "the march was excessively fatiguing." The rain continued to soak the already dampened men. In mid-morning, the sun began peeking through the clouds; a blessing for Zook's weary soldiers, who gasped a sigh of relief. Private Stewart of the 140th Pennsylvania wrote, "By this time the warmth of our bodies had dried the water-soaked clothing in which we had marched and slept and when the sky cleared, the discomforts of the way were speedily forgotten."[47]

After marching nearly eighteen hours, the men arrived at a pontoon bridge over the Potomac River, near Edwards' Ferry. They bivouacked by the riverside and awaited their turn to cross. Several hours later, near midnight, they finally began to cross the bridge.[48]

THE MARCH THROUGH MARYLAND

Charles A. Fuller (*New York State Military Museum*)

While awaiting their turn to march across the pontoon bridge into Maryland, the men of Company K of the 140th Pennsylvania received instructions to "take only the top rail" of a fence that ran near their location. Soon, campfires glowed in the darkness as soldiers brewed coffee and cooked their evening meals. The men began to relax after their fatiguing march as they waited on the repast. **LIEUTENANT CHARLES FULLER** remembered the slaughtered calf, which he had stored away earlier in the day for later usage. As he began to cook it, William Collins asked for a piece, which Fuller freely shared. It was then "fried... in the stew pan, which was the half of a canteen, and brought it on smoking hot." However, the meat was disappointing in that it was "deeken veal" and very "stringy," in Fuller's opinion. The men discarded it and feasted upon "Salt Hoss" (salted beef) for the rest of the night.[49]

Cross's Brigade finally received orders to march across the swaying pontoon bridge. Upon reaching the other side, the men learned they were now in Maryland. Many men began cheering and others shouted in joy. Some, thrilled to be back on Northern soil, hugged the ground. Most, however, were simply hoping for some much-needed rest after all the hard marching. Their joy, however, proved short-lived when word arrived that "Lee had crossed the Potomac and was heading directly for Pennsylvania." Lieutenant Fuller recounted, "Having been up and awake all of the night before, I was fearfully sleepy and hardly able to drag myself along." After crossing the pontoon bridge, the soldiers of the 61st New York were led to a ditch along the side of the road. Here, they were instructed to camp for the night. The men "plodded" into the ditch which, to their dismay, contained "two inches of mud, thick enough to encase me," as Fuller related. After attempting to climb his way out and failing, he just allowed his tired body to succumb to the wet, marshy, ground. "I was too near gone to speak bad words," another soldier remembered, "and so went on in silence, weighing five pounds more than before my descent."[50]

The time was nearing 2 a.m. when orders came for Zook's Brigade to cross. The men did so in the dead of the still, night air. Many of them, having crossed, were so exhausted from their days of marching that at this early hour, they literally fell onto the ground and slept soundly. Sweeney recalled, "All were practically asleep on march or halt. Oh, those plagued stops or halts through all that weary night!"[51]

Much of the following day, the entire Second Corps enjoyed a decent amount of rest. At 3 p.m., however, orders came to press forward from Poolesville to Barnesville in Montgomery County. On this day, the weather began to clear and the roads improved, making it a much more pleasant day for marching and catching up to "Marse Robert." Zook's aide, Lieutenant Favill, recalled in his diary, "Everybody was, of course, on the streets and showed us the greatest attention, looking in amazement at the interminable lines of infantry." As the troops passed through the small western Maryland villages, the townsfolk offered what goods they could spare, handing out cherries, bread, and other consumables. The march continued until 11 p.m. that night before the infantrymen finally camped near Barnesville.[52]

On Sunday, June 28, the men continue their march north toward the Pennsylvania line. The exhausted surgeon of the 148th Pennsylvania, Dr. Alfred Hamilton, admitted he was "so sleepy as to be scarcely able to remain in the saddle." Yet, the men were on an emotional high, and about noon, the division passed near Sugar Loaf Mountain. Here the men began "singing and shouting the 'Battle Cry of Freedom,'" according to Major St. Clair Mulholland, commanding the 116th Pennsylvania, "which resounded and filled the valley with music and was echoed from every mountain side—a grand tableau of war never to be forgotten."[53]

Caldwell's Division continued advancing toward the town of Urbana. The march was a constant reminder to the men that they were now not in the parts of war-torn Virginia that lay ruined and desolate. Instead, they were constantly enjoying the hospitability of the residents of this part of Maryland. Citizens lined the streets, in every passing town, with flags in hand—waving, shouting, and singing as the troops passed by.[54]

About that time, rumors began circulating among Caldwell's men that Maj. Gen. George G. Meade of the Fifth Corps had taken command of the Army of the Potomac, replacing General Hooker. The sudden change in leaders did not sit well with many soldiers, who hoped that George McClellan would be returning. Lieutenant Thomas Livermore recalled, "I do not think we greatly regretted the loss of General Hooker, but neither did we welcome General Meade with enthusiasm, since we knew little about him."[55]

Charles Hale (*Personal Collection of David Morin*)

Major Charles A. Hale of the 5th New Hampshire rode near Colonel Cross. They had just passed Sugarloaf Mountain and were in the vicinity of Boonsboro when an old friend, Capt. Frank Butler, approached them. Butler had been connected with the Signal Corps for some time, and the men caught up on lost time near the roadside. Hale recalled Cross telling of "the magnificent sword, spurs and watch that had been presented to him at Falmouth, a testimonial from the officers of his regiment expressing the sentiment of an injunction uttered by Captain [James] Perry as he lay dying amidst the slaughter of Fredericksburg. As he spoke of the matter in a pleased animated way, I saw that the colonel had been touched and gratified by this evidence of esteem from his loyal followers."

The conversation eventually turned to the battle that would, undoubtedly, be forthcoming. The colonel gazed at Butler and calmly stated, "It will be my last battle." The statement shocked the men who were riding alongside him and those within earshot of the conversation. Few of them attempted to downplay his remark, but Hale remembered, "He used the words in a grave decided way, and it gave me a shock, and also a feeling of resentment that he should speak in that manner."

Hale recalled that Cross had been, as of late, "in a sort of abstracted mood that was not usual with him." The officers continued to try to pass the conversation off, when Cross finally turned to the major and said, "Mr. Hale, I wish you to attend to my books and papers; that private box of mine in the headquarters wagon… After the campaign is over, get it at once, dry the contents if damp, and then turn it over to my brother," ending the conversation for the time being.[56]

Continuing onward, the Union soldiers passed through Boonsboro and encamped two miles outside of Frederick. The men of Caldwell's Division had strict orders not to molest any private citizens or their property. They could, however, by an earlier order burn any broken fence rails which they may come across for personal purposes. The 140th Pennsylvania's Robert Stewart recalled, "It was not so easy, however, to give up the privilege of appropriating the rails… One order was to the effect that we might take broken rails. This was literally interpreted and the man who could not find a broken rail to cook his coffee, straightway proceeded to break the first one that came to hand, and then carried it away in triumph."[57]

A suspected Rebel spy had been captured near Frederick. An inspection revealed that he was carrying documents showing the locations of Federal trains, troops, and their route of march. The spy confessed and "said that if he had not been caught, in twenty-four hours from that time he would have had possession of all our army train(s)." The outlandish statement drew the anger of the Federal troops standing around. Someone cried out to send the spy to Washington and let the government try his case. General Hancock exclaimed, "No! If you send him to Washington they will promote him." According to Father William Corby, the man "was suspended from a tree and left there, and while the army passed I saw him hanging by the neck."[58]

Winfield Hancock
*(Library of Congress
LC-DIG-cwpb-05828)*

GENERAL HANCOCK had a valid point in exclaiming this to be an inexcusable crime against the army and then hanging the spy on the spot, instead of sending him to Washington. Scores of men had been set free or exchanged for other prisoners, only to go back to their respective armies and continue killing their adversaries. Hancock was, however, just as hard on his own men. An example is upon crossing into Maryland, he warned his corps that "being in a loyal State, they had no right to molest or destroy private property." This statement was well respected around the camp, and very few soldiers disobeyed the order.

One evening, while on the march, the charismatic general rode along the line to observe his passing troops. At length, he noticed several soldiers attempting to run down a sheep. Hancock spurred his horse, reached the scene, and "swore at the supposed culprits: 'Blank, blank, you blank, blank, scoundrels! Did you not hear my orders? Send out the man that killed that sheep! I saw the animal drop! Do not try to evade, or I will have the whole company punished." When none of the offenders responded, he, again, renewed the threat "in still more vigorous language." While Hancock was railing about killing the sheep, it suddenly emerged from a nearby brush pile and ran off. Hancock wheeled his horse and said, "I take it all back. I'm glad you have not transgressed my orders."[59]

As night drew nigh, news circulated around Caldwell's camp confirming the army was now under Meade's command. Captain David Acheson again wrote to his loving mother, "Our marches are very fatiguing indeed and several times when it was raining the men at the end of a day's march would lie down in the water and sleep soundly. I never knew what a man was able to endure before… We do not get much news. All look anxiously for the news from Pennsylvania. It is rumored with us that Hooker has been superseded by Meade. I do not know how this will please the army but it seems to me that the Government is at a loss to know who is fitted for the command… I believe this to be the campaign of the war, and the rebs have staked their all upon it."[60]

At 6 a.m. the following morning, an orderly rode into camp and delivered an order directing the adjutant general to move the command in the direction of

Uniontown. The letter went unnoticed until nearly eight o'clock in the morning when the men were finally instructed to march.[61]

"The day was beautiful," Lieutenant Favill remembered, "but the sun much too hot for comfort." This march proved to be one of the longest by either army during the entire war. It covered nearly 32 miles and caused great exhaustion and dehydration, and a few deaths, amongst the soldiers. Despite the hardships of the march, many men marveled at the delightful scenery. Near Frederick, Father Corby noted, "We found the country very beautiful. The fields were like gardens in the highest state of cultivation. The fences were neat and well built. The buildings were not grand, but they had about them an air of comfort, and they looked like real homes."[62]

"In passing through these towns," Favill added, "we usually resumed the regular step, and with bands playing and colors flying make a stunning appearance. The Fifty-second, as in days gone by, although now with fewer voices, sing their memorable songs, which creates more enthusiasm than do the bands." Emory M. Stevens of the 148th Pennsylvania wrote that "the heat was intense and the dust several inches deep, rising and settling everywhere and filling eyes, ears, and throat." An officer said it was "a day of tremendous exertions." With few streams along the march, the men had difficulty in obtaining water for their empty canteens and most were becoming emotionally and physically drained. Youthful Pvt. Jacob H. Cole of the 57th New York stated, "The day was hot throughout, and halts were brief... There was complaint and grumbling and growling and worse." Some of the men shouted that "Hancock would not stop until he got to Harrisburg." Luckily for the men of the 57th, Lt. Col. Alford B. Chapman declared that "it was a soldier's privilege to grumble."[63]

"Straggling began early," remembered Lt. Gilbert H. Frederick, "and rapidly increased toward evening." Father Corby noted, "One man carried... about sixty pounds, including musket, cartridges, provisions, shelter-tent, and blanket... considering the load that the men had to carry, it was a marvelous feat." Yet, the men dragged themselves along the best they could along the "fearfully dusty" roads.[64]

General Zook marched in his proper place at the head of his column. After noticing more men beginning to struggle to keep up, he turned to his command and suggested "that every man be required to contribute something for the amusement of the party." He hoped that this might, in part, distract his men from focusing on their hunger, thirst, and boredom. Private Robert Stewart of the 140th Pennsylvania struggled to keep pace. He recalled, "The only drink we could take, without delaying the column, was the warm, insipid, and of times muddy water in our canteen, and the only solid food available was a mouthful of 'hardtack,' now and then." Lieutenant Favill took Zook up on his offer and, "made quite a hit by relating a lot of Ovid's metamorphoses, which some of them had never heard before and thought very wonderful." The ploy worked, at least for a time, and the men continued their march.[65]

There were a few bright spots along the line of march. The men paraded through town after town. Many of the citizens passed out food and water. Dr. Alfred Hamilton, the surgeon of the 148th Pennsylvania, remembered, "The people along the road sold and gave away all the eatables they had and seemed glad to see us pass and were surprised at our coming." Private Stewart recalled that "refreshments were freely offered at the gates of residences and by the side of the streets, and many a kind word and 'God bless you, boys,' rang in our ears and cheered our hearts."[66]

Meanwhile, Major Hale and Colonel Cross were riding side by side. Hale hoped that Cross had forgotten their conversion of the previous day in which he predicted his dire fate. Such was not the case, however. Cross, in the presence of his staff, again mentioned his premonition. Hale spoke up and "said something about the foolishness of entertaining such ideas." Cross would not hear anything of it. "He had rasped me also," Hale recalled, "and it finally led to his having some sharp words with me, that strained our friendly relations." The two men did not speak to each other again until the following evening.[67]

The heat of the march caused tensions even in the humblest hearts. Many of Caldwell's men began to grumble louder while others were so footsore they had to stop and rest. Still others continued onward with their respective regiments. For some, it was a life-and-death struggle. Private Martin Sigman of the 64th New York watched as man after man fell from the ranks. He remarked, "Some of us concluded that they wouldent [sic] come to a halt, and fell out of the ranks and laid down [on the] side of the road." According to Lt. Gilbert H. Frederick of the 57th New York, stragglers began pouring through other columns from regiments in their front. This caused confusion among the Emerald Staters and led to frustration among the various commanders. This stampede disrupted the continuity of the march. Frederick noted, "At the end of the column, when the last regimental staff had passed, there followed an army of the lame, the halt, the sick, and, last of all, the born tired. The ambulances were full of both officers and men."[68]

As the sun began to sink below the horizon, the column neared the Mason-Dixon Line. For the Keystoners in the 116th Pennsylvania, the thrill of approaching their home state boosted their morale. Major Mulholland noted that this "seemed to have a wonderful effect upon the spirits of the men of the Regiment, and frequent inquiries were made during the day for the State line from the farmers who lined the fences by the way and gazed in wonder at the passing column." At one point, one of the men from the 116th shouted to a nearby farmer, "Where does this road run to?" The farmer replied, "Oh, it runs right straight on!" Those were the only words the regiment needed to hear as they continued to march to the commonwealth's defense.[69]

In Patrick Kelly's Irish Brigade, some of the men declared "that they could not, and would not, go any farther." Some of their comrades responded to the grumbling by uttering, "Oh, come on!" Many others decreed, "Little Mac is surely in command." About this time, rumors spread that the army was now back in the hands of their former commander, George B. McClellan. This, of course, was a false statement. Someone had started it to "give more confidence to the rank and file." Father William Corby noted, "Fatigue and drowsiness, added to a rather weak and faint feeling, indispose men to converse, and by silent consent each one discontinues conversation. The click of a large spur, the occasional rattle of a sword, and other mechanical movements are the only sounds heard above the slow, steady tramp of the line and the heavy tread of the few horses that carry mounted officers. Even these mounted officers frequently dismount and walk to avoid being overpowered by sleep and to save themselves from falling from the horses... How men live through all this is a mystery."[70]

The column finally halted near Uniontown, Maryland, about 11 p.m., after more than fifteen hours on the road. Men fell in complete disarray as the order to "stack arms!" was finally given. Lieutenant Charles Fuller of the 61st New York wrote, "I know I was so completely tired out, that, as soon as arms were stacked, I stretched out without unrolling my blankets, and I knew nothing till the next morning, when I was awakened by the sun shining into my eyes. I was so stiff that it took some time to get on my legs."[71]

Exhausted men stretched all along the dusty road leading to the campsite. Private Martin Sigman of the 64th New York was one of those stragglers. Late in the march, he and a squad of soldiers rested their tired legs and feet. Soon, an officer rode up to him and said they "better get up and go on for our men had come to a halt and go[ne] into camp for the night." Sigman, and a few others, immediately rose and resumed the march. However, some of the soldiers stayed put, ignoring the orders to push on. After Sigman finally found his regiment, he immediately wished he had stayed with the stragglers, stating, "for I just got ready to lay down for the night to get a little rest and sleep, then I was detailed to go on picket all night."[72]

According to Private Stewart of the 140th Pennsylvania, "One of the most depressing and painful experiences of the forced marches which the troops were compelled to make, during these long summer days, was caused by foot sores in varying degrees of chafing and inflammation. Some of the men suffered so much from blistered and swollen feet that they could not wear their shoes, and there were many, as we neared the border of Pennsylvania, who had to be carried a part, or the whole of the time, in ambulances. The man who did not have a limp in his gait in those trying days was a rare exception among his fellows."[73]

On June 30, the men rested the entire day. Most of the remaining stragglers belatedly rejoined their respective regiments. Lieutenant Frederick of the 57th New York remembered seeing men coming up in clusters, "a motley, dirty crowd they were; for, having fallen in their tracks and slept, an early start was made to find their camps, mostly without washing or cleaning."[74]

Colonel Cross made a change in his brigade's organization during this brief stay. The newest regiment, the 148th Pennsylvania, did not find favor in his eyes. Major R. H. Forster, of that regiment, noted, "Now, because of his dislike, or prejudice, or whatever it may have been, officers and men of our regiment were almost daily... made to suffer wrong and injustice from him."

The culmination occurred on the evening on June 30. Lieutenant Colonel Robert McFarlane had for most of the campaign commanded the 148th in the absence of Col. James Beaver, who had suffered a severe wound at Chancellorsville. If McFarlane, according to Forster, "ever gave offense to Colonel Cross it was only in such efforts as he made to protect himself and those who served under him from imposition and injustice." Be that as it may, on this evening the company commanders of the 148th were called together to meet with **Col. Henry B. McKeen** of the 81st Pennsylvania. McKeen informed them that Colonel Cross had ordered McFarlane to be relieved so McKeen could lead the regiment. "To say that all were astounded and shocked at this sudden and unceremonious announcement is to give mild terms," Forster remembered, "Without a murmur of open complaint at the time, though the provocation was grievous, Colonel McFarland quietly bore this humiliation."[75]

Henry Boyd McKeen (*Photo courtesy of the Carlisle Barracks*)

While the troops rested, end-of-the-month duty rosters were reviewed and the men received their pay. During this break, Lt. Thomas Livermore decided to play a practical joke on Maj. Charles Hale. Contrary to standard protocol, Hale used a leather scabbard for his sword instead of the more common steel scabbards. Livermore offered his sword and scabbard for Hale's temporary use, saying "mine was more appropriate for him and his for me under the circumstances." Hale gladly accepted the offer. What he did not know at the time was that Livermore's sword had been broken in two places during prior events. Leaving a blade "about eighteen inches long which adhered to the hilt." Hale would not draw his blade until Gettysburg, where "it was considered very funny," according to Livermore.[76]

GETTYSBURG—THE FIRST DAY

On June 30, the infantrymen of Brig. Gen. James J. Pettigrew's Confederate brigade advanced into Gettysburg but withdrew when they spotted Brig. Gen. John Buford's Union cavalry. Pettigrew retired westward on the Chambersburg Pike without firing a shot. When Maj. Gen. Henry Heth later heard that Pettigrew had contacted Federal cavalry, some observers downplayed them as mere militia protecting the town. Heth famously asked his corps commander, Lt. Gen. A. P. Hill, "If there is no objection, I will take my division tomorrow and go to Gettysburg and get those shoes." Hill's casual reply, "None in the world," set in motion what would become the most famous battle of the Civil War.[77]

At 7:30 the following morning, July 1, Heth's Division was on the march from Cashtown eastward to Gettysburg. Unbeknownst to the Confederates, Buford had anticipated their morning arrival. He had deployed his men over a broad area to the west and north of town. One squad was deployed near the home of Ephraim Whisler, along the Chambersburg Pike. One of the cavalrymen noted a rising dust cloud and hastily sought an officer. Lieutenant Marcellus E. Jones of the 8th Illinois Cavalry was near Herr's Tavern. He rushed to the aid of the outpost, arriving just in time to grab Cpl. Levi Shaffer's rifle and fire it at the oncoming Rebels. The Rebels halted, deployed Marye's (Fredericksburg) Artillery of Pegram's Battalion, and fired several rounds.[78]

The Confederates eventually pushed Buford's skirmishers from ridge to ridge, until they came under fire of the main line of Federal cavalry. Here, the men of Gamble's Brigade stood fast against Harry Heth's Rebels, forcing them to deploy in line of battle, a lengthy process. This effectively bought Buford enough time for the arrival of the vanguard of the First Corps under wing commander Maj. Gen. John F. Reynolds.

Heth, despite orders not to bring on a general engagement, deployed Brig. Gen. James J. Archer's brigade on the right of the Chambersburg Pike and Brig. Gen. Joseph Davis's brigade on the left before ordering an advance. Partially up, they witnessed a brigade of Union infantrymen deploying in line of battle. The First Corps of the Army of the Potomac had arrived at last. A Rebel recognized some of the enemy and hollered aloud, "Taint no militia. It's the damn black-hatted fellows again. It's the Army of the Potomac."[79]

It indeed must have seemed like the entire Federal army was deploying into battle lines. Reynolds personally supervised the movement of Brig. Gen. Lysander Cutler's brigade across the Chambersburg Pike and deployed them in support of Hall's Battery along the railroad cut. Brigadier General Solomon Meredith's First Brigade, First Division, halted about three hundred yards in front of the Lutheran Theological Seminary. There, the Westerners of the Iron Brigade were ordered to lay down and await the enemy near the crest of the ridgeline.[80]

Soon, General Reynolds, still mounted on his horse, appeared in front of the 2nd Wisconsin. As he deployed the Badgers, he was near the edge of Herbst's Woods. He glanced back either to see if any of the other regiments from the brigade followed suit or to call for support. None did, and before he could turn around, a lead missile struck him in the back of his head, killing him. A few soldiers carried his body to the seminary and then to the house of a local man named George George and thence to the rear.

Meanwhile, Maj. Gen. Abner Doubleday assumed command of the Union forces then on the field. Some of the Iron Brigade advanced westward toward Archer's Brigade and captured the Maryland-born Confederate general. To the north, the Rebels found some initial success as Davis's Brigade successfully drove back Cutler's Brigade. However, the 6th Wisconsin, 95th New York, and 84th New York subsequently attacked and forced them to withdraw. After these actions, a midday lull fell over the battlefield.[81]

Doubleday took advantage of the lull and extended his lines, placing the Second Division, under Brig. Gen. John C. Robinson, on Cutler's right flank. He refused its flank along the Mummasburg Road facing Oak Hill, while the left faced the farm of John Forney. About this time, Maj. Gen. Oliver O. Howard's Eleventh

Corps arrived from the south. Howard soon learned that he, as the senior officer, was now in command of the battlefield, relieving Doubleday. He ascertained the prominent landscape in his front and chose Cemetery Hill as his fallback position for the First and Eleventh Corps if their lines were broken. He also instructed most of his own corps to take a position north of town while holding the division of Brig. Gen. Adolph von Steinwehr in reserve. Brigadier General Francis Barlow's First Division advanced beyond Howard's intended position to Blocher's Knoll. To Barlow's left rear, Brig. Gen. Alexander Schimmelfennig's Third Division stopped near the right flank of the First Corps. Major General Carl Schurz assumed command of the Eleventh Corps.

Meanwhile, the Confederate divisions of Major Generals Robert Rodes and Jubal Early were bearing down on this newly-formed line. Rodes deployed his men on or near Oak Hill and quickly formed his battle lines. About 1 p.m., the brigades of Junius Daniel, Alfred Iverson, and Edward O'Neal pushed against the First Corps, while the brigade of Brig. Gen. George P. Doles struck the gap near the Eleventh Corps.

Rodes' assault began before Jubal Early attacked down the Harrisburg Pike. Earlier, as he was coming to within earshot of the battlefield, Early could hear the sharp cracks of musketry and see the smoke of battle rising through the clear, summer air. Therefore, he deployed his brigades into lines of battle before they ever contacted the enemy. He quickly swung his right flank, Gordon's Brigade, around and struck Barlow's exposed division, driving them from the field. This set into motion a snowball effect of events that eventually led to much of the Eleventh Corps retiring from the field. Meanwhile, to the west, the bloodied First Corps, pressured by the brigades of Brig. Gen. Johnston J. Pettigrew, Col. John Brockenbrough, and a few regiments from Brig. Gen. Junius Daniel's brigade, also fell back. The men reformed on Seminary Ridge and deployed into line of battle.[82]

Once in front of the seminary, they came under attack from Brig. Gen. Alfred Scales and Col. Abner Perrin's brigades. The weight of the Confederate forces eventually proved too much for the brave men in front of the Seminary, and the Federal line soon broke and fell back to Cemetery Hill. The Eleventh Corps also broke about this time, and men from both corps were driven through the town and their designated position as well as Robinson's Division near Oak Ridge.

THE SECOND CORPS ARRIVES

The men of the Second Corps had camped nearly twenty miles to the south of Gettysburg the previous night. They had received orders very early on the morning of July 1 to move to Gettysburg. Lieutenant Favill remembered, "We fell in at daylight, took breakfast, and immediately marched, expecting to meet the enemy toward evening." The case would not present itself, however, and shortly after they started northward, the division was halted and ordered to return back to its original starting position. They were then redirected toward Taneytown and General Meade's headquarters.[83]

As the Second Corps continued moving forward, they noted an astonishing sight in the clear sky. Adjutant Charles A. Ramsey of the 148th Pennsylvania recalled, "Someone near, in looking upward, caught sight of a star. Immediately a number of us saw it, and then on looking closely we caught the dim twinkle of five or six more. We accepted it as auguring success for the undertaking, in which we were then engaged."[84]

After a brief march, the men arrived in Taneytown, where they halted near Meade's headquarters. The commanding general had sent out a circular earlier in the day, giving his plan for a defensive battle on ground of his choosing. He had not yet learned of the battle taking place fifteen miles to his front. Once General Hancock arrived, he immediately sought out orders from Meade. Hancock anticipated a northerly movement. Meade, instead, told of a plan that he and his staff had devised and that he "made up his mind to fight a battle on what was known as Pipe Creek… and that he was then preparing an order for that movement."[85]

While still there, Capt. Stephen M. Weld of General Reynolds' staff arrived with a message for Meade from Gettysburg. The note read, "The enemy were coming in strong force, and that he was afraid they would get the heights on the other side of the town before he could; that he would fight them all through the town, however, and keep them back as long as possible." General Meade stood straight as an arrow and shouted, "Good God! If the enemy gets Gettysburg, I am lost."[86]

By now, it was after one o'clock in the afternoon. A report trickled down to Meade that Reynolds was either killed or mortally wounded. Meade sought out Hancock and told him to place Brig. Gen. John Gibbon, Hancock's Second Division commander, in command of the Second Corps and for him to "proceed at once to the front." Meade also noted that "in the event of the truth of the report of General Reynolds's death or disability, to assume command of the corps on that field—the First and Eleventh, and the Third."[87] The announcement sent a shockwave throughout the camp of the Second Corps and among Meade's headquarters staff. His ideas of a solid defensive line in the Pipe Creek area had been dealt a crippling blow at the reported loss of Reynolds. The death of the popular general saddened all who knew him.[88]

Hancock recited to Meade that General Caldwell was senior to Gibbon and that Howard was senior to himself. Meade simply said that "he could not help it; that he knew General Hancock, but did not know General Howard so well, and at this crisis he must have a man he knew and could trust." At 1:10 p.m., Meade informed Hancock, "If you think the ground and position there a better one to fight a battle under existing circumstances, you will so advise the General, and he will order all the troops up." With those orders, Hancock put Gibbon in charge of

William Shallenberger (*Library of Congress 04304***)**

his corps, climbed inside an ambulance, and set off northward for Gettysburg.[89]

Soon, the Second Corps was on the Taneytown Road, heading toward Gettysburg. Southbound civilian refugees gave excited accounts of the growing battle. **First Lieutenant William S. Shallenberger** of the 140th Pennsylvania recalled that "wild stories of severe fighting and heavy losses came back along the lines." Lieutenant Favill recalled, "With few halts for rest to the music of the distant guns, we hurried over the dusty roads." As Caldwell's Division approached the field of battle, the men began to witness "white powder smoke of battle in great clouds far away to the northward and drift slowly along on the light breeze."[90]

The clatter of distant artillery and the rising smoke paid testament to the fact that they were heading into a heavy fight by late evening or early morning. Major Muholland mentioned, "It required no urging to keep the men up. The regiments moved solidly and rapidly, and not a straggler was to be seen." They quickened their pace forward. Along the way, the soldiers of the 148th Pennsylvania were ordered to move forward through the middle of a stream without removing their shoes. Colonel Cross, still carrying his vendetta against that regiment, overheard some of the men as they began to make "criticizing remarks." He sought the men that were speaking aloud. Looking about, he assumed the outlandish remark came from Cpl. George Duffy. Cross drew his sword and, according to D. W. Miller of the 148th, struck the corporal on the back of the neck with the flat of the sword. One of the bystanders disgustedly called out, "I'll bet if Colonel Beaver were here he would not dare do that." The bitterness between Cross and the Keystoners escalated as a result of the incident.[91]

Instead of heeding the order not to take his shoes off, Pvt. Lemuel Osman of Company C of the 148th Pennsylvania pulled them quickly off and tied them together just before dipping into the steam. "The current," he recollected, "was strong, every man was pressing forward for himself." As he continued to wade against the current, the laces of his shoes came untied and "away went my shoes. I was in a bad way but was compelled to march on without any covering my feet."[92]

About 4:30 in the afternoon, General Hancock arrived at Gettysburg. By then, the First and Eleventh Corps had been driven back through the town. Hancock met briefly with General Howard, explaining that Meade had sent him to take charge of the situation. Hancock asked Howard if he would like to see the written order that was given to him by General Meade. Howard replied, "No; I do not doubt your word… but you can give no orders here while I am here." Hancock agreed and said, "Very well… I will second any order you have to give." Howard conceded to this request and the two men conferred about the situation at hand. Before closing the conversation, Hancock remarked, "General Meade has also directed me to select a field on which to fight this battle." Hancock gazed at the heights of Culp's Hill and Big Round Top, and then continued, "But I think this the strongest position by nature upon which to fight a battle that I ever saw." Howard agreed, "I think this a very strong position, General Hancock, a very strong position." Hancock exclaimed, "Very well, sir, I select this as the battlefield." With that, Hancock swung his horse around and sent his findings to General Meade.[93]

By early evening, some of Caldwell's men were becoming footsore from the long march. Still not having much word from the front, they could only assume what they were to look forward to as General Reynolds' body passed through their ranks and was carried to the rear. Colonel George McFarland of the 151st Pennsylvania noted, "Many a tear fell at the sight of his stretcher."[94] Private George McIllhattan of the 148th Pennsylvania uttered, "Boys, if the rebels are killing the Generals they will not have much respect for us little fellows."[95]

About 9 p.m., the welcome orders came to halt and establish camp. Much to the men's delight, they formed a line of battle about two miles from the battlefield, thus alleviating any stress of a long march the next day. Josiah Favill recalled, "The moment the column halted the men dropped down on the road and most of them fell asleep immediately."[96]

Many other soldiers in the First Division did not have the luxury of resting. As soon as the men of the 61st New York were ordered to "stack arms," they were also ordered to establish breastworks. A soldier noted, "We went to a rail fence, took down the rails… spreading our blankets on the ground—we had staked up those rails and banked earth against them… they would have served quite a purpose as breastworks."[97]

Captain Henry V. Fuller and Pvt. George W. Whipple of Company F of the 64th New York, prewar friends from Little Valley, made arrangements to dine together that evening. When Whipple inquired as to the captain's preferences, Fuller "wished he could have some warm biscuit(s)." Whipple readily agreed. Fuller handed him a few bills to make the purchase and the private was off. Along the way, Whipple came across a house and witnessed "soldiers coming away loaded with good things." Whipple hurried over to the ladies that were dividing biscuits among the small group of soldiers assembled there. He arrived just in time to stuff his haversack full. When he offered to pay the women, they politely declined. The ladies, seeing the private's persistence, finally accepted his offer and gave him butter and a canteen full of milk in exchange for the cash.[98]

Captain Robert M. Foster of the 148th Pennsylvania bunked that night with Pvt. Lemuel Osman. While lying next to each other, Foster and Osman talked about the recent marches and the impending battle that surely would soon come. Finally, Osman's eyelids became too heavy to hold open any longer. He peered one last time at his friend, who was beginning an earnest prayer. Osman recalled after the war, "I can see him on his knees praying that God would be with him and the rest of us. I fell asleep, listening to his prayer."[99]

Sergeant Meyer of the 148th recalled, "We were now close up to the Confederate Army. We realized that we were upon the field of an impending great battle.

The battle had really already commenced… The boys became quiet and medita-
tive. We stacked arms, threw off knapsacks, accoutrements and coats… The sky
cleared and the moon shone brightly… The gray dawn of the coming day tinged
the eastern horizon, when we pronounced our work finished."[100]

Osman's and Foster's somber thoughts mirrored those of men throughout the
division. In the 140th Pennsylvania, two young soldiers from the same college,
town, and company spoke to one another. One of them asked, "Stewart, do you
think you will come out of this battle alive and someday get back to the old home
again?" "Well, Ben," his friend replied, "We're going into a great battle today.
Many must fall before it is ended. God only knows how it will be with us." After
a long silence, Ben spoke, "I've been thinking about this for some time and I have
a presentiment that I will see the end of this war and get back to old Canonsburg.
I would like to sing again in the choir of the old church on the hill and somehow
I feel that this desire of my heart will be realized." His friend acknowledged him.
Sadly, young Ben, like so many others from both armies converging on that small
Pennsylvania town, would "sleep his last sleep" in the fields of Gettysburg later
that day.[101]

CHAPTER 3

Saviors of the Wheatfield

"Brave boys are they,
Gone at their country's call;
And yet, and yet,
We cannot forget,
That many 'brave boys' must fall."[1]

AT THE SECOND CORPS' CAMP FOR THE NIGHT, just to the rear of Big Round Top, Major St. Clair Mulholland of the 116th Pennsylvania was awakened early on July 2 by Major John Hancock, the assistant adjutant general of Caldwell's First Division. He directed Mulholland to take nearly 400 men and "form a picket line beyond the Emmitsburg Road." Mulholland questioned him as to the exact position he wished his detachment to deploy, prompting Hancock to pull out a pencil and make a detailed sketch "on an old envelope by the light of a tallow candle."

Major Hancock's directions were vague, to say the least, which was understandable given the circumstances. However, before leaving, Hancock passed along the name of a local farmer that Mulholland could ask for assistance, if he needed to do so, for more accurate directions. About 1 a.m., a detachment passed to the south of Big Round Top, reached the Baltimore Pike, and came to the front door of the designated farmhouse. A soldier pounded forcefully on the door. Soon, the window slid open and the farmer appeared. However, he did not seem to welcome the Union squad. Instead, Mulholland found "considerable difficulty in getting him to answer (his) questions." The Irish-born major found no satisfaction in the knowledge he attained from the farmer, who seemed to doubt that the detachment was who they said they were. Frustrated, the old man slammed the window shut. A few minutes passed before Major Mulholland's patience wore thin. Finally, as a solution, Mulholland reported that he "had his door well battered with the butts of several muskets." Again, the farmer got out of his bed, put his head out of the second-story window, and began to attempt to justify his tardiness. At this time, Mulholland gave him "a short time, and a very short time indeed, to decide whether to come with me or be shot." With that ultimatum, the old farmer hurried down the stairs and led the men to their desired position. The detachment remained deployed for a short time after daybreak, when some of the Third Corps relieved them.[2]

Meanwhile, about 2:30 in the morning, the rest of the Second Corps soldiers were awakened from their slumber and ordered to fall in for "inspection arms," which "indicated very clearly what was ahead of us." according to D. W. Miller of the 148th Pennsylvania. After the inspection, the men were permitted to have breakfast. This was a welcome commodity because many of the men had been without such a pleasure since noon the previous day. Having been so tired the prior evening, they simply preferred rest over resolving their hunger.[3]

Captain Foster and Private Osman were also hastily preparing their meals. "Bring my haversack and we will see what I have." Forster demanded of Osman. Scrounging through it, the captain found some meat and bread. He then requested that the private fetch water to boil over a fire. With the new request, Osman was off. On his way back, he encountered a soldier who was coming from a nearby hospital bearing an extra pair of shoes. Remembering that he was without brogans because of the incident at the river, Osman asked for the extra pair. Much to his delight, the wounded soldier politely heeded his request. Now with fresh shoes, Osman made his way back to Foster to complete his breakfast.[4]

Soon, the men were ordered to fall in and advance the last three miles toward Gettysburg. Caldwell's Division was the lead element as the Second Corps headed to the battlefield. Shortly after beginning the march, Major Hale took his normal place alongside Colonel Cross. Hale had hoped that the colonel had forgotten about what he considered the nonsense premonition. That, however, was not the case. Shortly after the advance started, Cross turned on his saddle toward Hale and said "in a grave, firm, way, 'Attend to that box of mine at first opportunity." Hale remembered, "That was all, but it convinced me that he was in dead earnest and had firm conviction of impending fate."[5]

After advancing two of the three remaining miles, the column began to encounter fleeing citizens. Sergeant Meyer recalled, "Squads of frightened… men, women, and children, carrying bandboxes and packages of hastily gathered, valuables… were running by us to find places of safety to our rear." One of these "squads" was an elderly gentleman holding the hands of two small girls. "Good morning, father," Meyer said, greeting the older gentleman. The man responded in the negative. Meyer rephrased with "Fine morning." The gentleman then said, "Yes truly, but so full of terror and sorrow." Tears were streaming down his cheeks as he raised his hand toward the column of passing infantry and shouted, "God bless and spare you all!" and the small family continued to the rear. They had not gone too far when an artillery projectile exploded "with a frightful report over them." Meyer looked back, expecting the worse for the family, but instead found them retreating even faster "apparently all right."[6]

Soon, the soldiers were nearly upon the battlefield. They crossed into a small grove of open timber. There, doctors were posted in anticipation for the oncoming grim work. As Lieutenant Charles Fuller and his company passed by, he shook their hands. "We'll see you again later!" he called out. However, well after the war, he admitted, "I tried to say this with a jaunty air, but down in my shoes I did not feel a bit jaunty. I think we all felt that this should be a death grapple."[7]

By 7 a.m., the vanguard of the corps finally reached the fields of Gettysburg. Hancock formed his Second Corps on the left-center of the line. The Third Division was holding high ground near Ziegler's Grove, the Second was near an angle in a nearby stone wall, and Caldwell's First near the present-day Pennsylvania Monument, with the Third Corps beginning on their left and slight front. A calm stretched over the fields around Gettysburg. Lieutenant William Shallenberger later mentioned, "A most surprising quietness settled down upon the field and for hours you napped upon the grass, and otherwise enjoyed the summer day."[8]

By mid-morning, both armies had taken on a different shape as reinforcements were deploying at a consistent rate across the narrow valleys and plains. The First and the Eleventh Corps were already on the field, having been heavily engaged on the previous day. The Third and Twelfth corps had arrived before sundown on the 1st. The Sixth was at Westminster and the Fifth was drawing near the battlefield. The Army of the Potomac gradually began to take the general shape of a fish hook. Its right flank was bending around and toward Culp's Hill, where the First, Twelfth, and Eleventh Corps were deployed, and the left flank rested on Cemetery Ridge, a position held by the Third Corps.[9]

The men of the Second Corps were placed near the center of the line, where they overlooked almost a mile of open ground between them and the woods line on Seminary Ridge. Lieutenant Frederick of the 57th New York described his view: "There was a clear field in front, extending down a gradual descent to the bed of a stream called Plum Run, beyond which was the Emmisburg [sic] Road. Seminary Ridge, on which the Rebels had massed their forces, began to rise just beyond the road. Its crest was about a mile from and ran nearly parallel to Cemetery Ridge, along which the Union Army was posted. On our left-front was the Peach Orchard, in its rear the Wheatfield, and to the left-rear of these were woods and the two Round Tops."[10]

Colonel Cross, having just finished deploying his brigade on the field, noticed a few brigades of Union infantry to his front and left. He assumed that they had bivouacked there since the previous night. The colonel, eager for information, rode over in an attempt to find out the situation. Cross returned about twenty minutes later at a gallop. He halted his horse and said, "That is the Third Corps out there! The Second New Hampshire is over there beyond those buildings; the First Corps fought a tremendous battle away to the right yesterday, and were defeated; General Howard and his Eleventh Corps were again driven back." Major Hale noted that Cross's grave mood had completely disappeared as he was now "full of fire, showing the sharp impulsive manner that had always possessed him on former battlefields." Cross peered over the fields and knew that if a battle was to be fought today, it would be contested on those fields. He gathered his emotions together and stated, "Gentlemen: it looks as though the whole of Lee's rebel army is right here in Pennsylvania; there will be a great battle fought today."

Cross's speech, though patriotic, met with some skepticism within his ranks. Colonel Henry McKeen gazed at Cross "as though wondering how he had obtained that information." Cross dismounted from his horse, walked over to McKeen, and took him by the arm. The two officers walked away from the rest of the brigade, with both of their "heads bent in earnest conversation." They stopped a few yards away and grasped each other's hands for a moment, then turned and walked back toward the brigade. Cross peered over his men with admiration and pride as he exclaimed, "Gentlemen: Colonel McKeen will command the 148th Pennsylvania today; before night he will probably be commanding the brigade."[11]

Near Cross's Brigade, in the 116th Pennsylvania, Maj. St. Clair Mulholland remembered that the battlefield was in absolute silence and that "in a woods just back of our line the birds caroled and sang. Our horses quietly browsed in the rich grass, and the men lay in groups, peacefully enjoying a rest after the rapid march." Soon after the Second Corps reached its position, the Third Corps filed on their left and General Geary took his Twelfth Corps "White Star Division" to Culp's Hill. This series of movements left Caldwell's First Division on the left of the Second Corps.[12]

Thomas Livermore (*Library of Congress LC-DIG-Ppmsca-49722***)**

All was quiet, for now, with the exception of an artillery shot or an occasional sharp crack from a picket firing his rifle. Father William Corby wrote in his memoirs, "The two great contending forces watched each other keenly with beating hearts and anxious expectations of what result might follow the pending struggle. Generals are in a 'brown study', staff officers and orderlies are dashing along the lines from left to right and from right to left, carrying orders. On the flanks the cavalry and light artillery are on a sharp look-out, and all are astir." **LIEUTENANT THOMAS LIVERMORE** believed, "Our position was a fine one for defensive purposes."[13]

Having marched nearly fifty miles in the course of a week, many of the men of the division rested their heads on the ground. The hazy air was hot, the wind was still, and the smell of coffee and campfires loomed over the division. The soldiers chatted, slept, or prayed. The 148th Pennsylvania's Major R. H. Forster mused, "Whilst lying inactive in this position, I think every Pennsylvanian was inspired by the thought that he was on home soil, and that, with rare exceptions, each one nerved himself for the great struggle which he realized to be so near at hand, and in which he knew he would be called upon to bear a dangerous [sic] and it might be a fatal part." [14]

The time was nearly 9 a.m., and some of the men, thinking aloud, stated how odd it was for Hancock's Corps to be held in reserve. Not a moment went by when a nearby Irishman shouted in reply, "Yis, resarved it is, for the hard fightin'!" The men had to admire the Irishman's wit. Because of his heavy accent, he may have only been one generation out from his family having come to this country in search of peace and prosperity. Instead, he, like many other of the German and Irish immigrants, fought to preserve their adopted country.[15]

An hour later, Confederate skirmishers, spaced throughout the distant fields, began to take shots at some of Caldwell's men. Not long afterward, an artillery projectile was fired from a distant hostile battery that would "weigh mentally its course between mouthfuls." One unfortunate soldier had one of these artillery shell fragments find its mark when a piece of shrapnel went through the cartridge box of Pvt. George Osman of Company C, 148th Pennsylvania. Osman, who had been asleep at the time, let out a great cry when the fragment woke him. His screams shattered the calmness. Osman only lasted a few moments until he took his last breath, making him the first soldier from Caldwell's Division to be killed at Gettysburg.[16]

Largely ignoring George Osman's death, the veterans remained in their relaxed state. However, a much different situation was beginning to take place near the Second Corps' line. The commander of the Third Corps, **MAJ. GEN. DANIEL E. SICKLES**, attempted to gather as much intelligence as possible as to the enemy's whereabouts in his front. He was chilled to the bone as he glanced around at the high ground that could be easily afforded by the enemy, rendering it for a good platform to shell his entire line. About 7:30 in the morning, he sent orders to Col. Hiram Berdan, a famed marksman, to detach 100 men from companies D, E, F, and I of the 1st U. S. Sharpshooters to be sent forward "to discover, if possible, what the enemy was doing," according to Berdan's report. Brigadier General J. Hobart Ward, Berdan's brigade commander, also sent forward the 3rd Maine for support, while aligning the 4th Maine, 2nd U. S. Sharpshooters, and 99th Pennsylvania in reserve along the Emmitsburg Road.[17]

Daniel E. Sickles (*Library of Congress LC-DIG-stereo- 1802849*)

This unauthorized movement exposed the extreme left flank of the entire Federal army. Soon afterward, the 2nd U. S. Sharpshooters were recalled from their advanced position back to the main body of the Third Corps, where the marksmen deployed in a skirmish line near Little Round Top. The rest of Berdan's 1st U. S. Sharpshooters moved forward, anchoring their left flank near the Peach Orchard.[18]

Colonel Berdan realized that "it was impossible with this force to proceed far enough to discover what was being done by the enemy in the rear." This fact was reported to Maj. Gen. David Birney about 11 a.m., who ordered Berdan to send forward another detachment from the 1st U. S. Sharpshooters. The regiment's colonel, Casper Trepp, personally led the second detachment of 100 men in the same direction the initial detachment had traveled.[19]

The detachments linked up with one another and continued their march forward. As they advanced, they met a small boy. A soldier identified as simply "Comrade Buchanan" recalled, "As we approached these buildings a lad then living there, who had just returned from an errand to a neighbor's close by… remarked almost with a sneer… 'Look out! There are lots of rebels in there, in rows.'" The young man pointed toward Pitzer's Woods. The soldiers simply laughed off the warning and thought "that he knew nothing about war and was talking nonsense." Soon, however, the men received fire from three regiments of Brig. Gen. Cadmus M. Wilcox's Alabama brigade. The 8th, 10th, and 11th Alabama forced back the sharpshooter detachment despite the 3rd Maine coming forward to help Berdan's men.[20]

Meanwhile, Brig. Gen. Charles K. Graham arrived on the field with his Pennsylvanians of Sickles's First Brigade, First Division. His arrival, though welcome, put Sickles in a precarious position. Sickles knew that the enemy had been gathering in his front. He now also knew that with Graham off the Emmitsburg Road, the Third Corps' supply trains were "at the enemy's mercy," and there was still fighting along the high ground that seemed to encircle his position.

Sickles ordered a trusted staff officer, Capt. Henry E. Tremain, to ride to Meade's headquarters and "report the reconnaissance in progress, the arrival of General Graham, and the unoccupied road to the south; and… ask if there were any special orders about that road or the trains." Tremain dashed to Meade and reported his findings. The commanding general studied a map in silence for a few moments. Tremain later admitted that the general's brief pause was embarrassing. Finally, Tremain again requested what the general's orders were. Meade simply replied that he "would send cavalry to patrol it." With that, Tremain hastily rode back to Sickles to report his conversation.

Once he reached Sickles, Tremain relayed the message and exactly how the conversation took place. With the Third Corps being charged with holding the entire left flank, Sickles knew he must act on his own, if necessary. Not yet knowing that hostile enemy infantry was filing on Seminary Ridge (reflecting a similar maneuver Lee had done at Chancellorsville), Sickles had to make a decision whether to assume the aggressive or stay in his present questionable position. Quickly, he rode to the Emmitsburg Road to ascertain the situation there. Not much time passed before Berdan's detachment returned with its report of the fighting in Pitzer's Woods and how they "had been driven back at the point of contact." Tremain again rode to Meade's headquarters to discuss Sickles's findings.[21]

While his aide was off to report to the army commander, General Sickles began to advance his Third Corps under his own orders. The men of the Second Corps watched in astonishment as the line of battle emerged from the wood lot and neared the Emmitsburg Road. Major Muholland remembered this advance, "the boys dropped their cards, regardless of what was trump; and all gathered on the most favorable position to witness the opening of the ball."[22]

As they advanced forward, the entire Third Corps seemed to move as one. Alfred Hamilton recalled, "The sunlight reflected from thousands of highly polished bayonets and musket barrels. The 'broad stripes and bright stars' floated gayly in the breeze-altogether the scene was grand as the line of battle advanced."[23]

Indeed, the advance became a grand spectacle as the Third Corps began to halt near the Emmitsburg Road, near the home of Peter Sherfy and his famous peach orchard. Here, Sickles refused his line, bending it into an L shape. He formed this salient at the intersection of the Emmitsburg Road and the Wheatfield Road, with his line continuing onward toward a 25-acre field of wheat, later dubbed "The Wheatfield," and finally ending near Devil's Den. General Graham formed a line of battle along the Emmitsburg Road, in front of the Sherfy House. On his right flank was Third Corps, Second Division's commander, Brig. Gen. Andrew Humphreys, who continued to form his line up the Emmitsburg Road while placing his remaining brigade, under Brig. Gen. George Burling in support. Colonel William Brewster and Brig. Gen. Joseph Carr would be the two lead brigades designated to assail the anticipated Confederate line. French-born Col. Philippe R. de Trobriand soon deployed his regiments near the Wheatfield. To his left, running through Rose's Woods and across Houck's Ridge, was the brigade of Brigadier General John Hobart Ward.

This movement, however, was met with grave disapproval by **COMMANDING GENERAL GEORGE MEADE** as the enemy artillery began to fire a few shots at 3:30 p.m. Sometime after the advance, General Sickles was ordered to report to Meade's headquarters. Captain Tremain remembered, "The interview… between Sickles and Meade was brief. The artillery also had announced the commencement of the action. The Council of War had dispersed. General Meade met General Sickles in front of his quarters, and informed him he need not dismount; and that it was too late; that his presence was needed at his own front. General Meade said he would meet him there in a few minutes. We were off again in short order, because of the significance of the firing; and by the time we reached our starting point it was clear that the battle was thoroughly opened."

George G. Meade (*Library of Congress LC-DIG-cwpbh-01199*)

Sickles, unexpectedly in Meade's eyes and without orders, had moved his entire corps out of position. After Meade heard of the recent encounter with the Confederates in Pitzer's Woods, he decided to inspect the ground personally. Sickles watched as Meade and his staff approached. He rode over to them and graciously saluted "with a polite observation. Meade dutifully returned the salute, but began questioning Sickles's decision, declaring, "I am afraid you are too far out." The Third Corps commander replied, "I will withdraw if you wish, sir." Meade began to show his frustration and stated, "I think it is too late. The enemy will not allow you. If you need more artillery call on the reserve artillery." Meade added, "The Fifth Corps—and a division of Hancock's—will support you." It was too late. Lieutenant W. Shallenberger of the 140th Pennsylvania remembered, "Now, a shot is heard on our extreme right. Turning about we see the smoke rise and shot follows shot in quick succession. Battery after battery awakes out of sleep and succeed in hurling back the terrific onset of the enemy." and the entire line of Confederate artillery began to blaze away.[24]

Earlier in the afternoon, the Confederate divisions of Major Generals John Hood and Lafayette McLaws had formed on the right of General Wilcox soon after he confronted the Federal sharpshooters. The plan of attack was for Hood's Division to attack up the Emmitsburg Road, with his left connected with McLaws' right flank. McLaws was to have his left flank resting on the Emmitsburg Road and attack straight up toward the Federal center in a massive attempt to roll up the Federal left flank, just as they had done with great success at Chancellorsville back in May. Earlier in the day, Lee asked Longstreet for his opinion of utilizing Hood's men in directing him on the far right of the division. Longstreet replied, "I have great faith in General Hood's opinions and his ability to do whatever he plans to do."[25]

With the advancement of the Third Corps and several companies of Federal skirmishers deploying forward, circumstances now changed as the Union line extended much farther than what General Lee had initially realized. Therefore, the attack was thwarted, and locations such as Little Round Top, Big Round Top, and a portion of the Wheatfield, were all now in the equation in the minds of his men. According to one source, General Hood reported back to Lee and Longstreet about a plan of moving around to the right of the Federal Army and possibly taking them from the rear. Lee stopped, deep in thought for some time, and rose his head again after hearing the opinions of his lieutenants. "Gentlemen, I cannot risk the loss of a brigade. Our men are in fine spirits, and with great confidences will go into this battle. I believe we can win upon a direct attack." Lee extended his hand toward Longstreet and said "Good-by, General, and may God bless you!" He then proceeded to Hood and said, "God bless you! General Hood, drive them away from you, take Round Top, and the day is ours." With tears in his eyes, he turned "mounted the iron gray, and rode away."[26]

The men of Hancock's Second Corps watched as the Third Corps initially advanced to the Emmitsburg Road without any enemy fire being directed their way. However, the situation drastically changed. Standing all along Cemetery, someone from the 116th Pennsylvania cried out from Cemetery Ridge, "There!" as the unknown soldiers pointed directly across the field at puffs of smoke being emitted by the Confederate field artillery. Private Stewart of the 140th Pennsylvania recalled, "the dark masses of woodland beyond the Emmitsburg road were lit up with flashes of flame from the brazen throats of the guns." As the reports from the artillery blast began to ring in their ears, Major Mulholland recalled, "Another and another until the whole face of the forest is enveloped, and the dread(ed) sound of artillery comes loud and quick, shells are seen bursting in all directions along the lines. The bright colors of the regiments are conspicuous marks, and the shells burst around them in great numbers."[27]

Lee Plans His Attack

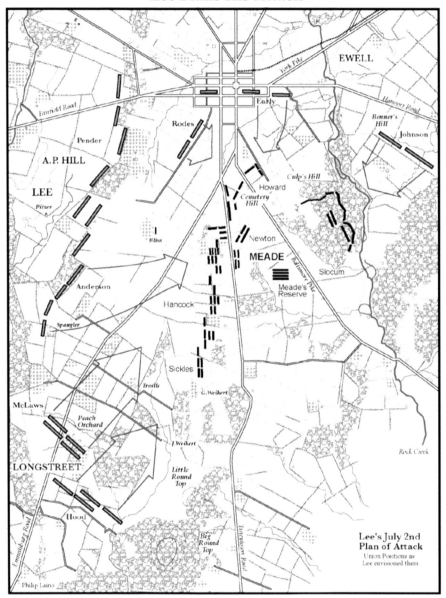

General Lee 's original attack plan on July 2.

About 4 p.m., one of Caldwell's staff officers rode along the lines as the artillery began to rain its deadly iron from the sky. At one point, he exclaimed, "Now, look out, we'll get into that, too!" Soon, the Confederate infantry began to advance on locations like Little Round Top, Devil's Den, and Rose Woods. Watching as the artillery barrage began, Colonel Cross stood on Cemetery Ridge. His heart was full when he addressed his men lying in wait for something to "turn up." "Boys," Cross exclaimed, "you know what's before you. Give 'em hell!"[28]

As Confederate artillery continued to slam into Sickles's exposed Federal line at the Peach Orchard, General Hancock witnessed the scene as he rode up to General Caldwell, Major Mulholland, Colonel Kelly, and Colonel Byrnes. Striding over, he rested one knee and leaned on his sword. He smiled and said of the Third Corps, "Wait a moment, you will soon see them tumbling back."[29]

Colonel Cross, meanwhile, could barely listen. He had been pacing in his usual manner as the time for a battle drew nearer, until a long line of worn grass created a path that could be easily discerned. With his hands clasped behind his back, he halted his nervous walk. According to Major Hale, "He drew out from an inside pocket a large new black silk handkerchief; arranging it in folds on his lifted knee, then handing me his hat to hold, he quickly swathed his head with it in turban fashion, tying the two ends behind… Again, he took off his hat, saying 'please tie it tighter Mr. Hale'; my hands were trembling as I picked at the knot; 'draw it tighter still' he said impatiently, and finally I adjusted it to suit him."

The manner which Cross tied the handkerchief around his head was not an uncommon occurrence. In prior engagements, the handkerchief was typically a red color. In the heat of battle, it made it easier to locate the commander when smoke filled the fields and woods. Another use was to shield the colonel's balding head from the sun's rays. At Gettysburg, instead of his usual bright red bandana, he displayed his premonition with the symbolism of the color black for his headpiece.

Soon after Hale tied the black bandana on Cross's head, General Hancock rode up. "Colonel Cross this day will bring you a star," Hale remembered Hancock stating to Cross "in his measured suave manner but the Colonel gravely shook his head and replied, 'No General, this is my last battle.'" The colonel's utterance was calm but with clear implications, given his recent premonitions. Hancock rode on and the attention, again, turned in the direction of the Peach Orchard.[30]

Meanwhile, the fighting had commenced on the southern part of the battlefield as General Longstreet sent forward the Confederate right flank division of John Bell Hood. Almost immediately, the action toward Devil's Den and Little Round Top began to become quite lively. General Hood sustained a serious wound from an artillery round near the Michael Bushman farm, resulting in his arm requiring amputation. His loss left Brig. Gen. Evander M. Law to command the already-engaged troops.

As the brigades of Law and Robertson pressed on, they began to take heavy artillery fire and skirmish fire from their front. This fire, along with the lay of the land, forced the troops to split. Part of Law's Brigade filed off to the right, and part of Robertson's filed off to the left. Thus, both brigades were divided in half. Attacking toward Devil's Den was the 1st Texas and 3rd Arkansas of Robertson's Brigade. General Law directed them "into the mouth of the beast," as Capt. James

Smith's 4th New York Artillery hurled deadly missiles into the oncoming troops. After pushing back the 99th Pennsylvania's skirmish line, placed directly in their front, the 3rd Arkansas attacked through Rose's Woods at the position held by the rest of Ward's Third Corps line. The 1st Texas eventually breeched the stone walls and rested near the base of the slope leading up toward the crest of Houck's Ridge. The "Orange Blossoms" of the 124th New York, held in infantry support of Smith's Battery, charged down the slope toward the 1st Texas. The result was catastrophic as they lost their commander, Col. Augustus Van Horne Ellis, and their major, James Cromwell, both killed in action.[31]

This attack was repulsed with the support of Benning's Georgia infantry coming up from their position on Seminary Ridge and breaking the line of the 124th. The Georgians fired into the New York men as they gradually attempted to regain the hill. Soon, the attack ranged across a broader spectrum, making their occupation of the crest of Devil's Den precarious and forcing them to leave.[32]

Earlier, in the Rose Woods, while the beginning of the fight for the den was taking place, the 3rd Arkansas attacked the 17th Maine, 99th Pennsylvania, 20th Indiana, and 86th New York. To say that it was a mismatch was an understatement. The veterans of the 3rd Arkansas rushed up the rocky, wooded slope at least twice, and both times were repulsed. The 99th Pennsylvania was moved from the right flank of Ward's line in support of the 124th New York on the crest of Houck's Ridge, thus weakening the line. Afterwards, the 3rd fell back to a rock ledge and spreading out its flanks to extend its battle line. Soon, the 15th Georgia joined in the attack and, in unison with the 3rd Arkansas and later the 1st Texas, began to drive the Federal regiments.[33]

As Confederate troops on the base of the rocky ledge were making a good fight, a fresh Rebel troops were readying themselves for an advance across the fields toward the Rose Woods. Brigadier General George "Tige" Anderson's brigade consisted of the 7th, 8th, 9th, 11th, and 59th Georgia.

Before being ordered forward, Captain George Hillyer of the 9th Georgia heard a patriotic comrade exhorting the men: "'Now boys, we are going to have a great battle and a great victory today. Suppose that by divine revelation, it was made known in a manner that we all believed it, that if one of us would walk across that valley and up to those batteries and be blown to atoms by one of those cannon, and thus sacrificing one life instead of many, the victory would be ours. Is there one of us that could do that?' I was just beginning to examine my own mind, and to wonder whether I would be equal to the task, but before the hasty thought found expression, Bliss rose up, and with his eye beaming pointed his finger to the enemy's guns and said: 'Yes if I could do that, I would walk straight across the valley and put my breast to one of the cannon and myself pull the lanyard.'"

Before being sent forward, Anderson's Georgians heard the Rebel yell emitting from their right and realized that Benning's Brigade had begun its advance, within moments, "Tige" Anderson ordered his boys forward. Like Robertson and Law, almost immediately Anderson's men began to take heavy fire from the enemy batteries. Captain Hillyer recalled that the line was held "which none but veterans could preserve under the fire we encountered as we passed through an open wheat field and across the intervening space to the enemy's position."[34]

In the general advance, Lt. Col. John C. Mounger led the 9th Georgia toward the enemy. Days before the battle, he had written a letter resigning from the Confederate army. It had not been accepted. Now, he led his men across "a full half mile of wheat fields, ready for the harvest, enclosed with stone fences intervene between our line and the rocky rampart where the enemy's bayonets glistened and cannons send forth their screaming, hustling and bursting shells," as a member to the regiment later recalled.

With such an artillery display, it was of little wonder that it wreaked havoc in Anderson's ranks. Mounger continued leading his men forward with "no sign of wavering." Then, within 300 yards of the enemy, "Lt. Col. Mounger fell, pierced by two grape shot, in front of the 9th." As he lay dying, he called out "boys, they've killed me now" and expired in the arms of his son, Thomas. Some accounts suggest that the fatal round was fired by Winslow's Battery positioned in the Wheatfield.[35]

Anderson's Brigade advanced into the Rose Woods and struck the main line of Colonel de Trobriand's Brigade in the Wheatfield. After descending down a "declivity" toward Rose Run, the Georgians then assaulted Hobart Ward's line in the Rose Woods. On the left of Anderson's line, the 9th Georgia began to blaze away at the 8th New Jersey and 5th Michigan, while the 8th Georgia confronted the 110th and 115th Pennsylvania of Col. P. Regis de Trobriand and Colonel George Burling.

It was in this phase of the battle that Lt. Alexander Tennille informed Captain Hillyer that he was now the highest-ranking remaining officer in the 9th Georgia and should take command. Before leaving, Tennille added that General Anderson's orders were for Hillyer to "change the front of the three left companies so as to face the enemy on our flank." Anderson's idea for this order was so that the part of the 9th Georgia, along with the entire 8th, could attack against the vulnerable 8th New Jersey and 115th Pennsylvania where a gap existed on the 115th's left between the 17th Maine. Hillyer promptly ordered, "Attention three left companies!" The men had no reaction despite Hillyer yelling it at the top of his voice "so great, at the moment, was the roar of musketry and artillery," as he recalled. Hillyer touched each man on the back and indicated the intended movement by the use of his hands.[36]

Meanwhile, the 8th New Jersey's position was precarious from the start. To the front, one member noted, was "a thick brush, big timber and rising ground, beyond which was a ravine with a hill on the other side. A few fence rails that were lying about were quickly seized upon and made to form a slight protection before the coming storm of battle should strike them." With the order given, the 8th Georgia and few companies of the 9th pushed hard into the two Federal regiments until they finally broke and retired across the field. As the 8th New Jersey fell back, "their colors became entangled in a tree. The remnant of brave fellows rallied around them with cheers and re-formed to meet the advancing foe." Finally, once the soldiers had recovered their colors, they retired off the field, while the 115th Pennsylvania moving to a ridge near Winslow's Battery and reforming their line there.[37]

Holding the far left of the brigade, the 17th Maine was formed along a low stone wall on the southern end of the Wheatfield. The Maine boys had been fighting hard with the 3rd Arkansas, 15th Georgia, and now the 11th Georgia, holding their own all the while. The collapse of the Union troops on their right flank put the 17th Maine

Preparing for Battle

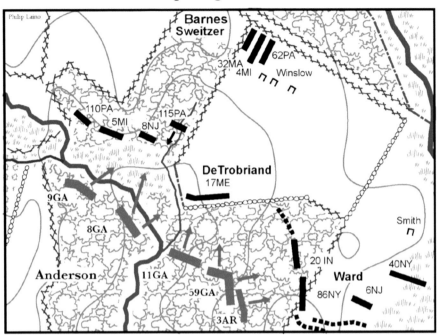

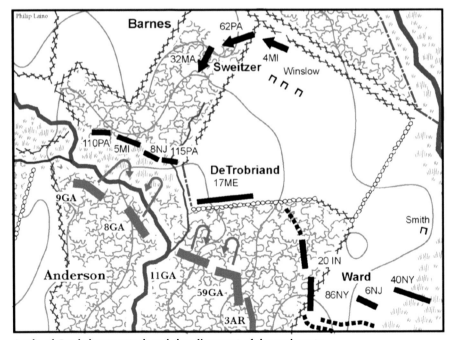

Angle of Confederate attack and the alignment of the regiments.

in a vulnerable position. Company B's Daniel Gookin recalled in his journal, "The Regts on the right of us had no protection but such as a rail fence afforded, in consequence of which they did not stand crowding so well as we did, and when the Rebs pressed them closely they gave way and left us exposed to a galling flank fire."[38]

Lieutenant Colonel Charles B. Merrill soon rectified the situation. Seeing that the enemy regiments were exposed as they crossed the open field to his right, he decided to refuse his right flank and pour a volley into the unsuspecting attackers. A 19th-century historian wrote, "At the salient angle was company B, with H, K, and C at the right; at the left of B was G the color company... All received a raking fire, particularly G, B, and H, but all remained steadfast, and routed the enemy, some of whom were taken prisoners, their color-bearer, who had advanced nearly to our line, narrowly escaping capture." These movements effectively stalled Anderson's attack. The two Georgia regiments had to fall back into Rose's Woods, where they reformed their line to the far end. As one Maine soldier recalled, "The fight had continued over an hour; many had fallen, but success inspired confidence." After being driven back, Anderson's Brigade reformed near the western end of what today is called the Triangular Field.[39]

Meanwhile, Kershaw's Brigade was finally advancing across the field. The Federal artillery at this distance, nearly 400 yards, rained effective fire down upon the South Carolinians. General Kershaw immediately noticed that neither Barksdale nor Wofford attacked in unison with his formation. Instead, he was left in the open with no support on his left flank. To rectify this, Kershaw sent the 8th, 3rd Battalion, and the 2nd South Carolina directly at the present-day Wheatfield Road to cover the gap. The three regiments sent were already under a terrific fire from the time of their advance. Now, they shifted toward the very guns which plagued their line. "We were at once," Lt. Alexander McNeil of the 2nd South Carolina recalled, "exposed (us) to a terrible fire from the artillery and we had proceeded but a short way before our men began to fall." Yet, Kershaw's men kept advancing toward their objective. The veteran general recalled, "I well remember the clatter of the grape against walls and houses as we passed [the Rose buildings]."[40]

As Kershaw's left flank continued to advance, several Federal batteries (Bigelow's 9th Massachusetts, Phillips's 5th Massachusetts, Clark's New Jersey Battery, Thompson's Pennsylvania Battery, Hart's 15th New York, and Ames' artillery) opened with canister. Massive holes began to form in the Rebel lines. Private John Coxe of the 2nd South Carolina remembered, "Just as our left struck the depression in the ground every Federal cannon let fly at us with grape. O the awful deathly surging sounds of those little black balls as they flew by us, through us, between our legs, and over us! Many, of course, were struck down, including Captain (Robert) Pulliam, who was instantly killed. Then the order was given to double quick, and we were mad and fully determined to take and silence those batteries at once. We had gotten onto level land of the Federal guns when the next fusillade of grape met us... We were now so close to the Federal gunners that they seemed bewildered."[102] With each shot, dust kicked up into a large cloud. McNeil lamented, "Our brave boys were mowed down by the score." [42]

The Wheatfield is Attacked

The advancement of Generals Kershaw and Semmes into the areas of Rose Woods, Wheatfield, and the Peach Orchard.

"We were, in ten minutes or less time, terribly butchered," Lt. Col. Frank Gaillard of the 2nd South Carolina recalled. "A body of infantry to our left opened on us, and as a volley of grape would strike our line, I saw half a dozen at a time knocked up and flung to the ground like trifles. In about that short space of time we had about half of our men killed or wounded. It was the most shocking battle I have ever witnessed. There were familiar forms and faces with parts of their heads shot away, legs shattered, arms torn off, etc."[43]

On the right flank of Kershaw's beleaguered line, the men of the 15th South Carolina had been marching at a leisurely pace as they crossed the field toward their foe. At the head of the regiment was Col. William D. De Saussure. George Anderson desperately sought support for another attack to follow the one that had just failed. He spotted the 15th South Carolina crossing the meadows, having been separated since the time of Biesecker's Woods, and requested their support. The request was accepted and the attack was ready to reform.[44]

Meanwhile, the Federal line was also being reinforced with the brigades of Col. William S. Tilton, 18th and 22nd Massachusetts, 1st Michigan, and 118th Pennsylvania, and Col. Jacob B. Sweitzer, 9th and 32nd Massachusetts, 4th Michigan, and 62nd Pennsylvania. The 9th Massachusetts being held in the area of Highland Springs Ave. and Hanover Road being in support. Both brigades belonged to Brig. Gen. James Barnes' First Division of Maj. Gen. George Sykes' Fifth Corps. After they filed into line of battle on the crest of Stony Hill, in the rear of de Trobriand's line, they deployed a line of skirmishers and faced toward the area of the Peach Orchard.[45]

The men noticed a change in intensity of artillery fire as the left of Kershaw's Brigade closed. Private John L. Smith of the 118th Pennsylvania recalled, "The increased activity of the guns, their loud and deafening roar, loud cries for canister, indicated, though his lines were still unseen by the infantry, that the artillery had discovered the enemy and were determined to inflict prompt and damaging punishment." Soon, the artillery began to slacken and the 118th's skirmishers returned to the main body after having been driven back. Not long afterward, according to Smith, "Across the unguarded space a column of the enemy appeared through the smoke, moving with shout, shriek, curse and yell, about to envelop the entire exposed and unprotected right flank of the regiment. They were moving obliquely, loading and firing with deliberation as they advanced, begrimed and dirty-looking fellows, in all sorts of garb, some without hats, others without coats, none apparently in the real dress or uniform of a soldier."[46]

Captain Francis A. Donaldson of the 118th Pennsylvania recalled that as Kershaw's Brigade approached the Federal line, a terrified rabbit appeared near the oncoming Confederates and raced for the rear. One of the Rebels cheered it on: "Go it, old fellow; and I would be glad to go with you, if I had not a reputation to sustain!"[47]

In the 3rd South Carolina, Color-Sergeant William P. Lamb proudly bore his regiment's flag in the face of the enemy. With four color guards already casualties, someone in the regiment called out, "Lower the colors; down with the flag," believing that Lamb's display was drawing enemy fire. Lamb simply quickened his pace and moved to the front of the regiment "where all could see" and exclaimed in loud, clear tones, "This flag never goes down until I am down."[48]

Meanwhile, Tilton's and Sweitzer's Union brigades began to pour hot lead at the 3rd and 7th South Carolina. Men soon lay strewn across the fields. John Parker of the 22nd Massachusetts recalled, "The still air hardly stirred the heavy clouds of smoke. The green leaves and twigs fell from overhead in a constant shower, clipped by the singing bullets. Indistinct masses of men across the run, with here and there the cross-barred Confederate battle-flag, were now visible. With the strong, resolute desire to check the living torrent, came a slight tendency to doubt one's self when the death-dealing missiles came so closely by without touching some part of the body, and an occasional flash of sadness as the pain-stamped face of some dying man was presented to view, when carried hurriedly to the rear... We were not there long."[49]

Kershaw's men, despite horrific casualties, continued to come forward. Private Smith of the 118th Pennsylvania recalled in a letter to his mother that the Rebels "advanced out and were formed in line of battle in the shape of a bent pin and finally the rebs came down the hill in front of us in droves and we opened fire on them very lively. I loaded and fired fifteen times. They were so thick that you could shut your eyes and fire and could hit them, and they jumped behind every tree and stump for cover and halted at the edge of the woods."[50]

While Kershaw's right flank pounded away at Tilton's and Sweitzer's brigades on the Stony Hill, his left flank continued with the attack across the Rose Farm and toward the Sherfy Peach Orchard. Casualties were high but the survivors continued onward, forded a small run, and began to ascend a small knoll toward the Yankee artillery. Directly in front of the 8th South Carolina and the 3rd Battalion were the infantrymen of the 3rd Maine. They were quickly swept aside and reformed behind the 2nd New Hampshire, which had been formed at the weakest point, the cornerstone of the salient of Sickles's angle and the 141st Pennsylvania. The 2nd New Hampshire had been ordered forward to support Thompson's and Hart's batteries.[51]

The determined looks on the oncoming Confederates' faces were more than the nervous artillerists could bear and some of them began to limber their guns. Yet, other batteries continued to fire with grave, decided, effect on their advancing foes. Sergeant William T. Shumate of the 2nd South Carolina recalled, "My face was fanned time and again by the deadly missiles."

Finally, Kershaw's left flank was now within the eighty-yard mark and began to see rest of the artillerists limbering up and flee from their guns. Soon, however, a command was heard "in a clear, ringing tone, above the din of conflict the command, 'By the right flank!" remembered one soldier. Each of Kershaw's regiments on the left began to face toward Sweitzer's Brigade and a gap that had just been created by the movement of the 62nd Pennsylvania and 4th Michigan, having been ordered to move from facing front (toward the Peach Orchard) to facing by the left flank (toward the southern end of the Wheatfield), where their help was most desperately needed.

As the Rebels made their movement toward the right, the Federal artillerists began to return to their guns. They soon delivered a devastating flanking fire down Kershaw's lines. The gray and butternut dead and wounded lay strewn across the ground. Very near to the 2ⁿᵈ South Carolina's Sergeant Shumate, the regimental adjutant was struck by a ball from a grape shot round in his foot. Shumate rushed toward his fallen comrade to see what could be done for him. The wounded soldier said, "Please cut off my boot." The sergeant removed the top of the fallen soldier's boot. With a "swift, eager look at the battery," the adjutant turned his back to the Federal gunners and "made the best time on record, until he reached a place of safety." Shumate recalled, "I can see him running now, with one foot naked, bleeding, and mangled, and the other encased in a long cavalry boot." After this deadly enfilading fire, much of Kershaw's left flank fell back to the area of the Rose buildings and awaited further orders.[52]

The attack continued on the southern end of the Wheatfield as Anderson's Georgians again pressed forward over the same ground where they had previously advanced. By this time, Brig. Gen. J. Hobart Ward's Union brigade had been pushed off Houck's Ridge. The 59ᵗʰ Georgia joined in the attack along with the 15ᵗʰ South Carolina, moving toward De Trobriand's, Sweitzer's, and Tilton's brigades. After a few minutes of fighting, General Barnes finally issued orders for his men to retire from the Stony Hill area. The decision to pull back proved to be heavily unpopular among his troops. When Tilton's aide, Lt. Col. James Gwyn, delivered the orders to the 118ᵗʰ Pennsylvania, the ranks took up the shout, "No retreat! No retreat! We're on our own soil!" Upon hearing this, Colonel Tilton proclaimed to Gwyn, "You see, sir; my men want to fight here." Though impressive, the reluctance failed to persuade Barnes and, soon, Major Charles P. Herring reluctantly shouted, "Change front to the rear," and the retreat was on.[53]

Colonel Sweitzer also received Barnes' order to fall back "and to take up a new position a short distance in his rear." Sweitzer was not fond of the order but dutifully instructed Col. George L. Prescott of the 32ⁿᵈ Massachusetts to fall back. Prescott stubbornly replied, "I don't want to retire; I am not ready to retire; I can hold this place." With Tilton's Brigade rapidly falling back, however, Prescott had little choice and he too fell back toward Trostle's Woods. After taking his new position, Sweitzer faced the Wheatfield directly, with Tilton facing toward the Third Corps line in the Peach Orchard.[54]

After Sweitzer and Tilton evacuated Stony Hill, Kershaw's men took up positions along the hill's wooded front. Many of them used the opportunity to test their sniping skills at the Federal batteries that continued to shell their position, particularly the 9ᵗʰ Massachusetts Battery under Capt. John Bigelow, while De Trobriand's Brigade also fell back to avoid being cut off from the Federal main body. His men also displayed the same negative reaction when the order was given to retire. Eventually, however, the 110ᵗʰ Pennsylvania and 5ᵗʰ Michigan fell back with Winslow's Battery, which was also beginning to limber. The 17th Maine remained in their advanced position only a short time until they were ordered back. Lieutenant Colonel William Luffman, who took over after General Anderson was wounded in the leg, saw the retrograde movement of their Federal counterparts. He ordered his Georgians to line up along the stone wall that the 17th Maine had just left. Luffman arranged his line from left to right: the 9th, 8th, 11th, and 59th Georgia. The 3rd Arkansas, 1st Texas, and 15th Georgia aligned on his right flank, thus extending his line nearly to the point of another stone wall on the eastern end of the Wheatfield.[55]

With much of the Union artillery having withdrawn from the field, the Federal infantry was left to confront the Confederate infantry coming from multiple directions. In their retreat, the 17th Maine halted near present-day Wheatfield Lane as Anderson's Brigade moved up and over the wall on the southern end of the Wheatfield, and also the west of it. About this time, Maj. Gen. David Birney, the commander of the First Division of the Third Corps, rode up and observed the 17th Maine's predicament. Having spent much of their ammunition, the Maine boys had no sooner replenished it when Birney called upon them to charge the Confederate position to protect Winslow's retreating artillery battery. Birney placed himself at the head of the regiment and "with a cheer and a rush it moved down into the Wheatfield." Anderson's Brigade again disappeared over the stone wall and awaited the Yankees.

The Maine men moved halfway through the field of trampled grain and haled on top of the crest of a small hill (near where Winslow's monument stands today). It was now about 6 p.m. and General Sickles, near his headquarters at the Trostle Farm, had just taken a wound that shattered his leg. That left General Birney in command of the Third Corps, a fact he learned just after he led the 17th Maine forward. As he rode off from the Mainers, Birney took measures to halt the Georgians who were advancing on them. Wisely, he ordered the 5th Michigan to the right flank of the 17th to extend its line to meet the attack. The fighting grew severe as the two almost isolated regiments began to slug it out with nearly two brigades of Confederates. The historian of the 17th Maine recalled that "the raking musketry fire of the enemy at short range, both from the stone-wall in front and the wood nearer and to the right, was making sad inroads upon the attenuated ranks… as there was no protection of any sort; occasionally the enemy would form a line and emerge from the woods as for a charge, but the firmness and confidence displayed… apparently disheartened him."[56]

With the Confederates beginning to bear down on the two regiments stranded in the Wheatfield and another full enemy brigade (under Brig. Gen. Paul Semmes) on its way, David Birney desperately sought additional help. That aid would soon come in the form of the First Brigade, First Division, Second Corps under Brig. Gen. John C. Caldwell.

Caldwell Moves

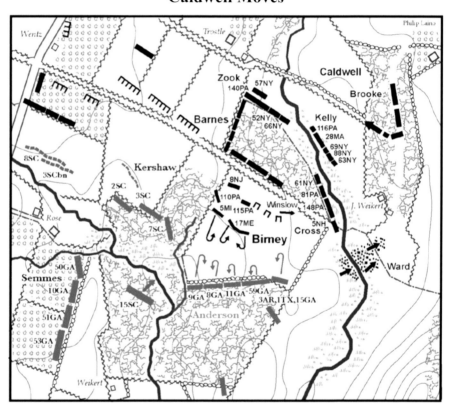

With Sweitzer and Tilton's regiments moving off Stoney Hill, Kershaw now takes possession and Anderson extends his flanks to cover more area. Anderson moves to attack the remaining elements of Barnes' men but is repulsed. General Caldwell's men are now moving in to position to overtake the field.

CALDWELL'S DIVISION ENTERS THE FRAY

Earlier, about 5 p.m. on the crest of Cemetery Hill, the soldiers of Caldwell's Division watched as the smoke from the battle emanated from Little Round Top, Devil's Den, and the surrounding areas. They knew that at any moment, they likely would be called upon to support the withdrawal of the Third Corps. First Lieutenant W. S. Shallenberger, 140th Pennsylvania, recollected that gun smoke rose "in dense clouds from Little Round Top. The rattle of musketry, the crash of grape and canister through the dense woodland tell the story of the conflict."[57]

As anticipated, soon a staff officer rode up to General Hancock and requested a division to report to General Sykes for support. Hancock glanced at Caldwell and announced, "Caldwell, you get your division ready." Within a moment, Caldwell ordered his men to "fall in," and, in grand unison, they began to form into a march column. On the far left of the division, Colonel Cross gave the command to his staff, "Mount, gentlemen." As he swung into his saddle, Major Hale recalled that "the ten hours of weary waiting [were] now forgotten."[58]

Father William Corby later mentioned that most of the men in the Irish Brigade had not practiced their religious duties for nearly three weeks, "being constantly on the march." He quickly sought an opportunity to address the troops while the "brigade stood in column of regiments, closed in mass." He mounted a large boulder as the men began to gather around. He began to address the troops: "My dear Christian Friends! In consideration of the want of time for each one to confess his sins in due order as required for the reception of the Sacrament of Penance, I will give you general absolution. But my dear friends while we stand here & in the presence of Eternity—so to speak with a well-armed force in front & with missiles of death—in the forms of shells bursting over our heads we must humble ourselves before the great Creator of all men & acknowledge… and conceive a heartfelt sorrow for the sins by which we have ungratefully offended the Divine Author of all good things. Him who we ought to love we have despised by sinning against his Laws—Him whom we should have honored by lives of virtue we have dishonored by sin."[59]

Father Corby remained on his rock as the men continued to file around the act of sanction. Major St. Clair Mulholland later wrote that Corby was "urging them to do their duty, and reminding them of the high and sacred nature of their trust as soldiers and the noble object for which they fought, ending by saying that the Catholic church refuses Christian burial to the soldier who turns his back upon the foe or deserts his flag." The brigade remained standing. Holding on tightly to every word the dear chaplain had spoken at "order arms." Corby ended his prelude by saying, "Rend your hearts & not your garments & I the consecrated minister of God will give you general absolution." With that, all fell on their knees, removed their hats, and extended their hands toward the chaplain, as Corby pronounced, *"Dominus noster Jesu Christus vos absolvat, et ego, auctoritate ipsius, vos absolva ab vinculo excommunicationis et interdicti in quantum possum et vos indigetis. Deinde, ego te absolvo vos a peccatris vestris in nomine Patris, et Filius, et Spiritus Sanctus. Amen!* (May our Lord Jesus Christ absolve you; and by His authority I absolve you from every bond of excommunication and interdict, so far as my power allows and your needs require. Thereupon, I absolve you from your sins in the name of the Father, and of the Son, and of the Holy Spirit. Amen!).[60]

As the men lifted their bowed heads, they noticed General Hancock standing near and that they were "surrounded by a brilliant array of officers, who had gathered to witness." The event must have been awe-inspiring. An officer recalled that he did not believe that "there was a man in the brigade who did not offer up a heartfelt prayer... What was wanting in the eloquence of the good priest to move them to repentance was supplied the incidents of the fight. That heart would be incorrigible indeed, that the scream of a Whitworth bolt, added to Father Corby's touching appeal, would not move to contrition."[61]

Caldwell's Division rapidly began to move by the left flank, toward the general area of the George Weikert farm. They filed off with Cross's Brigade leading, followed by Kelly's Irish Brigade, Zook's Brigade, and finally Brooke's Brigade bringing up the rear. The exact route they took has been disputed over the years; the men either marched on the Weikert farm lane or they marched past the George Weikert house and toward the Wheatfield via the Valley of Death and the John Weikert farm.[62]

CROSS'S BRIGADE ADVANCES TO THE WHEATFIELD

Earlier in the day, the 5th New Hampshire had been detached from the brigade. This left the 61st New York as the rear regiment until they reached the Wheatfield. Nearly three-quarters of a mile from their starting position, Cross's soldiers maintained their composure despite the rocky terrain through which they clambered. Major Hale remembered, "How well Cross rode; I can see him yet; tall in the saddle, straight as an arrow, lithe like an Indian, with a head on his shoulders and everything in the range of vision."[63]

Once Cross's Brigade approached the Wheatfield, the men halted briefly near a crossroad and formed their lines. Two aides approached Colonel Cross with orders telling of the disposition of the Fifth Corps and countermanding the previous order. They were now "to advance to the south side of the Wheatfield, drive the enemy back, and if possible establish the original line on the crest." In addition, they were to sweep the Confederates from the Wheatfield. One of the aides, who had been riding a young horse which plunged at every passing artillery round, shouted, "The enemy is breaking in directly on your right: Strike him quick!" just as the skittish horse ducked again. Cross wheeled his stallion about and spurred it along the line, shouting, "By the right flank! March!" This order caused instantaneous confusion amongst the ranks. Hale recalled, "for it brought the line of battle facing by the rear rank, with the file-closers pushing and crowding through, but in less than ten seconds the line was clear of the timber, and crossing the road, was advancing us steadily into the Wheatfield as though on parade."[64]

The brigade was deployed from right to left, facing from the rear as follows, the 61st New York (Lt. Col. K. O. Broady) 104 men, 81st Pennsylvania (Col. Henry B. McKeen) 175 men, 148th Pennsylvania (Col. Henry B. McKeen) 392 men, and the 5th New Hampshire (Lt. Col. Charles Hapgood) 179 men.[65]

For the moment, the 17th Maine was still in the middle of the Wheatfield attempting to hold the Confederate lines of Anderson and Kershaw back until reinforcements arrived. With Cross now entering the fray, Kelly making an appearance, and Zook beginning to take possession of Stony Hill, they were finally able to leave.[66]

Anderson's Confederate line extended nearly the entire length of the southern stone wall of the Wheatfield. With the fighting going well, they again advanced into the field just as Cross's Brigade came through a woodlot and into the area. The Federal motion was realized splendidly by General Kershaw, who refused the right flank of the 7th South Carolina to meet the threat presented by Cross's Brigade. He then rushed to the rear to call up the reinforcements of the 15th Georgia and the rest of his brigade and Semmes' Brigade. With Semmes still a few hundred yards to his rear, Kershaw ordered his brigade forward to the edge of the Rose wood line by a nearby grove.[67]

Meanwhile, a member of the 148th recalled his first contact of the enemy that day, "In front of us was a stone fence, behind which the enemy were gathered thick. Their guns were raised on the fence; the barrels of them glittered like a looking glass." Lt. William P. Wilson, one of Cross's aides, recalled, "The enemy in the meantime, elated with their success, and having reformed their line along the stone wall on the south end of the woods on either side, quietly awaited the attack."[68]

At this moment, no firing was taking place within the boundary of George Rose's wheat field. In the 61st New York, Lt. Charles Fuller remembered keeping his eyes to the front after being deployed and beginning the advance. Soon, two soldiers came toward Cross's line "on a run" and threw themselves over the stone wall in their front. Fuller recalled, "but a brief time passed when a solid line of men in gray appeared."[69]

Anderson deployed skirmishers who now began their deadly work on Cross's advancing brigade. Major Hale remembered, "As we emerged from the woods into the open ground, the bullets from the enemy's skirmishers came buzzing around like bees and we could see the puffs of smoke from their rifles in every direction, showing that we were about to encounter a heavy force." While Lieutenant William Wilson remembered that, "every rock, tree and bush concealed a sharpshooter and the moment the heads of Cross's line appear above the crest of the hill the edge of the wood along his entire front and right flank is fringed with a blaze of musketry" Yet, Cross's men continued to advance without firing a shot, with one exception. Private William C. Meyer, while advancing with the 148th Pennsylvania, took a shot at a frightened rabbit "which scurried along our front; he thought of the impoverished condition of his haversack and could not allow

Caldwell Storms the Wheatfield

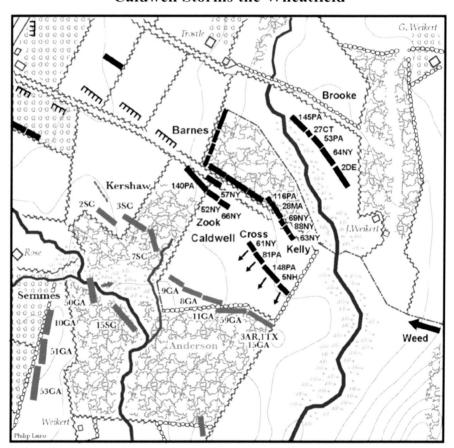

Anderson's skirmishers become rattled and begin to withdraw off the field as Cross moves
forward. Kelly is coming up behind him and is to link with Cross's right while Zook
moves to take Stoney Hill and support Sickles. Brooke is awaiting to attack near the John
Weikert farm.

this opportunity to replenish it pass by unimproved, though rebel bullets whizzed around his head," recalled a Private of the regiment.[70]

Cross's Brigade drove into the Wheatfield with such speed that nearly thirty of the enemy skirmishers had been swallowed whole by the rushing tide. Many of them, having been passed over by Cross's men, jumped up in the rear of the brigade and attempted to pass through Cross's line and back to their respective commands. Major Hale said that Colonel Cross shouted to him, "Get a file of men for a guard and hold them Mr. Hale. Look sharp, there's more in the edge of the woods by the wall; there's an officer; get his sword." Within a moment, Hale ran at the officer as fast as his legs would carry him. The Confederate officer, who had halted and faced Hale, laid the blade of his sword on the ground under his foot and "broke it short at the guard, and scornfully flung the hilt on the ground before me," Hale recalled. Fearing a hostile outcome, Colonel McKeen, who had been watching the situation unfold, ordered a sergeant and two privates from his command to assist him. Hale recalled, "We soon had twenty 'Johnnies' corralled back of a little sassafras thicket growing around an outcropping ledge."[71]

PRIVATE HENRY MEYER of Company A, 148th Pennsylvania, also had a brush with the skirmishers as he crossed the fence and rushed into the Wheatfield. "I remember having put a double portion of powder in the gun barrel the first load," he recalled, "and as I got on the other side of the fence, I took aim at one of the rebels not over two rods away, expecting to shoot him clean through the body and also hit with the same ball his comrade on the other side of him. But just as I was pressing the trigger, the Johnnies waved their handkerchiefs in token of surrender, and I desisted with some regret."[72]

Henry Meyer (*Personal Collection of Barbra Abbott*)

Many of the men tripped over the bodies of the 17th Maine while they were advancing. A general halt soon occurred while the 5th New Hampshire and the seven left companies of the 148th rested on the south end of the Wheatfield's woodlot, and the right three companies of the 148th and 81st Pennsylvania, along with the 61st New York, remained in the open field of grain. Then, without orders, Cross's Brigade opened upon their adversaries. Henry Meyer recalled, "I noticed how the ears of wheat flew in the air all over the field as they were cut off by the enemy's bullets." The commander of the 148th during the first portion of the battle, Col. Henry McKeen, proudly attested that the brigade's initial push as they "drove the enemy back to the far end of the wheat-field, a distance of over 400 yards. So quickly was this done that prisoners were taken by the brigade before the enemy had time to spring from their hiding places to retreat."[73]

"They are falling back boys!" exclaimed the frantic Captain R. M. Foster of the 148th; "Forward!" Though Cross's Brigade had been in the field for a very short time, being out in the open played an obviously significant downfall on the part of his brigade. Men were dropping by the scores from the well-entrenched Confederate troops even though Cross's boys had been dealing a heavy fire in response. Hale recalled, "Wounded men were staggering back to the rear, and the dead were getting thick along the ground." Lieutenant Colonel K. O. Broady of the 61st New York recalled that "the wounds received by my men seemed to be of an unusually severe character, and it is to be feared that the greater portion of the wounded will never be fit for active service again." Major R. H. Forster of the 148th Pennsylvania later reported that the "battle was desperate and sanguinary, the enemy endeavoring with might and persistency to drive us back, while the brigade held fast with marvelous valor and unyielding tenacity."[74]

It took but a short amount of time for a typical battlefield during the Civil War to become totally consumed in the sulfuric smoke emanating due to the high contrast of the rounds buzzing through the air. At the Wheatfield, on this day, the circumstances were no different. Men could scarcely see their commanders and barely make out what they were ordering. The black powder of the day also produced a thick soot on the inside of the barrel on their rifles. As the heat of the battle grew, in combination with this soot deposit, it became increasingly harder for a soldier to load and fire his rifle with effect. Such a case happened in the Wheatfield. According to Pvt. Lemuel Osman of the 148th Pennsylvania, "The barrel of my gun had got hot and dry and I couldn't force a ball down." Captain Robert M. Foster, of the same regiment, was in back of Osman who told him "to throw it down and hunt another." Osman obeyed the captain's orders, located one from company I, and went back to report to Foster. Upon his return, he found that the captain had been struck dead and "the blood was running down his cheek." Osman picked up the cap from his dead friend and gently laid it on his head. Ser-

61st New York Company K (*Library of Congress LC-DIG-cwpb-04045***)**

geant John Benner, a member of the color guard, retrieved the captain's sword and belt and carried them off the field.[75]

Colonel Cross looked about and realized the deteriorating circumstances. Stepping hastily back toward Major Hale and the few men around him, Cross uttered, "Boys: instruct the commanders to be ready to charge when the order is given; wait here for the command, or, if you hear the bugles of the Fifth New Hampshire on the left, move forward on the run." Hale watched as his black-bandana commander "strode alone into the woods where the right-wing of the 148th Pennsylvania and the Fifth New Hampshire, to judge by the sound were tearing things all to pieces. Standing by my prisoners, I looked after him sort of regretfully as he vanished among the trees." The last glimpse that Hale had of the colonel as he walked into the woods would haunt him for the rest of his life.[76]

Cross calmly walked into the bordering woodlot toward the commander of the 5th New Hampshire, Lt. Col. Charles Hapgood. He soon reached his former regiment and told the men to begin preparing to charge. From their position, they could barely see what was taking place in their front. Though they could see an occasional Confederate skipping from rock to tree, not much was known of the enemy's location or position. Thomas Livermore recalled, "In front of my regiment and on its left were many rocks, some of them very large, and the enemy were concealed behind."[77]

Edward Cross's Wounding Rock (*Personal Collection of James Smith II*)

Having already repelled "all advances" made by the enemy, Hapgood's regiment and the left of the 148th continued slugging it out with the 3rd Arkansas and 15th Georgia, along with the left flank of the 1st Texas and 59th Georgia (on the right), which only compounded the Cross's desire to charge. With bullets hissing and zipping around Hapgood and Cross, the duo briefly discussed the situation. Toward their front was a large egg-shaped boulder and, just before Cross could order the charge, Hapgood saw "a flash of a piece from that rock and the colonel fell." The round punctured Cross's naval and entered his bowls, nearly penetrating his spine. The mortally-wounded colonel dropped his pistol and slumped to the ground. Hapgood quickly glanced at the large rock that he witnessed the "flash" emit

Charles Phelps (*National Park Service, Gettysburg National Military Park*)

from and ordered **Sgt. Charles Phelps** of Company I to avenge the wounding of their brigade commander.[78]

The sergeant immediately took it upon himself to seek out the Rebel and kill him. Private Meyer also witnessed the wounding of the colonel, "I looked back and saw Colonel Cross… following down the slope, waving his sword…a moment later, he received another shot which proved fatal."[79]

Lemuel Osman had returned to his rightful place within the ranks of the 148th Pennsylvania after Captain Foster's death. No sooner had he found his place when he leveled his rifle at a nearby rebel. He felt the tension on the trigger, no doubt looking to avenge the death of his fallen friend. He prepared to fire when the Rebel surrendered. Instead of giving into temptation, Osman accepted the Confederate's gesture and sent him to the rear. The prisoner had not made it but a few paces "to the rear and," recalled Osman, "coming to the 81st Pennsylvania, drew a big revolver from his belt and shot a Sergeant through the body." Osman, infuriated as the treachery of the Southerner, turned and "struck him over the head with my gun and knocked him down," he related. An officer from the 81st, who witnessed the act, rushed to the scene and struck the fallen Rebel with his sword.[80]

By now, it was between 6 and 6:30 p.m. On the left flank of Cross's brigade, there was "no flinching or dodging," Lieutenant Fuller noted. This flank was positioned in the open ground of the Wheatfield and the men were continually subjected to the fire of the 11th, 8th, and 9th Georgia with help from the 7th South Carolina, firing from the woods on Stony Hill. While most of the men performed their duty, a second lieutenant, who Fuller did not name, was doubled over in fear. Captain Willard Keech went over to the frightened lieutenant and exclaimed, "Stand up! What are you crouching for?" The officer replied, "I'm not crouching." Keech did not accept this excuse and insisted, "Yes, you are!" The burly captain hit the lieutenant across his back, making "a sharp rap that made him grunt," in Fuller's words, and roared, "Stand up like a man!"[81]

Earlier in the day, before becoming engaged, Lieutenant Fuller informed his comrades "that when some one of them was knocked out I was going to take his musket and get into the firing line." Now, in the Wheatfield, Fuller had his chance. As the 61st continued to push forward, he recalled, "The Rebs had their slight protection, but we were in the open without a thing better than a wheat straw to catch a Minnie bullet that weighted an ounce. Of course, our men began to tumble. They lay where they fell, or if able, started for the rear. Near to me I saw a man named Daily go down, shot through the neck. I made a movement to get his gun, but at that moment I was struck in the shoulder. It did not hurt and the blow simply caused me to step back. I found that I could not work my arm, but supposed that hurt was a flesh wound that had temporarily paralyzed it, and that it was not serious enough to justify my leaving the fighting line… Sometime after this, I felt a blow on the left leg, and it gave way, so that I knew the bone was broken."

Fuller staggered to his feet and began to hobble to the rear until his foot became caught up in the tangled grain and he fell down at "full length." While lying helplessly in the field between the two lines "and hearing those vicious bullets singing over my head, I suffered from fear... waiting for other bullets to plow into my body," he recalled.

A life-long friend, Lt. Isaac Plumb, had watched Fuller fall. Plumb shouted in his direction, "Uncle Fuller, that's good for sixty days." He turned with a chuckle but was soon himself struck and fell to the ground. He was stricken with pain and "supposed a bullet had gone through him, and that he was done for." Plumb quickly threw his hands over the spot and held on tightly "with the thought that conscious existence might be a little prolonged," as his friend Fuller later related. Plumb fully expected to feel his life's blood ebbing from a gaping wound but, instead, found that he remained conscious. After a while, he cautiously lifted his hands in the expectation "to see an eruption of blood" but found none. He slowly moved about on the earth awaiting the shock of pain from being wounded but again, none came. He rose and resumed his place in the ranks. Plumb did not realize what had happened to him until that night when he "unbuckled his sword belt and discovered a strange formation in his vest pocket. In it he had a bunch of small keys on a ring. A Minnie bullet had struck his belt plate square and had glanced upward. Lodging itself under the plate into his vest pocket, where it met the bunch of keys." Upon further examination, he found that "there was enough force and resistance to bed the bullet into the ring and the key heads, and there the keys stood out held in place by the embedded bullet."[82]

Men continued to fall all along the Wheatfield and nearby woodlots. The once lush grain was now trampled and blood-soaked. The worst was yet to come. "Here," Private Meyer recalled, "the battle opened with great energy."[83]

Toward the center of the line, in the 81st Pennsylvania, Sgt. James "Reddy" McHale stood in line alongside his comrades. He was described as "fearless and audacious, freckled-face, pug-nosed country boy from nobody knows where." Still, "Reddy" proved himself trustworthy in the face of the enemy and he was given the honor of bearing the regimental colors. A seaman before the war, the 20-year-old had carried the banner in every conflict to this point, despite having been "deprived of the flag in time of parade because of his personal appearance, his soiled clothing, always burned round the heels of his trousers, his uncombed, uncut, shaggy red hair." At Fredericksburg, McHale not only successfully brought the flag of the 81st off the field of battle, he also rescued another regiment's colors that had been lying beneath several wounded men. Now, in Rose's Wheatfield, "Reddy" charged forward with his wooden flagstaff in his hands. His grasp tightened around it as the men of the regiment looked to him for guidance. When not fifteen yards from where the monument of the 81st Pennsylvania now stands, "he undertook to charge that stone wall alone and fell shot through the heart." McHale was mourned by the surviving officers and men.[84] Also falling about this time was Pvt. Frederick Gillhausen. The family man from Dauphin County, Pennsylvania, would linger 15 days until dying of his wounds. He is buried in the Soldiers National Cemetery.

Several other flagbearers in the brigade also fell in the savage engagement. The color sergeant of the 148th Pennsylvania was struck in the battle line. Private Lemuel Osman picked up the flag and waved it with all his might. He jumped across Plum Run and rushed forward but soon found himself within the stone wall concealing the Rebels. Halting, he stuck the flagstaff in the ground. He noticed that the enemy soldiers were busy reforming their lines. He handed the colors to John Benner, picked up a musket, and prepared to defend his position.

As Anderson's and Benning's Georgians prepared to charge, Osman believed that the Federals by now "were too weak to withstand it." He brushed aside his fears and continued to maintain a good fire, along with the rest of his regiment. During one of his loading cycles, he had just put a fresh percussion cap on his rifle when artillery round exploded above his head. The concussion knocked the young soldier to the ground. When Osman regained consciousness, he realized that the shell had "knocked the barrel off my gun," he recalled, "and I had nothing in my hands but the bare stock." Nearby, David Krebs was wounded. He handed his musket to Osman so he could continue the fight.[85]

Three-and-a-half regiments from Cross's Brigade were still on the firing line. The men began to huddle together under withering enemy fire on their front and flank. Some of the soldiers took the liberty to advance a few paces in front of their respective regiments, where they lay down to snipe at the concealed Confederates. A private from the 148th Pennsylvania recalled, "Thick smoke soon covered the scene, but lying on the ground, we had a better view than standing." Soon, the men in the rear ranks began to crouch to the earth to avoid the onslaught of Confederate lead. Meyer recalled that the rear rank "fired so close to our heads that the powder burned our faces. I watched the rebels as they moved from tree to tree, and shot at several with steady aim; whether any were hit, I could not tell."

"One of the men in the rear rank," Meyer later recounted, "had been sitting prostrate on the ground and firing his weapon as fast as he could possible in a forty-five-degree angle." Meyer asked the man, "Why do you shoot in the air?" The soldier matter-of-factly replied, "To scare 'em."[86]

ZOOK'S BRIGADE JOINS THE FIGHT

Shortly after 5:30 p.m., on Cross's right, Zook's Brigade was beginning its assault near Stony Hill. Earlier, during the Third Corps thrashing in the Peach Orchard and along the Emmitsburg Road, Maj. Gen. David Birney had called "loudly" for

Wheatfield 1900 (*Library of Congress LC-DIG-det-4911035*)

reinforcements for his embattled division. Staff officer Henry Tremain hastened to General Hancock to inform him "if Caldwell's division had not started, request it be sent at once, and that I should guide it directly to General Birney." Tremain would never make it to Hancock because Caldwell's Division was already well on its way toward the battle taking place in the Wheatfield.

Tremain soon encountered a column of advancing infantry, Zook's Brigade, the third brigade in the column marching forward. Tremain was stunned to find that the brigade he had just encountered was actually moving away from where Sickles most needed help, along the Emmitsburg Road. He immediately rode over and asked someone to whose command they belonged. Tremain was informed that they were from Caldwell's Division. He sat on his horse for a moment and pondered, "Why need I waste time to see Hancock?" He quickly glanced about attempting to locate the commanding officer. Seeing none in sight, he asked a nearby soldier "who his brigade commander was." The prompt response was "General Zook." "Where is he?" Tremain continued to question. "At the head of the brigade," the soldier matter-of-factly replied. Tremain thanked the soldier and rode to the front of the line.

There, Tremain encountered a small group of mounted officers. "Is this General Zook?" Tremain inquired. "Yes, sir." The response alleviated much of the distress that Tremain must have been feeling at that moment. He recalled, "The man was a perfect stranger to me and I realized that I might be mistaken for a demoralized straggler." To combat this suspicion, Tremain inquired as to where Zook's division commander had been located, while explaining his great urgency, "which indeed might have been clear to every soldier in the column," he recollected.

Tremain continued to glance over the scene before him. He surmised that if he rode on to the front of the division to locate General Caldwell, the rest of the division might bypass the position where they were needed. Tremain asked Zook, if circumstances dictated, if "he would not immediately detach his troops from the column and move into action." Zook replied with his accustomed politeness that "his orders were to follow the column." Again, Tremain repeated the question, this time with the added notion of "promising to protect him and to return to him as soon as possible with a formal order from the proper officer."[87]

Tremain's request was heartfelt and sincere. Both he and Zook could hear the fighting taking place toward the area of the Third Corps position and knew that, under the circumstances, the line could break at any moment from the continual Confederate pressure. "Sir," Zook replied in a calm, firm, manner, "if you will give me the order of General Sickles I will obey it." Tremain made the most of his opportunity and replied, "General Sickles's order, general, is that you file your brigade to the right and move into action here," and pointed to the area of Stony Hill.

Without a moment to spare, Zook wheeled his horse and gave the command, "File right." Later in his life, Henry Tremain opined, "Few men would have acted as Zook did. Yet, had he acted otherwise, it might have changed the fate of the day... What a splendid genuine soldier was this same Zook leading as he did his superb command straight into the jaws of mortal combat."[88]

Zook deployed his men into a battle line before they could sweep the area of the Stony Hill. From right to left, his regiments were the 140th Pennsylvania (Col. Richard P. Roberts) 515 men, 52nd New York (Lt. Col. Charles G. Freudenberg) 134 men, 66th New York (Col. Orlando H. Morris) 147 men, and in support was the 57th New York (Lt. Col. Alford B. Chapman) 175 men.[89]

Here, Colonel Roberts of the 140th Pennsylvania hastily addressed his troops, "Men of the 140th! Recollect that you are now defending your own soil and are fighting to drive the invader from your own homes and firesides. I shall therefore expect you to conduct yourselves as if in the presence of your wives, your sisters, and your sweethearts, and not disgrace the flag you bear or the name of Pennsylvanians." After the colonel finished, his men heartily cheered and began to advance.[90]

Soon, they encountered Third Corps soldiers beginning to fall back individually and in small groups. It was evident that a heavy fight was occurring to their front. Zook's infantrymen began to quicken their pace toward the front and the booming guns. They soon entered the Trostle farm. Here, the brigade came under sporadic fire from enemy batteries posted along Seminary Ridge. A few casualties occurred, but soon the brigade was on the edge of the Wheatfield-Stony Hill area. Zook briefly halted his brigade and ordered the men to load their weapons. Each soldier packed down their first round as tightly as they could seat and waited. The nervous sweat on their brows felt ice cold in the warm summer sun. Even with the brigade's experience in past fights, nerves still played on their minds. They were now in the North, fighting for their homes.[91]

In the 140th Pennsylvania, Lt. William Shallenberger gazed at his watch, noted that it was about six p.m., and readied himself for the order to resume the advance. That order came in a short time, and soon they reached the prone line of Sweitzer's Brigade. As Zook's brigade passed over them, "The boys picked their way gingerly," Shallenberger recalled. One of Sweitzer's men called out, "Don't mind us; step anywhere; step on us." Major Thomas B. Rodgers of the 140th Pennsylvania believed that "they enjoyed seeing us get between them and the enemy."[92]

Zook's Brigade began to approach the Wheatfield. Lieutenant Josiah Favill, Zook's aide, recalled, "The ground (here) was rocky, strewn with immense boulders, and sparsely covered with timber." The men attempted to maintain their line of battle as they crossed over these obstacles but, as they were attempting to reform their lines, Kershaw's South Carolinians began a withering fire. "The tumult became deafening," Favill remembered, "the mountain side echoed back the musketry, so that no word of command could be heard, and little could be seen but long lines of flame, smoke and struggling masses of men." William Shallenberger recalled in a letter to his brother, "The Brigade moved on to the music of the storm ahead, which, apart from the discharge of firearms, sounded like a hail storm among the leaves and branches." Still, the men maintained their oblique movement toward the enemy, attempting to drive them off of the smoke-covered hill. They eventually were in position directly in Kershaw's front as they "then rushed at a double quick boldly forward into the mouth of hell, into the jaws of death."[93]

As the rest of Zook's regiments filed into the wooded area, the Confederates unleashed their first volley at the 140th Pennsylvania. According to Pvt. Robert Stewart, "The balls rattled and crashed among the limbs of the trees behind and above us." This was not for long, however, because soon the enemy balls began finding their marks. Zook's Brigade had held their fire until this point. Now, they halted and were ordered to "load and fire at will." An officer in the 140th remembered, "Every instinct of self-preservation as well as of patriotic impulse nerved the men of that blazing line to obey it."

Forming a battle line on Stony Hill, the 140th Pennsylvania deployed in the wood lot, while the 52nd, 66th, and the left flank of the 57th New York were left exposed in the Wheatfield for a short time. Kershaw's 2nd, 3rd, and 7th South Carolina engaged the Keystoners on the low wooded, rocky hill.

By now, Zook's soldiers could hear increased activity directly in their front as the Irish Brigade became engaged. They soon began to advance in an effort to drive Kershaw off the field. Private Stewart of the 140th Pennsylvania recalled that while pushing forward, "Over and around the rocks and through a dense pall of smoke and stifling heat, until we saw a blaze of light in front, revealing the dark forms of a double line of men who were actively engaging the enemy." It was then that the brigade realized that it had veered too far to the left and their line now overlapped the Irishmen who had been coming up on their left in support.

Zook desperately sought to rectify this by a "right flank movement." This cleared the front of the exposed regiments and carried them to the open edge of woods. "With ringing cheers," remembered Stewart, "we gained this position and immediately came into close quarters with the enemy." Many of Kershaw's Confederates ducked behind cover and only exposed themselves as they fired ill-aimed rounds at Zook's and Kelly's Federals.[94]

Major Peter Nelson of the 66th New York marched with his regiment directly toward the Wheatfield. "Very soon we were under fire of musketry," he recalled. "Nothing daunted, we pressed steadily forward through wheat fields, woods, over rail fences 10 feet high, stone walls, ditches, deep ravines, rocks, and all sorts of obstructions, every one of which had served as cover for the enemy, and from which a murderous fire was poured upon us as we advanced, but without avail, as nothing could stop the impetuosity of our men." The men of the 66th rushed toward the enemy "their cry being constantly, 'Forward! Charge!'" With a rush, the men slammed into elements of Kershaw's Brigade on Stony Hill.[95]

For now, Zook's men knew they had to stick it out and hold off the enemy as long as possible. The 140th Pennsylvania's Private Stewart remembered, "In our front, and but a few rods away, there was an almost continuous blaze of light, behind which we could dimly discern the forms of the men who confronted us."[96] The fighting grew rapidly in their front. First Lieutenant Shallenberger of the 140th recalled it as being, "Terrible beyond words to picture the tempestuous rattle of the musketry as it sweeps over our heads in the heavy timber and plows through our ranks."[97]

While this melee was occurring, General Zook remained in the rear of the brigade's line with a mounted orderly and Lt. Charles H. H. Broom of his staff. By now, "the firing became terrific and the slaughter frightful," Lieutenant Favill remembered. "We were enveloped in smoke and fire, not only in front, but on the left, and even at times on our right apparently from men posted on the mountain sides. Our men fired promiscuously, steadily pressing forward, but the fighting

was so mixed, and rebel and union lines so close together, and in some places intermingled, that a clear idea of what was going on was not readily obtainable."[98]

Having sent the last of his regiments into battle, Samuel Zook urged his horse to jump a stone wall leading into the woods. Not long afterward, an enemy round glanced off of a nearby boulder and struck the general in his stomach before lodging in his spine. The stricken Zook glanced up at Lieutenant Favill, who was approaching him, and said "with an expression I shall never forget… 'It's all up with me, Favill.'" Zook was borne to the rear shortly thereafter, and Lt. Col. Charles Freudenberg temporarily took command of the brigade.[99]

Zook wounding site (*Personal Collection of James Smith II*)

The Irish Push Forward

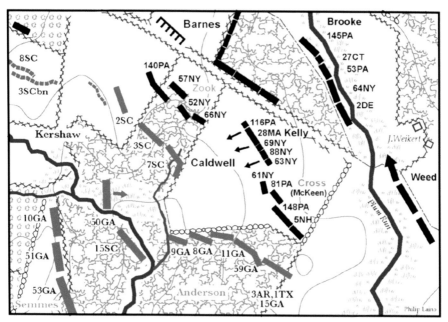

Cross and Zook are now fully committed to the fight and engaged. Kershaw begins to swing around and pull more of his men towards the Stoney Hill area. Kelly reaches Cross's right flank and begins to push towards Stoney Hill.

Freudenberg ordered the men to "cease firing" and then "forward, march!" to drive the enemy. He took position near the 52nd New York, which had moved to the center of the brigade line, and personally led the advance forward. After taking a few steps toward Kershaw's Confederates, he was "immediately disabled by three shots and carried off the field." For a brief period, the brigade was leaderless.[100]

The severe enemy fire began to decimate the brigade's ranks. In the 57th New York, Lt. Gilbert Frederick later reported, "As we pushed forward... man after man fell in his tracks, some instantly killed, others wounded." Lieutenant James J. Purman of the 140th Pennsylvania remembered, "The fight grew terribly fierce and bloody, we received a fire in both front and flank. Engaging the enemy here in close quarters, our ranks were soon thinned by their superior numbers and flanking fire."[101]

During this flanking fire, **Capt. David Acheson**, the loving family man from the 140th Pennsylvania, remained in position, urging his men to hold their ground. He had last seen Colonel Roberts in front of Company C preparing to charge the enemy. He prepared to do the same. His first lieutenant and personal friend, Isaac

George Laughlin, Alexander Sweeney, and David Acheson (*Photo courtesy of Washington and Jefferson College*)

Vance, was struck soon afterwards. Acheson turned just in time to see his comrade fall. Tears began to stream from his face.

Moments later, a Confederate round struck Captain Acheson in the chest. He fell in a heap. The pain showed on his face. Quickly, a squad of soldiers came to his aid and began carrying him to the rear. His life's blood was ebbing from the wound. Just a few rods toward the rear, a second bullet passed through Acheson's head. Either wound could have been considered mortal, according to most accounts. The hospital detail, realizing it was hopeless, gently laid down the stricken officer and retired to the rear. He lasted but a short time before he expired. Acheson's body would lie on the field for several days until he buried near the home of John T. Weikert.

Isaac Sharp, a veteran that served under the late captain, described him in the *Washington Observer* after the war: "He was truly a born leader. Many a captain in the service envied his power which he exercised to the complete control of his men. Though but a mere boy as regards years, and having youthful features in most respects, there was that something about him which shone from his eyes that left no doubt as to his ability as a commander and leader, Gray haired and grizzled enlisted men in the ranks were proud of him as their company leader. Nothing in the nature of praise can be said of Capt. Acheson's memory that would not be merited. He was a thorough soldier and a perfect gentleman at all times."[102] Acheson's initials D. A. were later inscribed on a boulder in the rear of the Weikert home.

A few moments before Captain Acheson's demise, **COLONEL ROBERTS** of the 140th had been leading his regiment on a right-wheel movement to clear his front and carry the right of his regiment out into the open edge of the woods. Before the battle, he had noted to one of his men that "he would be killed on that field and turning to his aide, asked him to send his horse home." Sergeant Ben Powelson of Company K, 140th Pennsylvania, noted that the sky "was growing dark. The air was hot and heavy with smoke and alive with death or his angels' screaming shells and hissing bullets… Here and there all along the line men were dropping and limping to the rear." When Colonel Roberts, flushed with victory, drew his prized sword that the citizens of Beaver County had given him upon his promotion. His name, engraved on it, shined in the sunlight of the clear day, and the sword flashed as he waved it forward. "Steady men," Roberts cried, "Fire low. Remember you are Pennsylvanians." An aide soon came forward and inquired of any orders. Roberts responded, "I have not seen General Zook nor one of his aides. I have no orders."[103]

Richard Roberts (*Personal Collection of Charles Joyce*)

He defiantly stood and shouted, "My brave boys, remember that you are upon your native soil. Your own Pennsylvania. Drive back the Rebel Invaders!" In front of Company K, he soon became a casualty of the Wheatfield conflict when a Confederate round ripped into the colonel's breast, killing him. "Loving hands carry him back a short distance and the fight goes on," remembered Lieutenant Shallenberger. He later commented that Colonel Roberts had earlier told him that "he did not feel at all well, and he felt almost sure he would not escape in the approaching battle." Roberts' premonition had come true.[104]

Near the left of Zook's line, Lieutenants Favill and Broom steadfastly sought to remove their fallen commander. Broom notified Favill that he would turn his responsibilities over to Captain Morris of the 66th New York and would soon be back to join him and Zook as soon as possible. With Zook, Freudenberg, and Roberts all down, Favill notified Lt. Col. John Frazer of the 140th Pennsylvania of Zook's condition and directed him to assume command of the brigade. He then began to accompany Zook from the field. Frazer begged Favill to stay, but Favill recalled, "I was personal aide-de-camp of Zook, and my duty was to him, and therefore I declined." The brigade would be without Lieutenant Favill for the rest of the duration of the conflict.[105]

In the front, not far from the 140th's colors, **SGT. THOMAS C. HAYES** of Company K suffered a dreadful wound and soon passed away. Nearby, in the same company, Thomas J. Carter also fell dead. The two would be buried together after the battle subsided. Powelson remembered, "I deeply felt the loss of "Clif" Hayes, my blanket mate, warm-hearted, noble spirited, ever faithful."[106]

Thomas C. Hays grave (*Personal Collection of James Smith II*)

In the 57th New York, youthful Pvt. Jacob Cole entered the fight with his comrades of Company A. An enemy round passed through his right arm. Cole, not realizing he was wounded, turned to a nearby soldier and inquired as to why he had struck him. His friend replied, "I did not hit you, but you have been shot and you had better go to the rear." Cole laughed and replied that he "was not hurt bad enough to do so." Soon after, a shell exploded directly in his front and shattered his right leg while killing two men standing near him. The concussion rendered him unconscious for a few moments. "The feeling was the same as though I had been struck on the elbow," Cole recounted, "A feeling of numbness came into the arm."[107]

Despite the pressure from Zook's and Kelly's Federals, Kershaw's three regiments stubbornly held their ground. On his left, the 2nd South Carolina advanced forward some fifty yards to confront the flank of the 140th Pennsylvania, while the 3rd South Carolina moved by its right to secure the middle portion of the wooded area on the Stony Hill. The 7th South Carolina continued its stubborn fight on the right of the brigade against the 52nd and 66th New York. Lieutenant Colonel Gaillard of the 2nd noted that the situation on the Confederate side was not an improvement over Zook's when he said that "the enemy's infantry came up and we stood within thirty steps of each other. They loaded and fire deliberately. I never saw more stubbornness. It was so desperate I took two shots with my pistol at men scarcely thirty steps from me." Gaillard noted that after taking two shots with his pistol, so great was the smoke from the battle that he could not readily see if his rounds did any damage to the enemy. However, when the smoke cleared, "there were some seven or eight dead lying just about where I was shooting."[108]

Confusion began to reign among the men of Zook's Brigade. Having witnessed the Third Corps advancing before subsequently calling for reinforcements, they fully expected to "join forces" with Sickles's beleaguered Third Brigade, First Division. However, the latter's main line had fallen back toward Caldwell's former position on Cemetery Ridge and toward the line of the Second Corps. No help was coming in the short term. Yet, Zook's men still clung to the belief that they would be fighting in conjunction with Sickle's troops until the 140th noticed the closeness of the Peach Orchard to their right and its current emptiness as "the smoke lifted for a moment." Zook's disheartened soldiers realized they were now alone and unsupported to their right.[109]

Colonel David Wyatt Aiken, the capable commander of the 7th South Carolina, recalled, "From the position of the Seventh, we could see the successive lines of the enemy as they advanced down the wheat field fronting the fifteenth and presenting their right flank." Aiken's front ranks were heavily engaged and began taking inordinate casualties. Among them was Lieutenant Colonel Bland, who was wounded in the thigh but refused to retire to the rear. He mentioned to Aiken that they "were then fighting a most gallant enemy."[110]

Aiken reported that he never saw a man from the enemy up to that point. His eyes always being fixed on his own line to urge his South Carolinians on in the direction from which the hissing, deadly enemy missiles came. At one point during this firefight, Bland called to Aiken, "Is that not a magnificent sight?" as he pointed "to the line of gayly dressed Union forces in the Wheatfield, whose almost perfect line was preserved, though enfiladed by our fire from the woods, decimating the front line, whose gaps of death were promptly filled by each file-closer stepping to the front as his file-leader fell." It was the famed Irish Brigade.[111]

THE IRISH BRIGADE'S STUBBORN BATTLE

Earlier in the action, when Zook's Brigade had deviated its course and initially pushed toward Stony Hill, Patrick Kelly's 530-man Irish Brigade had deployed just south of Plum Run, in the general area of the John T. Weikert farm. Their destination was the small wooded, stony hill to support Zook's and Cross's embattled soldiers. As the Sons of Erin neared the Trostle farm (just before Major Tremain encountered Zook) a woman "on horseback and in uniform" rode toward the advancing column. Anna Etheridge, a volunteer nurse with the 3rd Michigan of de Trobriand's brigade, had been involved in the melee near the Peach Orchard. She asked some of Kelly's officers for any information regarding orders for that division. She went back to take care of the wounded after her questions were satisfied. Major Mulholland of the 116th Pennsylvania remembered, "She was cool and self-possessed and did not seem to mind the fire."[112]

Orders for the Irish to advance through the Wheatfield soon spread through the ranks, the officers making it clearly known that the men were to either "fire or desist from firing as the broken nature of the ground permitted." The brigade moved at "right shoulder shift" toward the enemy, which lay thick within the boulders of Stony Hill and the northern end of Rose Woods.[113]

The Irish Brigade swept over the open fields just south of the Weikert farm, brushed the edge of Trostle's Woods, and deployed in a line of battle in the

Wheatfield. Their alignment from right to left was the 116th Pennsylvania (Maj. St. Clair A. Mulholland) 66 men, 28th Massachusetts (Col. Richard Byrnes) 75 men, 69th New York (Capt. Richard Moroney) 75 men, 88th New York (Capt. Denis F. Burke) 90 men, and the 63rd New York (Lt. Col. Richard C. Bentley) 75 men.[114]

This movement was not done without impediment, however. According to Second Lt. John B. Noyes of the 28th Massachusetts, the boulders were "prevent-ing the maintain[ing of a] regular line of battle." As the Irishmen crossed through the middle of the field, they passed Zook's Brigade (on their right) and Cross's Brigade (off to the left) on their way to engage Kershaw.[115]

The unfurled dark green banner of the 28th Massachusetts, proudly displaying the Harp of Erin, moved forward next to the red-white-and-blue colors of the United States. The men fixed bayonets as they pressed through the trampled wheat toward the enemy, all the while chanting their regimental motto, "Faugh a Ballagh" (clear the way). The 15th South Carolina had begun to fire as the Irish-men crossed the Wheatfield. The 50th Georgia, under General Paul Semmes, had advancing forward to support Kershaw's 7th South Carolina, which had bent its right flank back along a rail fence to meet the new threat. To the right of the 7th SC, the 9th Georgia of Anderson's Brigade also shifted position.[116]

The 116th Pennsylvania continued forward until reaching the small knoll recently vacated by Winslow's Battery, where the 17th Maine had earlier made their stand. Passing over this location and maintaining their line, someone from the 116th yelled out, "There they are!" Sure enough, toward the wooded line of Stony Hill, not even forty yards from their position, was a solid line of Confeder-ate infantry. Major Mulholland remembered that "no orders were given but in an instant every musket on the line was at its deadly work," as they formed on the left of Zook's Brigade.[117]

Soon, bullets from the 7th South Carolina and from Anderson's Brigade began clipping through the Wheatfield toward the left of the Irish line. Colonel Kelly ordered a brief halt and, according to Lt. James Smith of the 69th New York, the brigade "delivered one or two volleys, the enemy were noticed to waver, and upon the advance of our line the enemy fell back, contesting the ground doggedly." Smith added, "One charge to the front brought us in a lot of prisoners, who were immediately sent to the rear."[118]

Their line having been broken, it appears that the 7th and 3rd South Carolina fell back slightly to the crest of Stony Hill only to later advance again and regain their position. Kelly's Brigade soon resumed advancing in line of battle along with Zook's Brigade. According to Major Mulholland, they pressed forward "in good order."[119]

Many of the Irishmen, spoiling for a fight, welcomed getting closer to the enemy. The soldiers of the 63rd New York carried smoothbore muskets, which fired a large .69 caliber ball with three buckshot packed in behind a larger round ball. In close range, a volley from these weapons could wreak havoc on opposing troops. The regiment had earlier been issued nearly sixty rounds per man, allow-ing them to sustain the battle longer than the traditional 40 rounds if the need should arise.[120]

The Irish Push Forward

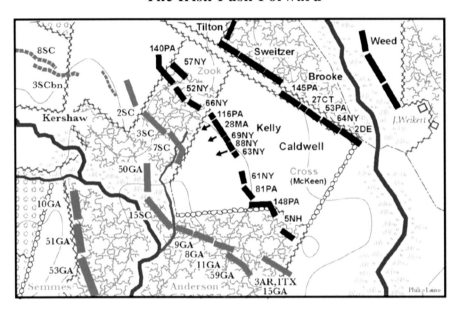

Cross and Zook are now fully committed to the fight and engaged. Kershaw begins to swing around and pull more of his men towards the Stoney Hill area. Kelly reaches Cross's right flank and begins to push towards Stoney Hill.

Zook and Kelly began outflanking Kershaw's 7th and 3rd South Carolina. A cloud of sulfuric smoke enveloped the hillside. Because of the rolling nature of the terrain, the Carolinians, in their elevated position, had to rise up and fire rather hastily to avoid being targeted. As a result, many of their shots passed over the heads of their Northern foes and flew harmlessly into the Wheatfield. The "buck-and-ball" shots that so many of the Irish had grown accustomed to using tore holes in the Confederate ranks. Major Mulholland claimed, "The effect of our fire was deadly in the extreme, for under such circumstances, a blind man could not have missed his mark."[121]

Peter Welsh of the 28th Massachusetts boasted proudly in a letter to his wife dated July 17, "It was a hot place, our little brigade fought like heroes." Captain Nowlen of the 116th Pennsylvania drew his service revolver and opened fire while maintaining the order in his company. Within a few moments, every officer of the brigade followed the young officer's lead and also opened on the enemy with small arms. As the Irish closed on Kershaw's line, Pvt. Jeff Carl of the 116th killed a South Carolinian with his bayonet.[122]

With the closer range, the Rebel fire began to strike down several of Kelly's oncoming Federals. Francis Malin, a towering Irishman in the 116th Pennsylvania attempted to shelter his tall, lanky frame. However, according to Major Mulholland, "He soon fell dead with a bullet through his brain." The ground on which they stood began to turn red with the blood of the brave men on both sides of the contest for Stony Hill. For almost ten minutes, the Irish Brigade stood toe-to-toe with the Rebels at a distance of less than fifteen yards.[123]

Zook's Brigade supported Kelly's soldiers but were losing more men in the process. Sergeant John F. Wilson of the 140th Pennsylvania was shot through the right arm, breaking the bone. His musket fell to the ground. Not wanting to leave the fight, Wilson made a motion to retrieve it when another Minié ball struck his left arm, breaking that bone as well. With both of his arms now "hanging helpless on either side," Wilson finally vacated the field.

Nearby, Private Stewart watched as Pvt. John McNutt was mortally wounded "and fell forward at his feet." A few paces away, Lt. Alexander Wilson and Hugh Weir, classmates of Stewart before the war, were stricken moments apart with mortal wounds. In the center of the line (near the site of the post-war monument to the regiment) Color Sgt. Robert Riddle was struck through the left lung. He instantly "fell with the flag in his hands." Company H's Cpl. Joseph Moody was at his comrade's side in an instant. He placed Riddle in a more comfortable position and passed the banner to Cpl. Jesse T. Power of Company E, who safely removed it from the field.[124]

The Federals were not the only ones losing manpower. Kershaw's Brigade was also taking significant casualties in the close-order firefight. The 2nd South Carolina lost W. G. Lomax, John Reynolds, William N. Riley, and William W. Waller, all killed while on the firing line. Of that regiment of about 350 men, 181 fell, a gruesome reminder of the brutality of the fight on that stony, wooded Adams County hillside. Maj. Robert C. Maffett of the 3rd South Carolina maintained his position "under a heavy fire of musketry at short range in front, and an enfilading fire of grape and shrapnel from the batteries that the left had failed in entirely silencing, until… we were ordered by General Kershaw back to another line a short distance in our rear.[125]

Kershaw's three regiments were in danger of being overrun by the two Federal brigades. "Now the voice of Kelly is heard," Major Mulholland mentioned, "ordering the charge; with a cheer, a few quick strides, and we were on the crest among the enemy." The two lines stood toe to toe without firing a shot. "We found there were as many of the enemy as there were of ourselves," wrote Mulholland. The bewildered soldiers looked upon one another without making so much a move in an attempt to drive or repulse. Finally, Mulholland mounted a boulder and loudly exclaimed, "Confederate troops lay down your arms and go to the rear!" He later admitted, "this ended a scene that was becoming embarrassing. The order was promptly obeyed and a large number… became our prisoners."[126]

In addition to driving elements of Kershaw's Brigade, Caldwell's two brigades also pushed back the 50th Georgia of Semmes' Brigade which had been posted in a ravine between Rose Woods and Stony Hill. Captain Hillyer, positioned in the natural rifle pit of Plum Run, later recounted, "I saw General Paul Semmes nobly doing his duty. He was one of the brigade commanders in McLaws' Division, and was standing in that branch just at that part of the line next to us, occupied by the… Georgia Regiment. General Semmes was killed or mortally wounded a few minutes later. We held this rifle pit, and whilst in it did our most effectual fighting. We met with some losses, and the water of the brook soon became red with blood, but the enemy in the front suffered far more than we did."[127]

The Irish Brigade's Major Mulholland challenged this claim laid by Hillyer when he wrote, "In front of our brigade we found that the enemy had suffered much more than we had. When engaged, our line was below theirs, as they stood on the crest of the hill. They fired down while our men fired upward and our fire was more effective. On their line we found many dead, but few wounded they were nearly all hit in the head or upper part of the body. Behind one rock we counted five dead bodies. This was some of the most severe fighting our division had ever done. While still yet finding five more behind another boulder." One of the men from Kershaw's Brigade "had torn his blouse and shirt open, exposing his breast and showing a great hole from which his heart's blood was flowing."[128]

The marshy terrain around the positions of the 50th Georgia and the 7th South Carolina held numerous dead or wounded Confederate soldiers. General Kershaw later penned, "I cannot tell how long we were engaged at that point. My impression is that it may have been a half hour, when the pressure upon the front and both flanks of the two regts., 7th and 3rd in that advanced position became too great." With little hope left and having taken on nearly four brigades from two different corps, Kershaw reluctantly ordered his survivors back to the relative safety of the Rose farm buildings.

Nearly fifteen minutes after the fighting ceased, Zook's and Kelly's brigades began to redress their lines in case of a renewed Confederate attack. In unison, both brigades had fought desperately to push Kershaw's Brigade off Stony Hill, a conflict lasting nearly a half hour. Once the hill was secured, Zook's Brigade reformed and wheeled to the left, forming a new line of battle (from right to left, the 140th Pennsylvania, 52nd New York, and 66th New York in the front rank, while the 57th New York went into a supporting position in the rear). Directly on the left flank of the 66th was Major Mulholland's 116th Pennsylvania of the Irish Brigade, followed by the 28th Massachusetts, with the 63rd, 69th, and 88th New York to their left.[129]

The dead and wounded on this portion of the battlefield were gathered in heaps. Some of the survivors broke their ranks to attend to them, while others simply stared across the blood-stained fields toward the distant enemy. With the field now quiet on his front, St. Clair Mulholland found time to walk around the field of carnage. It appeared that his day's work was not yet finished. He noted, "Over the little valley in the immediate front one could see the enemy massed and preparing for another attack." He noticed an injured soldier lying near him. It was youthful Pvt. Charles Gardner of the 110th Pennsylvania, one of de Trobriand's Third Corps regiments that vacated the area nearly an hour before Caldwell's division arrived.

Mulholland later described the gripping scene: "One young boy lay out-stretched on a large rock with his musket still grasped in his hand, his pale, calm face upturned to the sunny sky, the warm blood still flowing from a hole in his forehead and running in a red stream over the gray stone. The young hero had just given his life for his country. A sweet, childish face it was, lips parted in a smile—those still lips on which the mother's kisses had so lately fallen, warm and tender. The writer gazed upon the relics of a saint; but the little boy lying there with his blood coloring the soil of his own State, and his young heart stilled forever, seemed more like an angel form than any of the others."[130]

BROOKE'S BRIGADE IN THE WHEATFIELD

Earlier in the fight for the Wheatfield, while Cross', Zook', and Kelly's brigades all had been attacking their respective positions, Caldwell's Fourth Brigade under Colonel Brooke had entered the Wheatfield. Before the engagement, with the men drawn up in their usual order of battle, Brooke addressed his brigade. "Boys," he said, "remember the enemy has invaded our own soil! The eyes of the whole world are upon us! And we are expected to stand up bravely to do our duty!" After having been halted for a short period of time near the present-day Wheatfield Road, the soldiers stood by their arms briefly until Brooke ordered his brigade forward toward the field of ripe, golden wheat. Upon receiving the order, Pvt. George W. Whipple of the 64th New York recollected that his regiment "got over a stone wall after the rails on top were thrown off and started through a field of wheat up to our waists."

The order of the brigade, from right to left, was the 145th Pennsylvania (Col. Hiram L. Brown) 202 men, 27th Connecticut (Lt. Col. Henry Merwin) 75 men,

53rd Pennsylvania (Lt. Col. Richard McMichael) 135 men, 64th New York (Col. Daniel G. Bingham) 204 men, and the 2nd Delaware (Col. William Bailey) 234 men. Colonel Brooke later said that his brigade spanned the entire breadth of the Wheatfield.[131]

While pushing through the wheat, Brooke's men brushed along the side of Kelly's Irish Brigade on the right and Cross's boys on the left. Captain John C. Hilton of the 145th Pennsylvania reported that "the rebels, elated with their success, followed up the victory and came cautiously through the wheatfield until they met the veterans of the Second Corps."[132]

Captain Hillyer of the 9th Georgia remembered the moment he saw the Federal advance:

> Just then we noticed a fresh line of the enemy which appeared to be a reinforcement, and not to have been previously engaged in the battle. They were approaching us rapidly and directly in front of my regiment, but partly concealed by the smoke. I managed to call attention to them, and the word passed down our line to hold our fire. This new regiment of the enemy came within about forty yards. Some six feet in front of them was their color bearer, a splendid looking young fellow. We could see and distinguish his features... His flag was a bright new one, and he gallantly waved it over his head in front. I could not hear anything that he or others of them said, nor indeed could what we said to one another be well heard, so great was the roar of battle.
>
> Just then this color bearer stepped back into his line, and we knew that the volley was coming. With the precision of a dress parade, that magnificent line of Federals lowered their pieces and the volley came. But we had time to duck our heads and the sheet of lead passed harmlessly over us but I could see where the bullets cut and plowed the ground behind us. Every man of us then seemed to realize our tremendous advantage... I rose up and looked along our line, and I thought then and think yet, that that volley had passed entirely harmlessly over our heads, and that by it we did not lose a man. Our men rested their guns on the grass in front, and with the solid line of the enemy in easy, close range, returned the fire. It seemed that not a bullet went above their heads or below their feet. They fell right and left. There was a space below the smoke of a few inches just above the ground, and we in our rifle pit, having our eyes nearly on the level of the ground, could just see below the smoke the line of their feet. This line rapidly thinned... there was a long blue line on the ground, so close together that anyone could have walked over them as far as their front extended without touching the earth.[133]

Brooke continued his advance through the Wheatfield after the initial volley. Almond E. Clark of the 27th Connecticut stated, "We went forward with a rush firing as fast as we could, driving the rebels before us." By the time the brigade had advanced halfway through the Wheatfield, the entire line became "under the full sweep of the enemy's fire," according to the regiment's postwar historian, Pvt. Winthrop D. Sheldon. About this time, Sgt. Horace H. French of the 64th New York became one of the first casualties in the brigade when a Minié ball ended his service. Soon afterward, the 64th's Capt. Rodney R. Crowley also fell. The men were barely a third of their way to their target and they were already under a withering fire. In the 27th, **LT. COL. HENRY MERWIN** fell "while leading the command with this accustomed bravery." Colonel Brooke later lamented that "his death is a national loss."[134]

Henry Merwin Death Site (*Library of Congress LC-USZ62-98433*)

While in this position, the men were ordered to lay down so that Kelly's Brigade could overtake them "and rectify the line." General Caldwell had ordered the halt but, within a few minutes, the brigade was again ordered forward. Private Martin Sigman of the 64th New York recalled, "We was fireing [sic] as fast as we could, and it was a deafing [sic] roar and it was very difficult to hear the commands given, and took some efort [sic] to start the line forward into another charge."

The color guards of each regiment spearheaded the charge. During times of battle, the field became almost mass confusion while sight lines and hearing were greatly decreased. Various troops making various movements that were unknown from private to colonel attempted to maintain their lines under a galling fire on a typical Civil War battlefield, and the Wheatfield was no different in this analogy. Here, as on other battlefields, the regiments looked to the brave color companies to lead the regiment forward or withdraw safely. The 64th New York's color guards advanced forward as the regiment had stalled in the wheat. The sight inspired the regiment and the brigade, which advanced "with a cheer."

Brooke's soldiers continued on toward the southern end of the Wheatfield. Tall grass, large boulders, and an element of Rose's Run marked the area. In this sector of the field, Cpl. Edmund Stone, Jr. bore the 64th New York's national colors until he fell dead. He had earlier taken the flag after Cpl. Chauncey McKoon was wounded. Corporal A. C. Blackmore then carried it until the end of the conflict. Corporal Thomas J. Zibble carried the state flag until he was wounded. It would then fall into the hands of Cpl. Albert Empy, who also fell wounded, and ended up in the hands of Lt. Arnold R. Chase.[135]

Brooke Moves Forward

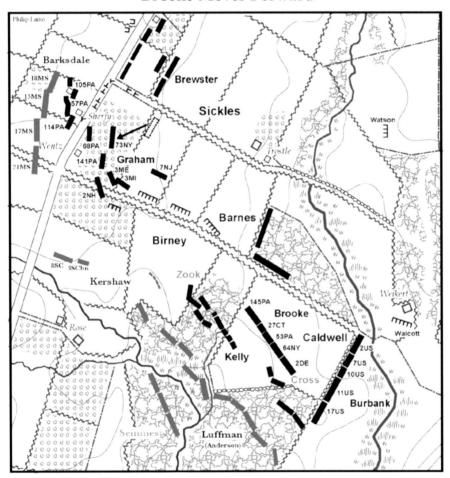

Cross (McKeen) pushes back Anderson's men considerably. Kelly and Zook overtake Stoney Hill and Brooke is beginning the final stage of the sweep. Awaiting them in Rose Woods are fresh Confederate troops poised to repulse them.

The brigade briefly halted again as it became intermingled with elements of Kelly's Brigade. Under a devastating fire, Brooke's Brigade attempted to sort out its ranks from that of Kelly's. Being out in the open did not bode well for most of the men, however. Private George Whipple sought the protection of a large clump of bushes in his front. There, he loaded his gun when "another soldier near [him] was struck by a bullet in the forehead and he fell against me," as he recalled. Captain Henry Fuller, of the same regiment, said, "Never mind George, forward!" but the attack had again stalled. This time, it would be rectified when Colonel Brooke "seized the colors of [his] own regiment (53rd Pennsylvania) … and carried them forward, that seemed to settle the business, for the men pushed ahead."[136]

Again, Brooke's brigade was on the move and driving Anderson's Confederate brigade through the Rose Woods and upon a steep, rocky, knoll on the opposite side of Rose's Run. Lieutenant Robert G. Smith of the 2nd Delaware claimed they "reached the farthest point gained by any of the Union troops during the day, capturing many prisoners," during the brigade's push. Private Sigman of the 64th New York recollected, "The line kept onward loading and fireing as we went across a creek [Rose's Run] into a piece of woods up to a ledge of rocks, and chased the Rebles up the ridge passed the rocks." The 27th Connecticut's A. E. Clark remembered, "Our number by this time was reduced to less than half that started in the fray but we had the flags with us." At the top, Brooke's Brigade found that Semmes' Georgia brigade was "drawn up in readiness just beyond, within pistol-range, opened upon them a withering fire."

"I think there is nothing that will cause a man to shoot so unsteady and wildly," Cpl. Stephen Osborn of the 145th Pennsylvania believed, "as to have the enemy charging down on him yelling like mad." A sudden Confederate volley immediately staggered the brigade. Colonel Brooke later reported the enemy position as being an "almost impregnable position on the rocky crest."[137]

Brooke quickly ordered his men to lie down to better withstand the oncoming fire. In addition to musketry from Semmes' Brigade to the front, the 1st Texas of Robertson's Brigade and the 15th Georgia of Benning's Brigade delivered a devastating enfilading fire along Brooke's line. Clark of the 27th Connecticut said that the brigade was taken by surprise by the Rebels who "poured a volley into us at short range." The flanking fire caused Brooke to bend both of his flanks back, eventually resembling a crescent shape, while the 2nd Delaware refused one end of its line to meet the new attack. Brooke was isolated for the moment, having outdistanced the rest of the division on the trek to Rose's Woods. Thus, both of his flanks were greatly exposed. The situation soon grew worse when Anderson's Brigade also opened after they had reformed on Brooke's left and Kershaw's South Carolinians, still by the Rose farm buildings, were on Brooke's right.[138]

The 50th Georgia, now with the 10th Georgia at its side, poured fire into Brooke's prone men. Private John Griffin received a round in his knee, shattering his femur. Sadly, his wife had passed away two years earlier on the same date.[139]

Brooke's beleaguered brigade continued its stand in its advanced, exposed position and bore the brunt of attacks by three veteran Confederate brigades. The 27th Connecticut planted its colors upon the top of the ridge, while "the men

Almost Surrounded

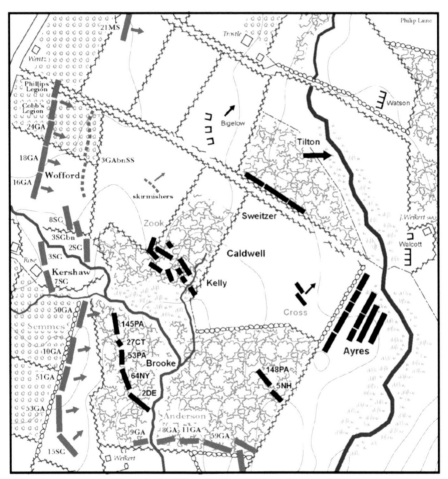

After Brooke sweeps through the Wheatfield and drives the remaining Confederate elements back, he is forced to hunker low on a ridgeline in the Rose Woods. Anderson begins to pepper his flank while Semmes, in his front, begins to fire and wipe out many of his men. During this time, Zook and Kelly face new directions while most of Cross's men now exit the field. The 148th PA and 5th NH advance to support Brooke's attack.

loaded their pieces under shelter of the brow of the hill, then, rising up, delivered their fire."[140]

Casualties began to rise as the men hugged the ground under the heavy fire from their Rebel counterparts on the crest. The flags of Brooke's regiments whipped and snapped as lead missiles passed by and often struck their shafts. In the Confederate ranks, Sgt. L. L. Cochran of the 10th Georgia stood in the thickest part of it. His regiment had been squaring off against the 27th Connecticut on the right flank of Brooke's Brigade. Both sides loaded and fired their rifles at will. Cochran remembered that one of his comrades, Gus Morrow, received a round through his shoulder. The stunned Morrow grasped his shoulder tightly for a moment. A few seconds later, a second Union round left Morrow dead at Cochran's feet.

Confederate Dead (*Library of Congress LC-DIG-cwpb-00865*)

Not far away from this incident, Cochran witnessed another comrade's demise. Private George Wilkinson was shot in the left knee. Cochran for the rest of his life remembered distinctly hearing Wilkinson's bone break as the round tore through it, making a sharp cracking sound.[141]

In the meantime, two of Cross's regiments, the 148th Pennsylvania and 5th New Hampshire, advanced into Rose Woods and engaged the 15th Georgia and 1st Texas in an attempt to support Brooke. Anderson's Brigade, along with Kershaw's 15th South Carolina, concentrated its fire on the 2nd Delaware and on enfilading Brooke's exposed flank. The 53rd Georgia attacked the right flank of the 2nd Delaware and the right of the 64th New York, who was also being engaged by the 51st Georgia. The 10th Georgia squared off against the 53rd Pennsylvania and the few small companies of the 27th Connecticut, while the 50th Georgia assaulted the 145th Pennsylvania.[142]

The subsequent fighting lasted nearly twenty minutes. Brooke "had an average of five rounds per man, or thereabouts." With their ammunition running low and his men exhausted, the colonel desperately sought reinforcements for his exposed flanks. He dispatched an officer to inquire of General Caldwell if any such troops were at his disposal. Before the courier could return, both of Brooke's aides lay wounded and Brooke, himself, received a painful bruise that hindered his walking ability. Yet, Brooke held his men in grand fashion. He reported, "I, with great difficulty, was able to maintain a proper knowledge of the enemy."

John Brooke Rock (*Personal Collection of James Smith II*)

Soon after being wounded, Brooke received information that his right flank was being turned, and it was losing cohesiveness under the well-directed fire of the 7th South Carolina. Had the brigades of Zook and Kelly kept advancing, this may not have happened. They had stalled on Stony Hill. The colonel again desperately sought the assistance of surrounding troops but there was none to be found. He maintained after the battle, "Finding unless I retired all would be killed or captured, I reluctantly gave the order."[143]

By this time, Brig. Gen. Romeyn B. Ayres's United States Regulars under Col. Sidney Burbank had formed a line of battle on the west side of the Wheatfield. Behind him was another reserve line held in support under Col. Hannibal Day. However, these fresh troops did not yet have orders to advance. Shortly before Brooke's line broke and ran for the rear, General Caldwell swiftly rode toward Colonel Sweitzer and his brigade, which was still posted at the edge of Trostle's Woods. Sweitzer noted the moment he saw Caldwell: "A general officer I had never seen before rode up to me, and said his command was driving the enemy in the woods in front of the wheat-field." Armed with this bit of information, he requested Sweitzer to move in to support Brooke's Brigade. Sweitzer denied the request to move without orders and quickly referred him to General Barnes, his division commander.

Caldwell dashed off to locate Barnes. Within a few moments, both generals rode back to Sweitzer's position. Barnes looked at Sweitzer and asked if he would take his brigade in. "I told him I would if he wished me to do so," recalled Sweitzer. Barnes replied in the affirmative and Sweitzer accordingly called his brigade "to attention." Barnes rode out in front of the brigade and "made a few patriotic remarks, to which they responded with a cheer, and we started off across the wheat-field," as Sweitzer recalled.[144]

Caldwell's men were not the only troops receiving reinforcements at this time. On Seminary Ridge, Brig. Gen. William T. Wofford's Confederate brigade was deployed in line of battle and ready for action at a moment's notice. They deployed from left to right as Phillips Legion, Cobb's Legion, 24th Georgia, 18th Georgia, and the 16th Georgia on the right.[145]

Near 7 p.m., the brigade was ordered forward at a double-quick while Brig. Gen. William Barksdale's brigade of Mississippians assailed the Peach Orchard to their left. Soon after the advance started, the 24th Georgia became tangled in the web of Alexander's artillery along the ridge, causing the regiment to lag considerably behind the rest of the surging Confederates. Yet, the artillerymen were not disturbed by the regiment being entangled, "Fire! Fire! Fire!" remembered Capt. William W. Parker of the Virginia Battery, "Each gun is discharging its leaden terrors into the ranks of the foe!" Soon, after General Wofford reestablished his lines, he rode up to the Georgians. With "his hat off and his bald head shining in the sun," he dashed through the belching battery. The sight caught the attention of many of the artillerymen. Captain Parker who drew his sword from his scabbard and shouted, "Hurrah for you of the bald head!" Parker wrote to the *Richmond Sentinel* after the war, "Oh, he was a grand sight, and my heart is full now while I write of it… Long may General Wofford live to lead his men." The rest of the battery repeated the same phrase as the Georgians swept down the hillside and began to drive their foes.[146]

In addition to driving the infantry, the artillery would be cleared from this area as well. Captain John Bigelow's 9th Massachusetts Battery was ordered to retire after the 21st Mississippi of Barksdale's Brigade crashed into them. Bigelow utilized the use of prolongs to accomplish this task. He testified, "No friendly supports, of any kind were in sight; but Johnnie Rebs in great numbers. Bullets were coming into our midst from many directions and a Confederate battery added to our difficulties. Still, prolongs were fixed and we withdrew the left section keeping Kershaw's skirmishers back with canister, and the other two sections bowling solid shot toward Barksdale's men."[147]

Confederate First Corps commander James Longstreet briefly led Wofford's Brigade into battle and across the Emmitsburg Road. He heard the disturbance from the cheers of his artillerymen and exclaimed, "Cheer less, men, and fight more!" His stern reply caused every artillery piece to begin firing again. Soon afterward, Wofford's aide, William Youngblood, beckoned for the general to dismount because of "the danger of being shot down by our own troops." Longstreet stubbornly denied the request and remained on his mount. Youngblood soon noticed that Barksdale's Brigade had begun to shift far to the left and away from the point of attack. Youngblood pointed this flaw out to Longstreet and asked, "Do you want General Barksdale to halt?" Longstreet said, "No. Go tell him to retake his position." With a dash, the officer located Barksdale and told him of the order. After he turned to return to Longstreet, Youngblood heard a dull thud as a bullet struck Barksdale. He watched as Barksdale fell from his horse. Youngblood went back and told Longstreet of what had happened, who responded by saying, "Go on beyond this orchard and tell… Alexander to advance his artillery and to keep in touch with Wofford's left."[148]

The sight of Wofford's Brigade advancing across the open plain was a sight for sore eyes in the ranks of Kershaw's Brigade that had been bogged down north of the Rose farm buildings. One of the men from the 2nd South Carolina noted upon seeing them, "That's help for us! Spring up the bluff, boys!" as they joined in on Wofford's right flank for the final push.[149]

The Confederate battle line now formed a giant horseshoe around Caldwell's division. On the ridge, Colonel Brooke ordered his men to retreat. Upon hearing the command, many of his men were hesitant to rise under such a withering fire. Captain John C. Hilton remembered that the order was made "not a moment too soon, as the brigade would have been outflanked and captured in five minutes more." The colonel, still unable to walk, was assisted off the field by "a burly fellow under each arm," he related, "though I did not give up the command or the fight until entirely off the field." Many of those who did choose to stand were quickly cut down by Rebel bullets.

The two men assisting Brooke apparently included his cousin, **Sgt. Samuel H. Rutter** of the 53rd Pennsylvania. He stayed with the colonel until a Minié ball struck him in his leg. He and Brooke assisted each other off of the blood-soaked field. Once off the field, Rutter acquired the assistance of **Dr. David Houston** of the 2nd Delaware who extracted the bullet.[150]

Colonel Brooke reported that, as he continued to urge his men to the rear he noticed, "In passing back over the wheat-field, I found the enemy had nearly closed in my rear, and had the movement not been executed at the time it was… all would have been lost by death, wounds, or capture." The realization justified his decision to pull out of Rose Woods.[151]

Samuel H. Rutter (*Personal Collection of Charles Joyce*)

David Houston (*Personal Collection of Charles Joyce*)

Still on the knoll, **CAPT. HENRY FULLER** of the 64th New York was in front of Company F when he heard the call to retreat. He quickly looked over his shoulder and asked, "Who sent the order?" No one seemed to know, so Fuller and his group stayed a few more moments. Men were retiring all around them when, finally, one of Colonel Kelly's aides rode to the squad of hunkered men "calling out to us to fall back," remembered Private Whipple, "and to get out of there." The ensuing moments would plague Whipple's mind for the rest of his life. "We started back," he later wrote. "As Fuller rose to his feet to move with us he fell wounded near my feet. I helped him up. One of his legs seemed useless. I had hold of him on the left, and some one assisted him on the right side and thus we made several rods to the rear followed by the enemy when a bullet struck him in the back and came out in front just under my arm.[152]

Henry Fuller (*Scienceviews. com SIA2413*)

A few other soldiers—Pvt. Martin Sigman of Company C, Pvt. Ephraim Russell, and Pvt. Charles Clock— initially helped Whipple take Captain Fuller off the battlefield. However, with bullets zipping past them, they soon left and made their way back as fast as possible through the Wheatfield to the rear. Now alone, Whipple grasped his captain tightly and continued to carry him to the rear. When they reached the banks of Rose's Run, Whipple carefully laid Fuller on the ground in as comfortable position as he possibly could. The stricken captain looked up and said "George, keep up good courage." Whipple later recollected, "I shall never forget that look," as he finished his work by moving Fuller behind a bush and "straightened out his limbs for he was dying."[153]

Several Confederate soldiers soon swarmed toward Whipple and his incapacitated captain. Drawing near, and taking no heed to the private's dying friend, they demanded his surrender "with awful threats." Whipple claimed that "it was hard to leave my best friend and captain," but he did what he had to do and surrendered. Before being brought to the rear, Whipple requested to be allowed to retrieve some trinkets out of Fuller's pockets as mementoes. The captain, apparently expired, lay by his feet. Unwilling to comply, the Confederate officer angrily responded, "Go to the rear you d----d Yankee son of a b---h," and two Rebel soldiers hoisted the New York private away.[154]

On his way to the Confederate rear, Whipple had the chance to repay the injustice. Reaching the top of the rocky ledge, he encountered a wounded Rebel lieutenant who "sat on the ground leaning against a rock." He asked Whipple, "Yank, got any water?" The question momentarily struck a nerve in the young private. He had just been captured and not allowed to collect Fuller's personal effects, and now one of the enemy had the audacity to beg for water? Whipple, with compassion outdueling his anger, drew his canteen and looked upon the man with great sorrow. After the Rebel officer received a drink, he asked to "be carried to the ambulances." Two guards, along with Whipple, fabricated a makeshift stretcher out of Whipple's shelter tent and carried the wounded man nearly a half-mile to the rear. The private recalled that after he brought his new friend to his destination he "seemed very grateful, took my name, company and regiment and gave me his name etc." The two expressed wishes to cross paths again someday.[155]

During Brooke's retreat, Sgt. Joseph Charlesworth and Pvt. Leroy Shippey, undoubtedly friends during their time in camp, were wounded at the same time. As they fell back, the popular William Wemple was taken prisoner along with several others. With comrades falling all around them, there would be another casualty in Brooke's Brigade that would send a shock wave through the ranks.[156]

LIEUTENANT WILLIS "WILLIE" G. BABCOCK had been through the thick of it. Before the orders had come to retreat, he was "very active in directing the men how and where to shoot," according to Maj. L. W. Bradley of the 64th. "I saw him standing by the side of Sergeant Peterson of his own Co. tearing cartridges for the Sergeant." After their retreat, the Confederates drew hotly on their tail. Pushing into the Wheatfield, all hope for a successful escape seemed to have disappeared. Babcock, however, kept urging his men toward the rear, hastening them to reform on the opposite side of the Wheatfield into a line of battle. The Confederates were swarming through, as Wofford now made his presence known, having pushed most of Zook's and Kelly's brigades off Stony Hill. Lieutenant Babcock only made it a short way before a Confederate ball broke his collarbone. The shot appeared to have come from an elevated position such as from Kershaw's or Wofford's brigades. The round severed the main artery and Babcock bled out in minutes.[157]

Willis Babcock (*Photo courtesy of the Carlisle Barracks*)

Brooke's Brigade continued to fall back under the galling fire before reforming near the northern edge of the Wheatfield, along the present-day Wheatfield Road. They had made it farther than any other brigade in Caldwell's Division, but at a drastic cost. Of the 851 officers and men Brooke brought into the fight on the second of July, he had lost 45.7%, 389 men. It could truly be said that not many other brigades would have stood the test of fire as long as Brooke's Brigade had under such a destructive fire. Private Martin Sigman said it best in his account, "I think that was (the) hottest place we came across that day. I think that if we had stayed at the ledge of Rock just a little longer, they were closing in upon us, and we would all have been taken prisoners. It was useless for us to go so far ahead of the other troops, on our right and left, and have nothing to protect our flank."[158]

ZOOK AND KELLY ALSO FALL BACK

Having procured the assistance of Sweitzer, Caldwell looked to boost his line further with the use of Ayres's Regulars, still in their position along the western wall of the Wheatfield. Caldwell conferred with Ayres about supporting his First Division. The two talked for a few moments before Lt. William H. Powell of Ayres's staff noticed Zook's lead elements beginning to break. He remarked to Caldwell, "General, you had better look out, the line in front is giving way.' Caldwell turned and said, in rather a sharp manner, 'That's not so, sir; those are my troops being relieved.' With this assurance, Caldwell and Ayres continued their conversation, while Powell continued to watch the line in front. In a few moments, he again said, 'General Ayres, you will have to look out for your command. I don't care what anyone says, those troops in front are running away.'" At this remark, both generals scanned the battlefield. Without a word, Caldwell spurred his horse and rode off to the right, along the stone wall, to tend to his command.[159]

Just as Brooke's Brigade had broken and headed for the rear, some of Zook's and Kelly's men had also had enough of the firefight. They had taken the brunt of Kershaw's South Carolinians and, now, with Wofford's Georgians closing in and around their flank, they too began to fall back toward the rear. Lieutenant Colonel John Fraser, who now commanded the 140th Pennsylvania, remembered, "I observed a great many to the left of this brigade moving rapidly to the rear, and the rebels, apparently fresh troops, in large numbers and in good order marching to outflank us on the right."[160]

Wofford's Brigade outflanked Zook and Kelly by nearly 150 yards. The 24th Georgia, along with Cobb's Legion and Phillips' Legion, were attacking down what is modern-day Wheatfield Road without any significant resistance. Lieutenant Gilbert Frederick of the 57th New York recalled the scene as the Confederates "were marching steadily, with colors flying as though on dress parade, and guns at right-shoulder-shift." The fresh troops caused confusion in the Federal troops and, after noticing the fresh Confederate brigade, Fraser sent an aide twice to Zook. He later recollected, "I did not know at the time, nor until after the fight was over, that General Zook had been mortally wounded when leading the brigade into action."[161]

Fraser soon noticed that men began to fall back all around him, and bullets were zipping through the air striking down many in the process. Fraser concluded, "I judged it necessary for the safety of those who had wheeled considerably into the enemy's ground to maintain my position and keep the enemy at bay as long as possible", but it was not long before Fraser joined in the retreat.[162]

The 57th New York's Gilbert Frederick recalled that Lt. Col. Alford Chapman, upon seeing that his regiment was being flanked, called out "About face!" After marching a short distance, the regiment "turned and gave the enemy such a volley of lead as, for a time, disordered his advance." While the rest of the regiment fell back, a few of the men remained at the edge of the woods and awaited the Confederate tide to resume their fire.[163]

First Lieutenant W. S. Shallenberger recalled the scene years later when he spoke at the 140th Pennsylvania's monument dedication: "Sweeping across the Wheatfield, in shattered detachments, almost surrounded by the exultant foe, the remnant of our strong, proud regiment is seen to fly, in the dusk of that eventful day. Where our line would rally we dared not guess. The wounded in large numbers were soon collected at a little farmhouse skirting the Wheatfield [John T. Weikert house], and the rebel soldiers passed on."[164]

Another of Caldwell's soldiers later admitted, "It seemed miraculous that any one came out of that wood alive, so terrible was the fire when we entered it. The fighting in this locality continued through the afternoon, each side charging and falling back alternately."[165]

As the Confederates advanced over Stony Hill, Jacob Cole, the young 57th New York private who had earlier been wounded by a shell, awoke "surrounded by the enemy." He panicked, knowing that at any moment he would likely be instructed to go to the rear as a prisoner. Suddenly, a sharp pain emanated from his injured leg. Cole looked down to find a Confederate officer standing over him with his foot firmly planted in his leg wound. Cole begged the officer to have mercy on him and to step off his leg, but instead of consent, he received hatred. The officer drew his sword and exclaimed, "You d—n Yankee, I will cut your heart out." The officer raised his sword to strike him when, according to Cole, "A ball came… and cut him through the throat, and he fell beside me dead."[166]

In the 140th Pennsylvania, **Lt. James J. Purman** was one of the last men to retire from Stony Hill. He and his orderly sergeant, J. M. Pipes, fled the hillside together and came under a deadly Confederate fire. Purman later mentioned, "We suffered dreadfully, losing more, I think, than on the advance," yet fled they did until they stopped after becoming exhausted. Purman exclaimed to his sergeant, "We must get out of this, or we'll be gobbled up." Pipes agreed in the affirmative and the two were off again.

The Confederate shots were beginning to strike around them closer and closer as they chased Purman and Pipes, all the while shouting, "Halt, halt, you damned Yankee, halt!" "Visions of Libby and Andersonville filed through my brain," Purman remembered. "If I halt, some careless brutal fellow may shoot me after I have thrown up my hands. They can't hit me, anyhow, on a double-quick. These thoughts determined my will, and I refused to halt." Soon, however, they came across a fellow soldier calling out, "Comrades, carry me off!" The sad sight of the soldier, Pvt. John Buckley of Company B whose leg had been crushed by a shell, was

James Purman (*Photo courtesy of the National Archives and Records Administration*)

too much for the men to bear and they slowed for a few moments. Purman told him, "We can't do that; I doubt if we can get away ourselves, but we'll do the best we can for you," as they rushed over to their wounded comrade. With the assistance of Sergeant Pipes, he hoisted the wounded soldier up and carried him to the rear some distance. There, the two brave men sat the injured soldier down between two rocks. Purman grasped the man's hand tightly, looked into his eyes, and said, "Goodbye, comrade."

Purman fixed Buckley's legs in a comfortable position and again began to retire off the field. Within a few steps, the 24th Georgia opened a volley that brought down Purman. A round pierced through his left leg, breaking the bone. "I'm struck!" Purman cried out to Sergeant Pipes who was nearly a full rod ahead of him. Soon, Pipes was hit and fell in the bloody wheat. Purman recalled, "Many have attempted to tell how it feels to be shot. At first there is not pain, smarting nor anguish. It is very like the shock of an electric battery. But that delusion soon passes, and the acute pain follows, and you know that a missile has passed through the tender flesh of your body."

As the missile struck Purman, the sword he was carrying flew a few feet in front of him. Its tip stuck in the ground with its handle upwards, until it dropped down with its tip still imbedded in the soft earth. While the Confederate regiment continued to charge over him, Purman read "from the floating colors, 'Twenty-fourth Georgia.'" For the first time, he examined his wound and noticed he "was hit about four inches above the ankle, the ball passing through, crushing in both bones." Though his act would eventually earn him the Medal of Honor, he and his comrade lay helplessly on the field, for now.[167]

During the 140th Pennsylvania's flight from their position on Stony Hill, young Cephas D. Sharp also headed toward the rear. It proved to be a perilous journey. An account in the *Commemorative Biographical Record of Washington County, Pennsylvania* recalled:

> A bullet passed through both of his thighs, and at the same instant another lodged in one of his knees, the latter proving fatal. He fell and soon after received another terrible shot which paralyzed him for a time. Regaining consciousness, he supposed a ball had passed through his breast, but found a Minnie-ball deeply imbedded in the pocket Bible which was carried in his breast pocket. Night threw her mantle over the bloody tragedy as the dying soldier lay where he fell among the others. Listening he heard the familiar voice of Bedan Bebout in prayer. He spoke, and they succeeded in dragging their bodies together... Slowly, painfully, the night passed on, and morning found them helpless in the hands of the enemy. They hired rebel soldiers to carry them to a place of greater security..."[168]

Cephas and Bebout were soon dead. The last words that Cephas uttered were, "Oh, God, cut me loose, let me go."

Wofford's Brigade swept over the area so fast that many of Caldwell's infantry-men were taken prisoner. Lieutenant Shallenberger recollected, "For fifteen minutes perhaps, visions of southern prisons flitted before many of us." Major Thomas B. Rodgers and his comrades in the 140th Pennsylvania had been making their way back "in splendid style." As they broke the wooded hillside and entered the Wheatfield, "Three Confederate battle flags flashed by us, and we were in the hands of the enemy." The squad of men were taken to the rear where a Confederate sergeant demanded Rodgers's sword. He declined, stating that he

Cephas Sharp (*Personal Collection of Ira Dennis*)

would only deliver it over to an officer. The two men got into a heated argument until it was concluded that Rodgers was right in his contention.

As Rodgers was led to the rear, one of Longstreet's staff officers witnessed the procession of Yankee prisoners. He hastily rode over to the squad and demanded, "Sergeant, what is that officer doing with his sword on?" The sergeant explained the situation, to which the officer replied, "Very well, I am an officer and he can give it to me." Rodgers handed his sword to the young staff officer. Toward dark, he again spotted the young staff officer "exhibit my handsome sword with the remark that he had captured it from a Yankee officer. Of course, I remained discreetly silent."[169]

William Shallenberger was not immune to the desperate struggle. When Lieutenant Colonel Fraser ordered the regiment to retire, Shallenberger quickly ran to the right side of the 140th and gave the order to fall back. He recalled, "[I] had just given it and turned to move off, when I felt a shot through my boot in the calf of my leg." The brave lieutenant began to limp to the rear, but the Confederate tide came too fast. "(I) found I should fail," he said, "Several steps had been taken when my sword which had been drawn, and which I was using as a cane, was knocked out of my hand and broken in two." When the entire regiment began to retire from Stony Hill, Shallenberger, along with the rest of the wounded, had to fend for themselves. The Confederate brigades of Semmes, Wofford, and Kershaw all converged near where Zook's Brigade had been stationed and advanced over the ground they had occupied. Shallenberger kept hobbling toward the rear and somehow avoided enemy detection. "I could not stop," he recalled, "much less turn back." Soon, several members of his regiment assisted him off the field. However, it did not last long and Shallenberger insisted for the men to leave him in a "little log house… or they themselves would be taken."

Two of the men, from Company H, however, refused to leave the officer by himself and remained with him until the enemy passed by. Phillips's Legion passed through the area where the men rested, and two of their number remained outside the cabin as a guard. "They did not offer to molest us," said Shallenberger, "but talked in a manner which showed they were utterly tired of the war." There, they would stay until friendly troops could retake the area.[170]

In Company K of the 140th Pennsylvania, Benjamin Powelson had been fighting with the rest of the color company. He had fired some 17 rounds at the enemy when David Boyd called out, "Orderly, they are falling back." Powelson fired the round he had just primed and turned to find that Boyd had disappeared. Powelson went into a panic. He found himself alone and began to fall back. He soon came into contact with unfamiliar troops, probably from Brooke's Brigade, "all running for dear life and Johnnie bullets rattling all about us," remembered Powelson. Crossing over an open space, he could see the Rebels closing in on his left. They immediately order him to surrender. "I'll run the risk," Powelson said aloud, and he ran as fast as he could muster toward the friendly lines that had reformed in some timber just a few rods off. He was one of the few men in his company that made it off of Stony Hill unscathed.[171]

Nearby, Lt. Col. Alford Chapman and his 57th New York were holding their line with great effect against the Confederate attack. With Wofford's and Kershaw's brigades pushing in on their flanks, Chapman "held [his] men together until the greater part of the front line had broken through." Yet soon, "A staff officer rode up to me," Chapman reported, "and stated that the right of the line had broken, and that the enemy were coming in rapidly on that flank, advising me to move my regiment to the rear to avoid being taken." He briefly attempted to protect his flank by changing his front forward to the right, but it was not to be. With the Confederate pressure proving to be too much, he then moved this command to the rear in line "in good order," while the Confederates continued their close pursuit. Several times, the lieutenant colonel halted his men and ordered them to fire a volley into their pursuers, staggering their line and halting their advance, but had little success in doing so. They continued this maneuver until reaching the rest of their division and reforming their line there.[172]

The last reported unwounded soldier to leave the crest of Stony Hill was the 140th Pennsylvania's Sgt. John A. Burns of Company A. During the call to fall back, Burns did not hear the order, or just plain ignored it. He stood his ground and, before he knew it, he was surrounded by the enemy. He quickly made the determination to leave as quickly as possible. Discarding his knapsack and retaining his rifle, he began to fall through the tangled wheat stalks. He recalled that "it was like descending into hell. The enemy were yelling like devils. Our men were falling back. It was terrible confusion-smoke, dust, rattle of musketry, the roaring of cannons and the bursting of shells." Burns heard Confederates shouting from the rear, "Halt, you damned Yank!" but the wily young officer kept up with the pace until wheat tangled around his ankle and tripped him. He listened as the "bullets whistl(ed) lively around him." He decided his best option was to lay in this position until the enemy had passed. Soon, he looked forward and noticed a Union line of battle. It was the Pennsylvania Reserves of Crawford's Division. They had been lying down and "concealed by the standing grain." After catching his breath for a few minutes, he stood up and "plunged forward and fell exhausted just behind the battle line," thus making back to friendly troops safely[173]

After the battle, much animosity circulated around Caldwell's Division. The men of Zook's Brigade were not exempt from this feeling. The men, veterans of the army, hated to retreat in the face of the enemy and doing so put a bitter taste in their mouth that would last even after the war was long over. One soldier of the 140th was very outspoken about his feeling when he stated that his regiment "would never have come out if the officers had let us alone. But we would not surrender. We were completely flanked and cut our way out."[174]

The Irish Brigade's line also broke during the attack from the three Confederate brigades. Just before the enemy advance, Major Mulholland witnessed what he "believed to be a column of the enemy passing through the Peach Orchard and to the rear of our division." The major quickly alerted Colonel Kelly to this chain of events "but could not convince him that the column… was a Confederate force, the smoke and distance preventing our seeing accurately." About this time, a regiment of Zook's Brigade, probably the 140th Pennsylvania, had filed on his right flank and formed at right angles to his line for support. Mulholland went to Kelly and again requested permission to be relieved from command of the 116th Pennsylvania and be allowed to take the regiment of Zook's Brigade forward to ascertain as he had a "feeling…(of) uneasy and anxious in regard to the character of the… force." Kelly granted permission of the major's request and, after placing Capt. Garrett Nowlen in command of the 116th, went to the other regiment's officers to tell of his mission. He was immediately informed that "the colonel had been killed and that there was no field officer present with the command."

Mulholland, "pointing to the column that for a full ten minutes had been passing to our rear," beckoned the regiment to follow him to the Peach Orchard so they might learn the nature of the troops. He later recalled the bravery of the regiment, "The command had just lost its heroic colonel and on another part of the field fifty of its members lay dead and two hundred wounded, and now an officer who was a stranger to almost every man in the ranks, asked them to go forward and attack, if necessary, a whole brigade of the enemy. Yet every man in the most noble command responded to the call and promptly followed me toward the advancing hosts."

The regiment had only marched about fifty yards when Wofford's Brigade could be seen with their "flags unfurled in the breeze and we saw distinctly that the moving column consisted of Confederate troops," Mulholland noted. At that moment, the major knew that furthering his advance would be useless. He quickly instructed Lt. Col. John Fraser to place his command on his right flank and extend his line to bolster against the enemy attack. Just as Fraser began to give the order, a staff officer rode up to Mulholland, who was by now walking back toward his own regiment. He called out that "we were surrounded and to fall back and save as many of our men as possible."[175]

Undoubtedly, Mulholland did not know what to make of this order. He had no idea that, in the time that he was gone, Kershaw's Brigade had renewed their attack toward his position and began to drive his brigade off of the field. While there is little collaborating evidence to support Mulholland's claim of taking command of the regiment, it is very interesting to know what might have happened had the regiment remained in line and was able to confront Kershaw's Brigade.

Mulholland, when he peered back through the woods he realized that every regiment, with the exception of the one he had just commanded and his own 116th Pennsylvania, had pulled off of Stony Hill. He immediately told his men of the dangers that were quick to come their way and pointed in the direction of Little Round Top, ordering his squad to fall back to that point. The flags were quickly rolled up and the few remaining men ran down the slope, through the woods, and into the deadly Wheatfield. Little to their knowledge, they ran directly into the oncoming Confederates. A soldier in the brigade recalled, "The slaughter here was appalling, but we kept on, the men loading and firing as they ran."[176]

In this mass attack delivered by three enemy brigades, Lt. John Noyes of the 28th Massachusetts remembered, "Suddenly the brigade on our left (Brooke's) in the vale gives way in quick confusion. We hold our ground firmly, however, though enfiladed by a severe fire on our right flank." The Irish Brigade found itself surrounded under this fire being delivered at them on both flanks and front. Noyes remembered, "No alternative was left but to fall back irregularly, and in great haste." Several members of the brigade were taken prisoner. The enemy had advanced to the point they were nearly on top of them. As they too broke into the Wheatfield, they came under "a terrible flank fire from the advancing rebels." Noyes recalled, "That plain as I came over it, close to the green flag of the Regiment was rapidly becoming cumbered with the bodies of the dead and wounded men."

While in his haste, a Confederate prisoner, close to the lieutenant, received a round in his foot. "He hurried by falling with a deep groan," Noyes recalled. The wounded man continued on and was soon beyond the reach of the enemy rifles.[177]

Lieutenant James J. Smith of the 69th New York added, "Suddenly [we were] under a very severe fire from the front, most probably another line of battle of the enemy." The attack began to drive the Federals, who were now ordered to fall back. Smith went on to say, "We had scarcely got this order when we were attacked by the enemy on our right flank in strong force, and extending some distance to the rear, evidently with the intention of surrounding us." There, Smith attempted to rally his men, but found his effort in vain and impossible to achieve. So great was the Confederate pressure on his troops that "great confusion that prevailed at the time." They continued to fall back to the rear and reformed near Brooke's 53rd Pennsylvania.[178]

Major Mulholland was one of the retiring Federals that stumbled into the Wheatfield with his regiment. He, and his men, soon reached the middle of the field, where a Union brigade had been placed and where the Confederate brigades had ceased firing on the fleeing troops. Yells from the brigade's commanders came barreling in, directed toward Kelly's Brigade, "Come here, run this way!" Within moments, Mulholland and about ten of his men were over the stone fence and into the awaiting arms of friendly troops. From there, the men continued farther back, reforming on the Taneytown road, to the rear.[179]

Sergeant George Halpin of the 116th Pennsylvania, along with a few comrades, were captured during the retreat. Halpin was shot and unable to get away. Captain Teed of that regiment had been running alongside the sergeant when he was struck. Unlike Halpin, Teed went unwounded, but so confusing was the moment when they raced through the Wheatfield that they ran into the wrong line of infantry and were captured by the enemy. Halpin would remain behind enemy lines, wounded. Mulholland later said, "The fire, as the men passed through the wheat, was severe and destructive, and so close were the lines of the enemy between which the men ran, that they finally had stopped firing, as they were hitting each other." Another man from the 116th regiment running the gauntlet was Martin Gallagher. He was making haste, as witnessed by Mulholland, when he fell with a ball through the leg. He was unable to move it because the bone was badly broken. He was left on the field and by the end of the conflict had received six wounds.[180]

In due time, three of the four brigades that Caldwell had brought to the fight had now been pressed into the Wheatfield, swarming with Confederate troops. Many of Caldwell's men were confused as to where to go and whose command was where. The confusion allowed many of the Confederates to close on their adversaries. A soldier in the Phillips' Legion mentioned, "We went into them with our bayonets and clubbed them with our guns. It was here that I went after the flag; and after shooting one man, and clubbing five others, I was in the act of reaching for the flag when a fellow named Smith jumped in ahead of me and grabbed it. I came very near clubbing him, but he put up such a pitiful mouth about having a family of small children that he wanted to see so bad, I let him have it so he could get the furlough."[181]

With Zook's, Kelly's, and Brooke's brigades in full retreat, the bulk of the
Confederate advance now struck three regiments of Sweitzer's Brigade and two
of Cross's regiments. Cross's Brigade had begun to fall back just as Wofford
and Semmes began their attack. Still lying wounded on the field was Lt. Charles
Fuller of the 61st New York. He had earlier been struck by one of the Confederate
deadly missiles and had lost the use of a leg and arm. Soon, Fuller spotted two
comrades, making haste toward the rear of the brigade. "I yelled out to them," he
later mentioned, "Drag me back!" The two men stopped, grabbed Fuller on either
arm, and began to haul their officer to the rear "not on any funeral gait, but almost
on a run." The two men continued to pull Fuller back a few rods and over a slight
elevated piece of ground when he cried out, "Drop me." Wordlessly, they dropped
Fuller and continued on their way.

Fuller drew a tourniquet from his haversack and began to apply it as best he
could with his "one serviceable arm." He later recalled, "I did the best I could to
get it around my leg, for anything I knew I was bleeding to death, and, if possible,
I wanted to check the flow of blood. I think my effort did not amount to much."[182]

Elements of Brooke, Kelly, and Zook were streaming through the hotly contested Wheatfield at this point. The 61st New York and 81st Pennsylvania had
recently fled from the field, leaving only a few companies of the 148th Pennsylvania and the 5th New Hampshire still in position in the woods. They were finally
compelled to fall back. Colonel McKeen noted in his official report, "The Fifth
[New Hampshire] and the One hundred and forty-eighth [Pennsylvania] remained
in position, steadily holding the enemy in check, until every round of cartridge in
this portion of the brigade was expended, and even then held their position until
relieved by a brigade of General Barnes' Division of the Fifth Corps. Pass the
relieving brigade by file, they retired in splendid order, as they were enfiladed by
a galling fire from the left flank."

After the battle, much of the credit was given to those troops that stayed in
their position and endured the heavy fire of Anderson's Brigade. Major Forster
reported that while Colonel Brooke had been driving the Confederates from Rose
Woods, Brooke's "position here was an exposed one; and he was repeatedly told
to look out for his left flank.... contrary to expectations, he experienced no trouble
from that direction. Hearing afterwards of the portions of the First Brigade that
remained in place by Colonel McKeen's order, Brooke freely acknowledged that
it was their fire that kept the enemy off his threatened flank," for the most part.[183]

General Caldwell stated in his official report: "The division on the afternoon of
the 2d fought with its accustomed gallantry, and performed everything that could
be expected of either officer or men. The large number of killed and wounded
attest its desperate valor. That it fell back was owing to the breaking of the troops
on the right, permitting the enemy to get on its flank and rear."[184]

Major R. H. Forster reported afterwards that Caldwell "falls into a slight inac-
curacy of fact," in that "when he came to speak of 'falling back,' he should have
excepted the First Brigade from his general statement, because in no sense should
it be understood that this brigade was forced to fall back from any cause, and not
a single man, unless wounded, left its line until it was regularly relieved by other

troops." Whatever the case, the First Brigade took a pounding by both artillery and infantry fire, losing 38.7% of its number during the three-day battle, nearly all on July 2.[185]

Nearly half of the 148th Pennsylvania had fallen back, while the other half remained on the firing line. One of the men left behind was Pvt. Henry Meyer, still observing Anderson's Brigade streaming from boulder to boulder through the Rose Woods. Soon, he realized that his comrades on his left had begun to fall back. He rushed through the woods and, finally, back to the stone wall that most of his regiment had defended moments before. There, he found Cpl. Jacob Lanich "lying dead, being shot through the head from ear to ear." Sergeant G. W. Leitzell was not far from Lanich, having been shot through his knee. The injured sergeant, feeling the rush of the oncoming Confederates, beckoned Meyer to assist him to the rear. With all the strength he could muster, the young private got the sergeant to his feet and attempted to assist him. However, the exertion from fighting for nearly an hour in the hot July sun fatigued Meyer. He could only bring the sergeant part way to the rear until he had to lay him down. Meyer, "then gave him my canteen which was filled with water in exchange for his, which was empty. Half an hour later he was in the hands of the enemy."[186]

Private Meyer continued to fight. Apparently, he fell in with Ayres' counter-attack, eventually linking up with Cpl. Manassas Gilbert of his regiment. He had been severely wounded in the shoulder blade "and was quite weak, being hardly able to walk." They both, with the assistance of another soldier, reached the summit of Little Round Top.[187]

In Company I of the 148th, R. M. Wadding received a "bad gunshot wound in [his] groin." He lay on the field for several hours. Near him, Pvt. Samuel Shaw of the same company was shot dead. His comrades Privates Thomas McCullough, Harrison Long, Frederick Gillhousen, and Andrew Hagerty were all mortally wounded in the Wheatfield. Wadding witnessed Hagerty "start to walk off the battlefield, while the enemy were between us and our lines, and that seems to be the last known of him." Privates Edward Pyler, John Howard, John Shuster, Hugh Barr, and many others were wounded, yet were eventually able to rejoin the regiment.[188]

Another soldier in the 148th Pennsylvania, Pvt. Lemuel Osman, who earlier had his musket literally blown to pieces in his hands, realized the regiment was running out of ammunition and it would not be long before the order would come to fall back. Within moments, they fell back to the stone fence bordering the Wheatfield where the command was given to "Lie down." A brigade of Bucktails then passed over the men and were compelled to march farther to the rear.[189]

In the 5th New Hampshire, Major Hale continued watching over his prisoners even while his beloved colonel lay bleeding only a few rods away. After the order to charge never occurred, Hale's prisoners became "troublesome." Therefore, he started them to the rear while trying to keep them "as clear of the woods as possible for fear they would make a break." One of the Confederate officers kept his eye on Hale while looking at his surroundings for a chance to escape. Hale responded by keeping him on the left of the line and in the open ground for as long as possible. The group soon crossed a fence near the Trostle house and came to a spring where wounded men were resting in the sun and drinking its fresh water. Hale noticed that Lieutenant Gove was among them. He had been wounded in the shoulder and that "his clothing was drenched with blood." The ghostly-looking officer soon drew himself upward and continued to the rear unsupported.[190]

The wounded of the 148th Pennsylvania included Pvt. Jacob Carter, who was at the tender age of 19 when he enlisted on August 19, 1862. During the charge for the stone wall, he was struck in his right hamstring by one of Benning's or Anderson's Rebels. He fell to the ground in great agony. He lay in this position "under both fires and the Rebels carried their flag over me twice," he recalled. Carter twice fainted because of the pain and loss of blood in the Wheatfield, only to again regain consciousness while the Confederates rushed wildly around him. Fearing for his life, the young private smeared blood from his wounded leg onto his face and hid himself in a furrow until the Confederate squad had passed by his position. He then commenced to pull out a leather strap that his uncle had given him before leaving for the war and used it to make a makeshift tourniquet. He would lay on the field of battle for days before being gathered to the rear and placed in a field hospital where he would receive treatment from nurse Mary Jane Ledy in Gettysburg. The two hit it off and, after making a full recovery, they were married the following year.[191]

Many of Caldwell's soldiers hastily regrouped in Trostle's Woods. Soon thereafter, they fell back farther toward the Taneytown Road where they continually heard and saw the sounds of battle still raging from the area they just vacated. **SWEITZER'S BRIGADE** still held its position on the far end of the field, while Ayres remained deployed along the eastern breastwork. These brigades were all that were in the way of the Confederate tide from bearing down on the men. Colonel Sweitzer recalled that he "observed… that there was considerable firing diagonally toward our rear from these woods, which I then thought were shots from our troops aimed over us at the enemy in the woods beyond and falling short." That was not the case, however, as Anderson's Brigade, supported by Semmes' and Kershaw, began to pound away at the remaining Federal defenders.[192]

The Confederate onslaught soon turned into a full-blown inferno. A soldier of the 4th Michigan recalled the opening moments of phase two of the Wheatfield conflict, "Then commenced that terrible harvest of our brave men." Another man from that regiment recollected, "Rebels to the right of them, rebels to the rear of them, and rebels in front of them, volleyed and thundered." The fire enveloped Sweitzer's Brigade in a cloud of smoke, dust, and fire causing confusion. Still, Sweitzer's men kept up their fire until a color bearer near Sweitzer turned and exclaimed to him, "Colonel, I'll be damned if I don't think we are faced the wrong way; the rebs are up there in the woods behind us, on the right." Almost immediately afterward, Sweitzer was informed that the 4th Michigan and the 62nd Pennsylvania were beginning to take a blistering fire from the direction of Stony Hill, causing their flank to waver. Sweitzer's quick thinking allowed him to refuse the two regiments and buy time for reinforcements to come up and support his stand.[193]

A Perfect Storm of Confusion

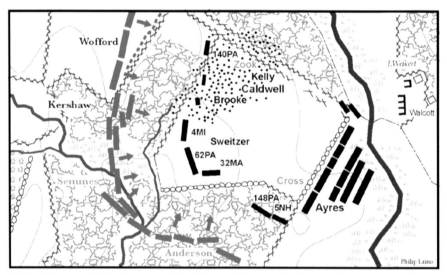

Caldwell's attack is broken up as Confederate brigades begin to make a strong push back. As they retire off the field, Ayres begins to send his men forward to confront the attack.

Above the roar of musketry and exploding rounds, the colonel of the 4th Michigan, Harrison Jeffords, could be heard shouting, "Stand firm, my brave boys; my brave 4th Michigan, stand firm," and they did so with utmost tenacity. Jeffords directed his men with great zeal and was loved by the entire regiment for doing so. As they crossed into Pennsylvania, just days before, he had halted his men and exclaimed, "Men you are now standing on free soil once more now give three cheers for the free States." Now, here, in this small Pennsylvania farm field, he was prepared to give his all for the cause of the Union.[194]

With one problem addressed, Sweitzer then sought to solve the other. He dispatched Lt. John Seitz, his aide-de-camp, to find General Barnes to tell him of their situation. In a mad dash, the lieutenant was off and reached the point where he had last seen Barnes. The general could not be located, however, and it was found that "the enemy [Wofford's Brigade] was in the woods on our right as far back as where we had started from, and along the road in rear of the wheat-field." Therefore, finding that they were completely surrounded, Seitz rushed back to report to Sweitzer.[195]

On his way back, his horse was killed. Seitz raced on foot to locate the colonel to direct "the command to fall back." It was too late, however, and onward came the Rebels in a thick band. The mass of gray and butternut tide, "Yelling like demons… [as they] rush[ed] upon our little band, crowding us back by sheer force of numbers, step by step, into the murderous wheat field, and pressing right into the heart of the regiment," one soldier reported. [196]

While this was the ultimate outcome, this was not the only time that the brigade was ordered to fall back. Not long into their stand, the 32nd Massachusetts' commander, Col. Luther Stephenson, received an order to fall back from an officer from Sweitzer's Brigade. Stephenson assumed that the order must have come from Colonel Sweitzer and began to withdraw his men from the Wheatfield. Sweitzer became "fighting mad" at the withdrawal, which he had not ordered, and immediately sought the reasoning behind their retreat. The commander of the 32nd merely stated that he was carrying out orders and halted his men, turned about, and began to fight the enemy again. Not for long, however, as soon as the command to retire came, he was heard above the din of battle, "Left face, and every man get out of this the best way he can."[197]

Jacob Sweitzer (*Library of Congress LC-DIG-cwpb-05579*)

General Barnes watched from a secure position to the rear of Sweitzer's Brigade. He watched in horror as they became "nearly surrounded and in a very perilous position," as remembered by one soldier. Barnes spoke as Sweitzer began to break, saying, "There goes the Second Brigade, we may as well bid it good-bye." However, they would get off the field by retiring "diagonally" and suffered "heavily" as they fell back, occasionally halting to fire on their pursuers.[198]

During the withdrawal, color-bearer Thomas Tarsney of the 4th Michigan abandoned the flag that he had sworn to protect, with his life if necessary. It was almost immediately seized by Confederate troops once they infiltrated the area. Stunned by the chain of events, Col. Harrison Jeffords shouted for the assistance of Adjutant Richard W. Seage and Lt. Michael Vreeland. Jeffords with his "hat off, his eyes flashing with the light of battle, with drawn sword, rushes full upon them." Within a moment, the trio confronted the Rebel holding the banner. Jeffords reached for the flag staff, after just firing his revolver directly into the surging Confederate soldiers. Just then, Seage struck the flag-seizing soldier with the blade of his sword. The impact sliced through the Confederate's neck, severing the main artery. "Rally round the flag, boys," Jeffords called aloud. Then, more Confederate soldiers came to the assistance of their fallen brother-in-arms and, "literally pin[ned] the gallant Jeffords to the earth with bayonets."

A desperate hand-to-hand fight ensued for possession of the coveted flag. Michael Vreeland fought off several Rebels until he received a bullet in the chest and was bashed over the head with the butt of a musket. Seage was shot through his breast and stabbed in the left leg with an enemy bayonet. Colonel Jeffords had another bayonet run through his body, inflicting a mortal wound less than two rods away from James Johnston, his tentmate who had been shot earlier. It was remembered by one soldier, "No grander hero fell on this dreadful field than Harrison H. Jeffords, the only officer of the army killed with the bayonets of the foe. There, on that low ground... is the spot where that fight for the flag took place and where the soil drank the blood of our hero chief, and of many of our bravest comrades."[199]

The colonel crashed to the ground in a hard thump and shouted, "I am killed!" With nobody to come to their aid, the three badly wounded Union soldiers lay still as the Confederate tide swept over them and recaptured their flag. All they could do was helplessly watch as it disappeared to the rear. Colonel Jeffords, Seage, and Vreeland were captured and carried to the rear where they were placed with many of their comrades.[200]

The Confederate that delivered the fatal blow to Jeffords did not have long to live. After the war, a member of the regiment stated, "The man at whose hands he lost his life was a moment after gasping in death. A bullet from Major Hall's revolver had entered his brain. Conspicuous for gallantry in the hand to hand conflict was Capt. William Robinson. He killed six rebels with his navy revolver and was then one of the officers to snatch the musket and cartridge box of a dead soldier and kill others." Another account validates the claim. James Houghton of the 4th Michigan's Company K remembered a few days after the battle: "...on the bank near the trench lye [sic] a large Rebel Sargent [sic] one of our mineys [sic] balls had passed through his head so quick that it dislocated all the Confederacy there was in it and it was gradualy [sic] oozing out onto the Ground for the flies to Diagnosis. It was said that He was the man that Stabed [sic] Colonel Jeffords."[201] Jeffords died the following morning. His last reported words were, "Mother, mother, mother."[202]

THE REGULARS ADVANCE

With Sweitzer's Brigade beginning to fall back under the Confederate pressure, General Ayres sent Colonel Burbank forward with the first line of the United States Regulars. Their alignment, from right to left, was the 2nd U. S., 7th U. S., 10th U. S., 11th U. S., and 17th U. S. Almost immediately, the brigade made a right wheel maneuver that spanned nearly halfway across the Wheatfield, sweeping aside Confederate skirmishers along the way. The 61-year-old Col. Sidney Burbank had been a classmate of Robert E. Lee at West Point and had graduated in 1829. He received his baptism by fire in the recent Battle of Chancellorsville, a month earlier. There, he performed well under the circumstances. Now, in the Wheatfield at Gettysburg, he would again perform well under much of the same pressure, as he thrust his U. S. Regulars against four brigades of surging Confederates.[203]

As the Regulars advanced forward, broken elements of Sweitzer's Brigade moved through his ranks, occasionally disrupting his lines. The men had to watch where they stepped or faced tripping over the men that were fleeing or had fallen, with exception of Lt. Col. J. Surrell Greene's 17th U. S. Infantry. They closed in on the woods where the 5th New Hampshire and the 148th Pennsylvania had earlier advanced and fired into the flank of Anderson's Brigade. The 17th U. S. began to take fire from Confederates ensconced in Devil's Den and on Houck's Ridge. Greene's men remained stationary in this position for some time as they battled back and forth with the posted enemy. Greene recalled, "At this time the left flank was much exposed to the enemy's sharpshooters, and the left company… was thrown back to confront this fire and to a more secure position under a slight rise of ground."[204]

As Burbank's Regulars moved forward, Col. Hannibal Day's brigade of Regulars also moved forward. They held the stone wall on the west side of the Wheatfield, just as Burbank had before. Day's alignment, from left to right, was the 14th U. S., 12th U. S., 6th U. S., 4th U. S., and 3rd U. S infantry regiments. Almost immediately after getting into position, Day heard the commotion between Burbank and the Confederates. His left flank, by this time, was also beginning to take fire from the area of Devil's Den. Therefore, he shifted the 14th U. S. by changing much of their line to face in that direction. It was a wise decision. Within a few minutes, it looked like the men of Anderson's Brigade were going to break through the area of Rose Woods and deliver an enfilading fire. Now, he had soldiers in position to counter the enemy move.

Meanwhile, as Burbank continued his wheeling movement toward the southern end of the Wheatfield, his men came under attack from Wofford's Brigade. The Regulars continued past the point where Lt. James Purman of the 140th Pennsylvania helplessly lay. "Come and cut my boot off my foot," Purman shouted to the passing tide. One of the Regulars hurriedly knelt down and commenced cutting. His knife, however, being dull put pressure on the lieutenant's wound. Purman quickly asked the soldier to cease.[205]

The Confederate line formed on Burbank's flank and fired down his line. The 2nd U. S. bore the brunt of the attack and men began to fall. This caused the regiment to lag behind the rest of the wheeling motion, eventually causing them to stall entirely. Major Arthur Lee, in command of that regiment, recalled, "A fresh column of the enemy at this time appearing upon our right… [there were] three lines of the enemy, elevated one above the other on the slope to our right, poured in a most destructive fire, almost decimating my regiment and cutting off the color-staff, causing the colors to fall into the hands of the color-bearer." However, this had to either be a misrepresentation or Lee was the victim of a fading memory because only two lines at any time were formed by the Confederates and only one by Wofford. Whatever the case, the 2nd was soon ordered to withdraw. As they "retired slowly to the shelter of the woods, again they crossed the stone wall, rocky rising ground, and marsh in good order as the ground would admit, under a most withering fire."[206]

During this time, Lt. William Fisher of the 10th U. S. and his fellow infantrymen had halted near the southern end of the Wheatfield. They remained in this position in the attempt to buy time for additional support to be brought up. Within ten minutes of the beginning of the Regulars' fight, Fisher received a bullet in the chest. Lieutenant George Hamilton, who was standing a few feet from Fisher at the time, said that the stricken officer raised his left arm to try to drape it around his neck. Soon, other soldiers came to their assistance. Sergeant Terrance McCabe recalled, "[Fisher] grasped a tree while falling and was carried to the rear by Lt. Hamilton, Welles, and myself. He rolled his eyes full of gratitude toward us but already he was speechless. He never uttered a word after being wounded." They carried Fisher to the rear, toward Plum Run. A smile appeared on his face as he gazed upwards. Not a man of the detail could hold back the tears. McCabe said of his fallen officer, "In all… general engagements he behaved… with a coolness, intrepidity and personal bravery, almost unequalled during my long time of service. While in the Army he was always of a sedate, contemplative character and never did I hear a profane word come from his lips."[207]

Lieutenant Hamilton noted that McCabe was wounded in the side while carrying Fisher. Unable to carry him on, the detail continued to the rear. Soon, Welles, too, was wounded in his leg and unable to continue as well. The hopeless struggle finally subsided and they lay the dying Fisher down. Hamilton remembered, "After I had left him a few paces I returned and took possession of his watch which was turned over to Capt. Bush of the 10th Infty along with all his effects. You wish to know if he lingered after he was struck or if he seemed to suffer with pain. Now to the best of my opinion he did not live five minutes after he received the wound nor did he seem to be in the least pain for when I stooped over him to take his watch their was seemingly no life and there was a smile on his countenance."[208]

The Confederates Fall Back

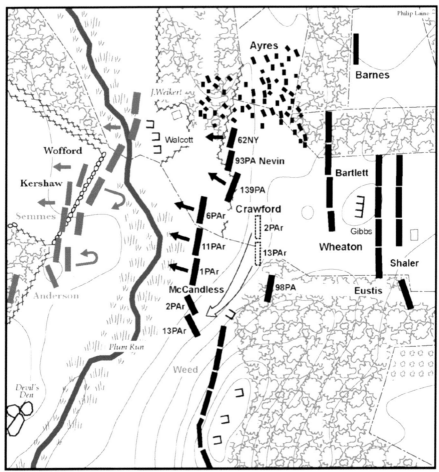

The remaining Confederates that broke through the counterattack are now met with a heavy wave of counter-resistance themselves and are swept from the field.

With the 2nd U. S. now retiring, the 7th became the right-most regiment as the brigade continued its stubborn advance. It, too, came under this destructive flanking fire, which caused the men, like those of the 2nd, to fall back toward the stone wall. After the 2nd broke, the rest of Burbank's Brigade retired from the right-most rank and on. The Confederates were now in full possession of the Wheatfield, at least temporarily.[209]

Colonel Day, who had just come into position near the stone wall, barely had time to finish forming his brigade before Burbank's Brigade broke in front of him. Almost immediately, the Rebel brigades of Wofford, Kershaw, Semmes, and Anderson advanced in a long line of battle spanning the length of the Wheatfield, through Rose Woods to the south, with two regiments of Wofford's Brigade supporting them in Jacob Weikert's Woods to the north. As Day watched this enemy force in front of him, he received an order from General Ayres telling him to withdraw his men to Little Round Top. Lieutenant Colonel John H. Page was near Day at the time. He later described the incident in a letter:

> I saw General Ayres with some staff officers about fifty yards to our right. I also saw our troops… to our right and front, retiring with their colors drooped. I ran to where General Ayres was and heard him say: 'Those regiments are being driven back.' Some one said they were retiring to a new position. General Ayres replied: 'A regiment does not shut up like a jack-knife and hide its colors without it retreating.' I ran back to my company. General [Colonel] Day was right behind it. A staff officer came to him and told him to retire to the base of Little Round Top, just as soon as our 2nd Brigade in the woods came out. General Day asked me to strike a match, as he wanted to light his pipe. I did so, and he bent over, his horse was shot through the neck.[210]

Within moments, Ayres's Division broke across the soon-to-be-named "Valley of Death" toward Little Round Top. Federal artillery had previously been deployed throughout the area in anticipation of the Confederate attack. Lieutenant Aaron Walcott's 3rd Massachusetts Light Artillery was positioned next to the John Weikert farm, with a two-gun section of Capt. Frank Gibbs's Battery near Little Round Top. Four other guns of that battery were unlimbered near the Valley of Death facing the Wheatfield. Four guns of Charles Hazlett's Battery D, 5th U. S. Artillery had been hauled to the summit of Little Round Top.[211]

While Barnes' and Burbank's retreats were in progress, Gibbs's Battery opened upon the advancing Confederate infantrymen. Captain Gibbs later explained, "Our front was hardly clear when the irregular, yelling line of the enemy put in his appearance, and we received him with double charges of canister, and were used so effectively as to compel him to retire. So rapidly were the guns worked that they became too hot to lay the hand on."[212]

Near the base of Little Round Top, the situation was much the same. Lieutenant Page was caught up in the charging Confederates. He recalled, "As we were falling back, we saw the battery officers at the base of Round Top waving their hats for us to hurry up. We realized that they wished to use canister, so took up the double-quick. As I was crossing the swampy ground, Captain Freedley… was shot in the leg, fell against me, and knocked me down. When I got the mud out of my eyes, I saw the artillery men waving their hats to lie low. I got behind a boulder with a number of my men when the battery opened with canister. The rebels came from all directions for the guns, and lost all formation. They waved their battle flags."[213]

The shock of what Day's and Burbank's men had endured was reflected years later when a soldier of Brig. Gen. Stephen Weed's brigade famously wrote, "For two years the U. S. Regulars taught us how to be soldiers, in the Wheatfield at Gettysburg, they taught us how to die like soldiers."[214]

The valley between Little Round Top and the Wheatfield turned into a sight of terror. Dead, dying, and wounded men were piled on top of each other. The once-clear waters of Plum Run now ran thick and muddy with a red tinge from the blood of fallen soldiers. Spent and dropped balls lay on the ground. Shirks, gasps, groans, and sighs could be heard throughout the field. Yet, the Confederate infantry still pressed forward. A soldier recalled this surreal scene, "A few hundred yards to the foot of little Round Top, already strewn with our disabled comrades, became a very charnel house, and every step was marked by ghostly lines of dead and wounded. Our merciless foes from their vantage ground on our right, poured in volley after volley." Another soldier recalled, "[Our] attention was attracted to the solid, raining, regular tramp of firm, determined men. Concealed by the smoke of the irregularities of ground, the sound of approaching mass was heard before the line appeared in sight."[215]

The Rebel attack wave soon began to pass through the remaining sections of the Wheatfield into the open plain of the Valley of Death with Little Round Top in their front. Captain Hillyer of the 9th Georgia recalled that it was "a rocky hill and about a hundred and fifty or two hundred feet high, sloping so that a person could climb it, but with difficulty." The newly positioned Fifth Corps division of Brig. Gen. Samuel W. Crawford awaited them on the summit of Munshower's Knoll, just north of Little Round Top.[216]

Crawford had earlier placed elements of his division from right to left: the 6th Pennsylvania Reserves, 11th Pennsylvania Reserves (Fisher's Brigade), 1st Pennsylvania Reserves, and the 2nd Pennsylvania Reserves in the rear. The 13th Pennsylvania was held in a second line in temporary support but soon would form on the left flank.[217] To the right of Crawford was the 3rd Brigade, 3rd Division of the Sixth Corps under Col. David Nevin (taking over for Brig. Gen. Frank Wheaton). Their line was to the rear of Walcott's Battery and John Weikert's house. Quietly, they awaited their orders to move forward. Their alignment was, from right to left, the 62nd New York, 93rd Pennsylvania, and 139th Pennsylvania.

The Yankees on Little Round Top joined with Crawford's men to pour lead into the Rebels. Hillyer noted, "Their combined fire was almost resistless. Our line emerged from the stumpy brush through which we had charged… and the elevated plateau which stretched away on our left… We had then been fighting for over three hours… I could see to the right and left… thirty-five or forty battle flags, and only from thirty to fifty men with each. On crossing this opening and going a little way up the rock slope, we saw that no one of the entire line was nearer the enemy's position than we were."[218]

A soldier in the 11th Georgia believed, "Nothing but the exhausted condition of the men prevented them from carrying the heights… this rout was vigorously pressed to the very foot of the mountain, up the sides of which put the enemy in greatest confusion"[219]

The Confederates applied steady pressure to Gibbs's Battery and pushed partially up Little Round Top's steep rocky slope. At one point, an officer of the battery rushed toward the 11th Pennsylvania Reserves and said, "Dunder and Blixen, don't let dem repels took my batteries." A soldier in the regiment remembered "his earnest words of appeal, as the enemy hurried up to the positioned." Immediately, Col. Samuel M. Jackson yelled to the artilleryman to "double-shot his guns, hold his position, and we would see to their safety." A Pennsylvanian responded, "Stand by your guns, Dutchy, and we will stand by you." Jackson remembered, "This seemed to put new confidence in the captain, who returned to his guns and served them most heroically, inflicting frightful execution upon the foe, as he poured the shot and shell into their very faces."[220]

On the right flank, Walcott's Battery was in trouble. Most of the infantry supports had been pushed off the field, and ammunition was becoming scarce. Soon, Walcott ordered that his guns be spiked but only one gun was successfully disabled. Under tremendous pressure from Wofford's Georgians, Walcott was forced to abandon his other five guns without spiking them. He and the surviving artillerymen fell back toward Cemetery Ridge and the guns fell into Confederate hands.[221]

Finally, Crawford decided that he could wait no longer and ordered his Pennsylvania Reserves forward. He realized that "the enemy were coming over the wheat field, I saw their red flags very plainly & I appreciated the fact that something need be done." With a rush, his men began to drive the Confederate attackers backward down the hill and toward the Wheatfield. Evan Woodward recalled:

> Most gallantly did the brave fellows dispute the ground, but the overpowering masses of the enemy swept victoriously on, and their wild shout of triumph rang through the valley. Our battery to the right belched forth its sheets of flame and smoke, hurling its missiles of death over the heads of the flying mass into the enemy immovable and firm stood the Reserves, resting on their arms, silently gazing on the magnificent and grand sight, until our broken masses had passed to the right, and the enemy had advanced within fifty paces, when the gallant Crawford, seizing the standard of the First, whose bearer had been shot down (Color-Sergeant Bertoless Slott), waved it aloft and cried out, "Forward, Reserves." With a simultaneous shriek from every throat, that sounded as if coming from a thousand demons, who had burst their lungs in uttering it, on swept the Reserves, delivering, as they started, a solid volley, and careering vicariously over the field.

As Crawford reached to grab one of his regiments' national flags, Cpl. George Swope protested, "I can't give you my colors." The stunned Crawford replied, "Don't you know me, I am your general, give me your colors." Swope handed them over with a reluctant huff. Crawford hoisted them high and began to charge the enemy as his brigade followed. All along, little Swope held tightly on to the trousers of the general.

Nevin's Brigade from the Sixth Corps advanced on Crawford's left flank. Together, the two brigades pummeled the exhausted Confederates and drove them back across the Valley of Death into the Wheatfield. All along, Crawford's diminutive companion Swope held tightly on to him. Near the end of the charge, Crawford handed the colors back to the brave young man, who continued to carry them throughout the rest of the battle.[222]

Crawford's Division swept forward with a rush and a cheer. Not halting for a single moment, they reached the stone wall separating the Wheatfield from the Valley of Death where the Confederates made "their last desperate rally to retrieve the day." It was not to be for the Confederate force, however, as "standard bearer after bearer was shot down, but with empty muskets the column pressed on, and leaping over, bayonetted and scattered in flight the proud foe," recalled Colonel Jackson. He had also recalled the counterattack, "I gave the command to fix bayonets and charge. This order was obeyed with a will and, with that familiar yell peculiar to the Pennsylvania Reserves, we rushed upon the foe with a determination to either drive the invaders back or sacrifice ourselves on our native soil." With the enemy soon in full retreat, Woodward remembered, "One loud shout of triumph rang through the valley and over the hills, and it was with the utmost difficulty the men could be restrained from following the enemy further."[223]

Lieutenant Charles Fuller of the 61st New York was still lying on the ground during the Confederate retreat. Moments earlier, he had witnessed the enemy line of battle pressing over him. Now he watched as "the officer in command was mounted and rode by within a few feet of me... Shots were exchanged at about that distance to the rear of me. This fighting was not severe and a short time after these gentlemen in gray moved back in the same manner they had advanced, greatly to my relief. I did not fancy remaining their guest for any length of time."[224]

The Confederate force must have been amazed when they saw the Pennsylvania Reserves charging toward them. After such a push as they had made in the Wheatfield, driving Union brigade after Union brigade back, they were now routed. Captain Hillyer remembered, "I heard no order to retreat and gave none, but everybody, officers and men, seemed to realize that we could not carry the position, the enemy outnumbering us probably ten to one, and we exhausted, and our ranks thinned as they were. By common consent we fell back to a point where there was a stone wall." After briefly rallying at that position, the Rebels continued farther to the rear.[225]

Lieutenant Fuller continued to lay in his position when a young Confederate soldier came forward "whose face was smutted up with powder and smoke." He demanded from Fuller, "Give me that scabbard!" Fuller responded, "Johnny, you will have to excuse me, as my arm is broken and I can't unbuckle my belt." With not a moment to spare, the Confederate lifted the sword out of the sheath and rushed away from him.[226]

After the conflict had begun to die down, General Crawford sought out Samuel Jackson. He approached him with the compliment, "Colonel Jackson, you have saved the day, our regiment is worth its weight in gold; its weight in gold, sir." Captain Gibbs of the Ohio battery soon approached the regiment to thank the infantrymen. Bringing himself to their attention, he uttered, "The Pennsylvania Reserves saved mine pattery, by god. I gets you fellers all drunk mit beer."[227]

Meanwhile, Captain Hillyer and his Georgia comrades continued to fall back. They, eventually crossed paths with the 11th Georgia. Lieutenant James Morrow of that unit came rushing toward Hillyer and was heard to exclaim, "If you have been in there any further and could not do anything, there is no use for me to go." The two men quickly jumped over the stone wall and began to call for the halt of their troops. Major Henry McDaniel of the 11th Georgia, farther to the right of the two officers, called for the same. Hillyer remembered, "It is my testimony that every man who heard his voice or mine, or was near enough to see, be attracted by our words and gestures, stopped at once and formed a line behind that wall." In less than a minute, the officers reformed what was left of their entire line, and soon it "was well in hand just as much as before the charge began." From this position, they continued to move to the rear and rested near the gorge of Plum Run to the same position they had held earlier.[228]

The final leg of the charge of Anderson, Semmes, Kershaw, and Wofford had failed. Almost immediately after the conflict, blame of who was at fault for the failure began to circulate through the Confederate camps. General McLaws stated, "I accordingly formulated a series of questions which would cover the claim made by General Crawford, and sent a copy to General Wofford, whose reply was never received." Colonel Benjamin Humphreys of the 21st Mississippi, one of the men also questioned, later answered with the statement that "Wofford's Brigade was not driven back, nor did they go back because they were afraid to fight. Wofford must have gone back by order from some superior authority… I did not know of the Pennsylvania Reserves under Crawford." Likewise, Col. Goode Bryan answered the question by stating, "I can and do most positively assert that my command was not driven back… and I further assert that I received the order to fall back from a courier of General Longstreet. I also positively assert that there was no enemy on our right or front to cause us to fall back."[229]

Nobody ever forgave General Longstreet in Wofford's command for making such a decision in the moment. However, a quick glance at the position of the Federal batteries and infantry would most certainly make one see that the possession of that hill would most likely have not succeeded. Longstreet attempted to attribute his decision to withdraw his men due to mistakenly identifying the Sixth Corps as being in position and performing a counterattack. The Confederate ranks were reformed in a position fronting Stony Hill and the Rose Woods. The Wheatfield, therefore, became a no-man's-land for the duration of the battle.[230]

By twilight on July 2, the fields and woodlots of the battlefield were scarred by the horrors of battle. John Caldwell's soldiers continued to lick their wounds as they reformed south of their initial point of advance. While, off to Caldwell's right, Willard's Brigade of the Second Corps formed against Barksdale's Mississippians and battled while they were engaged in the Wheatfield. They were soon ordered forward into the Plum Run gorge to halt his advance. During the ensuing melee, both William Barksdale and Col. George Willard received mortal wounds. Farther on their right, the 1st Minnesota was thrust into battle against Wilcox's Brigade, stopping the Alabamans at the cost of most of the men in the Second Corps regiment.[231]

After Confederate Brig. Gen. Ambrose Wright's assault had been repulsed, most of the battlefield reined in silence until a general engagement ensued to the right rear of Caldwell's position involving Howard's Eleventh Corps against two of Jubal Early's brigades on East Cemetery Hill. Farther to the right, and at the same time, Wadsworth's First Corps Division, along with Brig. Gen. George S. Greene's brigade held their line on Culp's Hill against the forces of Maj. Gen. Edward "Allegheny" Johnson. The attack on East Cemetery Hill was repulsed, but Johnson's Confederates did capture some vacated breastworks on Culp's Hill.

Throughout the fields of Gettysburg, the Federals successfully held their lines. Though, in some intervals, they were broken a time or two, they remained in their "fish-hook" position to face the Confederates another day. On Seminary Ridge, Robert E. Lee contemplated his next move. He concluded to attack Meade's flanks at first light the following day. Both flanks of the Federal line had held this day, but General Wright did break the line in the center. With Pickett in reserve and coming up, he determined his division would lead the attack the following day.

Likewise, Meade had to make a determination as to what he desired to do. He called together his Corps commanders to his headquarters at the home of Mrs. Lydia Leister on Taneytown Road. There, Meade's chief of staff, Maj. Gen. Daniel Butterfield, proposed three questions for the corps commanders to ponder:

1. Under existing circumstances is it advisable for the army to remain in its present position, or to retire to another nearer its base of supplies?
2. It being determined to remain in its present position, shall the army attack or await the attack of the enemy?
3. If we await to attack how long?

The vote only took but a minute and was found to be "unanimous to remain and fight it out," too much of the approval of General Meade. On question three, it was decided not to attack "until Lee moved." Brigadier General John Gibbon of the Second Corps remembered, "I never heard General Meade say one word in favor of a retreat, nor do I believe that he did so, being confident I should have heard it… I recollect (that) there was a great good feeling amongst the corps commanders at their agreeing so unanimously, and General Meade's announcement, in a decided manner, 'Such, then, is the decision.'"[232]

Meanwhile, agents of the Bureau of Military Intelligence under the direction of Col. George Sharpe interviewed various prisoners taken during the two days of fighting. The findings were astonishing. The intelligence officers learned that they had captives from every known division in Lee's army with the exception of Pickett. Given that insight, they suspected that if Lee resumed his attack on the following day, he would use his fresh division and would probably attack the center, held by elements of Hancock's Second Corps with supports in reserve.[233]

CHAPTER 4

The Bloody Aftermath of July 2

"Like the day star in the wave
Sinks a hero to his grave,
Midst the dew fall of a Nations tears,
Happy is he on whose decline
The smiles of home may soothing shine.
And light him down the steep of years;
But oh how grand they sink to rest
Who close their eyes on victory's breast."[1]

THE WHEATFIELD, AND ITS ENVIRONS, RESEMBLED SOMETHING out of a horror film. General Crawford, after sweeping the area and ordering his men to halt, noted in his official report, "The dead of both sides lay in lines in every direction, and the large number of our own men showed how fierce had been the struggle and how faithfully and how persistently they had contested for the field against the superior massed of the enemy." Veteran Robert Carter described the scene in his book:

> The picket duty having been performed, we were relieved and going still further to the front…we made a tour of the blood-soaked field… In every direction among the bodies was the debris of battle—haversacks, canteens, hats, caps, sombreros, blankets and every shade of hue, bayonets cartridge boxes—every conceivable part of the equipment of a soldier of the blue or grey mingled with the bodies of Yankee and rebel, friends and foes… They were in every possible position, with arms uplifted, with clenched fist and menacing attitude, some with the smile of peace as though death had come gradually and without pain. Others, and the majority, had a settled and determined expression as though filled with revengeful thoughts. Some were in the act of tearing a cartridge, others just loading or reaching for the rammer—all called forth in a moment in the twinkling of an eye—though the mysterious hereafter… Our tour extended well to the front, across the swale inside our picket lines, now held by the Pennsylvania Reserves… Masses of Kershaw's and Wofford's Brigade advancing up to the muzzles of these guns, which had been loaded either with double shotted canister or spherical case, with fuses cut to one second—to explode near the muzzles—had been literally blown to atoms and in a moments brief space into eternity. Corpses strewed the ground in every step. Arms, legs, heads, and parts of dismembered bodies were scattered all about, and sticking among the rocks, and against the trunks of trees, hair, brains, entrails, and shreds of human flesh still hung, a disgusting, sickening, heartrending spectacle to our young minds. It was indeed a charnel house—a butcher's pen—with man as the victim.[2]

Many men from John Caldwell's Division lay strewn over the blood-soaked ground that they had tramped over. Major Robert Forster of the 148th Pennsylvania noted that the division was "weary and worn by the toil and excitement of the afternoon, all sank to rest for the night upon the crest of Cemetery Ridge, while many of our comrades were sleeping the long sleep of death in the Wheatfield and woods where they had fallen." The assistant surgeon of the 148th Pennsylvania, Dr. Alfred Hamilton, established a temporary hospital at the modest home of Jacob Hummelbaugh. "The family had just left a partially eaten meal on the table," Hamilton noted. "A half barrel of flour was in the attic… the flour tided us over in the 'slapjacks' made by Davy McIlhattan." The house was soon flooded with wounded from the Third Corps and other soldiers who were too weak to make it to their respective field hospitals. One of these injured men was **CONFEDERATE GENERAL BARKSDALE**. Hamilton described his injuries:

> He was shot through the left breast from behind, and the left leg was broken by two missiles… he was brought by some staff orderly to my temporary hospital. I gave him what I had to relieve him. He asked several times whether I considered his wound necessarily mortal. I told him I did. He desired peace, but only upon terms that would recognize the Confederacy. He was large, corpulent, refined in appearance, bald, and his general physical and mental make-up indicated firmness, endurance, vigor, quick perception and ability to succeed whether as politician, or civilian or warrior… He asked about our strength and was answered that heavy re-enforcements were coming. Said he, 'Militiamen under McClellan?' He said that Lee would show us a trick before morning; that before we knew it Ewell would be thundering in our rear. He was dressed in the jeans of their choice. His short roundabout was trimmed on the sleeves with gold braid. The Mississippi button, with a star in the center, closed it. The collar had three stars on each side next to the chin. Next his body was fine linen or cotton shirt which was closed by three studs bearing Masonic emblems. His pants had two stripes of gold braid half an inch broad, down each leg.[3]

William Barksdale (*LC-USZ62-100480*)

General Barksdale died soon after being taken to the house. He was buried in the yard and later reinterred in his native state of Mississippi.

Lying on the field, exposed to the elements, many of Caldwell's wounded men could not make it to the field hospitals. As they awaited assistance, thoughts of home, sweethearts, wives, sisters, brothers, fathers, mothers, and other loved ones began to creep in. The stillness, only being broken by a shot from a picket rifle or two, was all that some men could handle. Soldiers attended to the wounded; a few robbed the dying that littered the Wheatfield during the proposed temporary truce.

One of these men still lying about was Lt. Charles Fuller. To him, the field seemed to calm a bit as the sound of battle gradually died. However, soon the incessant moans and groans of the injured began to fill his ears. He attempted to move several times, but each time he found the pain to be severe and had to give up trying to find a more comfortable position. Fuller remembered, "I had heard that wounded men always suffer from thirst, but I was not specially thirsty, and I wondered at it."

He continued to listen to the stricken men around him. Moans, shrieks, and shouts filled the mid-summer night air, to the point that Fuller took it upon himself to try it. He remembered, "I did not have any desire to groan… So I wondered if I were really badly hurt, and if I could groan, if I wanted to. I determined to try it, and drew in a good breath, and let out a full grown-man groan. I was satisfied with the result and then kept quiet." After this incident, he realized that a picket line was beginning to form to his rear. He successfully drew the attention of a sergeant who told him the number of his regiment. Fuller then called to the officer, stating that he "wanted to get back out of this debatable belt of land between the skirmish lines." The sergeant replied that he would go to his officer and seek permission to retrieve the fallen lieutenant. Within a few minutes, the sergeant came back with his lieutenant. Both men conversed. Fuller cried out that "[his] present anxiety was to get to the rear of our skirmish line-that where I then lay was likely to be fought over again, and any little thing, would… set the pickets firing at one another."

The officer still expressed doubt as to whether they would succeed in getting Fuller off the field safely. Confederate skirmishers were all through the woodlots. Fuller then suggested that the two men could create a makeshift chair with "their hands, as children often do." The two officers, at once, hastily made their way to the lieutenant and placed their hands under him. They started to lift him "but the broken leg hung down, and caught in the trampled wheat." Fuller screamed in pain that he could not go on. However, not to be deterred, the officer suggested that he would carry Fuller on his back. The two men struggled to get the lieutenant on his back which they, eventually, succeeded. Fuller remembered, "Then he attempted to raise me up, but my weight and the tangled foot were too much, and we all went down in a heap together, I under." In the fall, Fuller had the wind knocked out of him. He desperately gasped for air, eventually coming to, and said that "if they would straighten me out and cover me up with my blanket, I would excuse them with thanks for their kind intentions." The two men did and were back over their lines within a few minutes.

The darkness now settled in all around Fuller. He lay on his back and gazed up at the stars in wonder of what was yet to come. As he described it, "my thoughts went on excursions the wide world around." For hours, he lay there, hearing "no sound but the groanings of the men lying on the field about me." He soon recognized the voice of a private in Company A, Phil Comfort. "Phil had always been one of the incorrigibles. He would get drunk, and brawl, and fight on the slightest provocation… I do not know what Phil's business was… I suspect he may have been there for the purpose of accommodating any corpse that was desirous of being relieved of any valuables he was possessed of, fearing they might be buried in an unmarked grave with his dead body." The private had a knack for helping the wounded on every battlefield that he had ever been involved in. Soon, the lieutenant shouted for the private to draw near to him. He recalled:

> I never asked Phil about the orders, or from whom they came, that sent him in to hailing distance of my place of repose, but I made haste to call Phil up to me. He responded to my call, and in a moment was staring down on me in the starlight. He said, 'Why, Lieutenant that's you ain't it!' I admitted the allegations, and said I wanted to get out of here. He replied that he would go for a man and stretcher.

Within a few minutes, Private Comfort arrived with the help necessary in taking Fuller off the battlefield. Soon, he and others carried the lieutenant to a field hospital slightly to the rear. There, Fuller found that most of the wounded from his regiment had already been taken to this location. He received immediate attention from surgeons who cut open his trousers. They found where the bullet had entered and quickly put a strip of adhesive plaster over the wound to slow the bleeding. Fuller told the doctor that he believed that his leg should come off at once so inflammation might not set in. At his earnest request, the doctors promised him that he would be the first to see the operating table. However, this was not to be, and Fuller watched impatiently as one soldier after another were brought onto the surgeons' table and examined before him. Time passed and July 2 turned into the third. Eventually, with the assistance of Pvt. Porter Whitney and another man, Fuller had them take him down to the table, setting him down right under the noses of the doctors. Shelling soon began for Longstreet's Assault and the place of operation was moved.

Later the next day, at a different field hospital, Fuller encountered one of his men from Company G, **FRANKLIN GARLAND**, who had been struck by an enemy round in the Wheatfield. Fuller noted that "his breathing was painful to hear. A bullet had gone through his lungs and every time they filled a portion of the air went through the wound with a ghastly sound." Fuller asked his friend, "Are you badly wounded, Frank?" He replied, "Oh, yes!" After a few moments, Fuller was moved to the official Second Corps field hospital and immediately placed on the operating table. Where, under the use of chloroform, the operation was successful. Unfortunately, Garland did not survive his wound. The 21-year-old died on July 4. He was later re-buried in the New York section of the Soldier's National Cemetery.[4]

Lieutenant James Purman of the 140th Pennsylvania continued to lay on the ground during that terrible night. He recalled, "The dead and wounded of both armies lay thickly strewn over the field, which was still disputed ground." Purman slowly placed his leg in as easy a position as possible to help alleviate the pain radiating throughout his whole body. He went on to say, "Never shall I forget that midsummer night. The almost

Franklin Garland (*Personal Collection of The Thanatos Archives—Jack Mord*)

full moon was shining, with drifting clouds passing over her face. At intervals with its covering the trampled and tangled grain, boulders and wounded and dead men, then passing off revealed ghastly scenes of cold, white, upturned faces. It was indeed a field 'Covered thick with other clay, heaped and pent, Friend and foe in one red burial blent.'"

The night wore on for the men lying in the field. Purman was no exception. The quiet was frequently broken by the cries and groans of the wounded, lying in a seemingly endless field of pain and sorrow. Not far from Purman, an injured soldier repeatedly cried for his regiment, "Oh, Seventh Michigan!" His pitiful manners strained the nerves of all lying nearby.[5]

The next morning, July 3, a sharp skirmish broke out in the Wheatfield and the wounded were caught in the middle of it. "As the sun rose higher, the firing grew hotter," wrote Purman, "our wounds more swollen and thirst more intense… the prospect of our relief became exceedingly hopeless." During the fray, Lieutenant Purman noticed the Michigan man who had been begging for his regiment to save him. He was a sergeant. He hoisted himself off the ground as best as he could and asked Purman, "Have you any water?" Purman replied, "No, but I have a little whiskey." "For God's sake give me some," the man replied. "I am dying from thirst." Purman, as best as he could, rose to his good leg and threw the canteen with all the force he could muster toward the soldier. It fell about half-way between the men as shots from nearby Confederates began to hiss around them. Purman recollected, "I heard a ball make that peculiar thud, and the sergeant cried out, 'I'm struck again! My right hand was resting on my left arm and the ball passed through my hand and arm.'"[6]

The two wounded men lay under the storm of lead passing over them. The sergeant called to James again, "Are you a praying man?" When Purman replied in the affirmative, the Michigander said, "Then pray for me." There, on the field of blood, sweat, tears, and battle, the two men prayed. "If ever there was an earnest, sincere petition sent up to the Throne of Grace it was then," recalled Purman.

Hours passed and the restless men grew tired of lying under the blistering sun. Occasionally, they rose up and attempted to reposition themselves to keep from becoming too sunburned on one side or the other and to assess their surroundings. "Nothing could be seen except a line of blue on one side and gray on the other," Purman later wrote, "and nothing heard but the crack of the rifles and the zip of bullets in the wheat, or their well-known thud in the ground or the body of a wounded man." About 2 p.m., the men were listening to the opening of the cannonade that preluded Longstreet's Assault when Purman again adjusted his position and hoisted his leg at an angle, exposing it above the trampled wheat. That proved to be a mistake. Another ball struck him between his knee and ankle. With a shout to his Michigan friend, he cried, "I've got it again through the other leg."

They both agreed that they must get off the field by any means necessary and, by lying closer to the Confederate lines than their own, they decided heading toward the Rebels was the best route. They searched for any movement by their Rebel counterparts. Soon, they spotted a nearby Southern soldier, who turned out to be Thomas P. Oliver of the 24th Georgia. Purman cried out, "I am twice wounded and dying out here. Won't you bring me a canteen of water?" Oliver replied, "I can't do it. If I attempt to come out there your sharpshooters will think I am trying to rob you and pick me off." The lieutenant answered with a groan, "Crawl through the tangled wheat, and you will not be seen from our side. At Chancellorsville I saved the lives of many of your men, who would have died from thirst." Oliver was moved by the plea of the fallen Union officer. He quickly filled his canteen in the bloody waters of Plum Run and began to crawl to Purman. "When he reached me," Purman recalled, "I drank and drank, and thought it was the sweetest water I ever had tasted." The Rebel then poured some of the water on Purman's wounds and cut his boots from his legs.

These simple acts of kindness gave Purman a rejuvenated hope for life. He told his Confederate companion just as he was about to leave him, "This is a pretty hard place for a man to lie, between two fires. Can't you carry me out to where your line is posted in the edge of the woods?" Oliver stopped for a moment and answered, "The way the balls are flying, if I should attempt to lift you up we would both be killed." Eventually, he agreed to hoist Purman on his back and carry him from the field.

Halfway to the Confederate lines, Purman shouted, "I can't hold on any longer" and fell to the ground unconscious. His Rebel partner went back to Plum Run and, refilling his canteen, threw water on the face of Purman. Thus revived, Purman asked, "Where am I? What is the matter?" Oliver explained the circumstances and again picked up the Federal officer. They continued forward until they reached the outcropping of woods near the Stony Hill. There, Oliver placed his new friend on a rubber blanket and gave him some water and a Confederate biscuit. Purman gave Oliver his watch as thanks for his effort but insisted, "Please don't take my sword belt, as it is a gift from friends at home. Oliver affirmed, "It shall not be taken."

After drinking a little more water, Purman again felt like himself. He asked to be taken to the rear so that a surgeon could look at his leg. He was told that the Confederates were too tired to move so far to the rear and that it was best that he stayed there with them. Soon, however, they noticed that the Pennsylvania Reserves were again forming to attack. Purman stated, "You need not trouble carrying me off—our boys are coming." Crawford's Reserves moved forward and poured a heavy volley into the Rebels as they crossed the Wheatfield. The retreating Confederate troops fired a few shots and fell back in great haste. One of the wounded men still in the field called out, "Fire high! Fire high!" Purman remembered, "Although the balls rattled among the rocks and trees about me, I enjoyed that charge hugely, for it meant victory." His smile broke into laughter as Purman saw blue-clad soldiers coming to his aid. Purman was taken to the rear, where he would lose his leg to a surgeon's knife.[7]

The misery south of Gettysburg did not end with the wounded. Portions of whole commands were assigned to the grim task of burying the dead and tending to the dying during the night of July 2. One of these men was the pioneer, Sgt. Thomas Meyer of the 148th Pennsylvania. It was about eleven o'clock at night when they were ordered "with picks, shovels and sperm [whale oil] candles" to the field to help accomplish the task. To their dismay, they "found acres of ground covered with wounded, and among them, many who died after being brought here from the field." They scanned the ground. "This was an awful place," admitted Sergeant Meyer, "the most able writer could not give the slightest shadow of an idea of this dreadful charnel scene; the awful sights in the wheat field and death valley thickly strewn over with weapons, cannon, broken gun carriages, thousands of dead men and horses, mutilated in all manner of form and degree."

The ghastly scenes on the battlefield chilled the bones of even the most hardened soldiers. Cold forms that had passed lay strewn among the barely able. The burial crews separated the Confederate and Union dead in long rows. They "lay promiscuously side by side, and close together… on the bare wet ground, the feet of one row nearly touching the heads of the next row."

The dim flicker of candles could be seen all over the Wheatfield. Many of the wounded, and their assistants alike, questioned why there were no surgeons near this point in the battlefield. Meyer noted, "The men in hundreds of cases dressed each other's wounds, making bandages out of their drawers taken from their bodies for the purpose… Men wounded in the legs had the pant legs cut off, some close to the body, leaving the leg entirely naked; in the same way arms, chest, all parts of the body naked and uncovered."

In the open fields and woods, the wounded laid exposed to the harsh elements. "Many lay entirely helpless," recalled Meyer who continued through the bloody wheat, "till the skin was scalded and burned into pealing blisters in the face." Comrades stumbled upon one another in the dying light. Meyer and his pioneers encountered Amos Erhart of Company A of the 148th Pennsylvania. He had few clothes on and sported "a nasty hole through the thigh just grazing the femoral artery." The men looked at Erhart and noticed that his pant leg had been cut off, a shoe and stocking were gone, and "the naked leg [w]as cold as ice." They began to fear the worst for their comrade but found that the wound had been nicely dressed and was no longer bleeding. Erhart "remained asleep in the darkness, as soundly as anyone could in the best bed."

Manassas Gilbert, also of Company A, sat a few feet away on the ground with his back leaning against a tree. A bullet had entered his shoulder, causing so much pain that the pioneers found him awake. Meyer stopped at this point and listened to the "deep moans of agony in continuous chorus," which made this position a real "Hell on Earth." Graves only about a foot deep were prepared for the dead. To save time, Meyer said that "a shallow grave [was dug], against the first man in a row, and he was then laid down into it; a similar grave was dug where he had lain. The ground thus dug up served to cover the first man, and the second was laid in a trench, and so on, so the ground was handled only once." This practice saved both time and limited work.

The time was about 3 a.m. when the candles were about burnt out and signifying that their work would soon cease. Meyer and the others in the burial crews quickly packed their belongings and regrouped at their respective field hospitals. When they arrived, Meyer found "the wounded… in greater distress. The endless and louder moans were indicative of intense suffering." Meyer recalled:

The voice of a boy was heard in prolonged loud wails and screams, high above the rest. His voice became hoarse and husky, but as morning came he was more quiet, and a little later entirely still. I imagined he had fallen asleep. As soon as it was light enough I went over and asked the wounded lying near, 'Where is the boy that was in such agony during the night?' A wounded soldier raised himself on his elbow, pointed over a few others and said, 'That is him; he is now dead.' I went over to him. He was a boy about sixteen, smooth faced as a woman and handsome. He was dead; one of his feet was torn into an unrecognizable mass of flesh, bone and sinew. Gangrene was evidently the immediate cause of death. Early amputation would have saved the boy's life. Here many had died of their unattended wounds during the night… When the operations were finished they were carried away, and laid out on the ground. There was no time to assist them in resuscitation, and many never woke again. Many strangled to death for the want of a little assistance at the proper time.[8]

SAMUEL ZOOK'S LAST MOMENTS

The wounded Brig. Gen. Samuel K. Zook was brought from the field with the aid of his friends, Josiah Favill and Charles H. Broom. Zook was clearly in great pain. Broom examined the wound and declared that the general was shot through the bowels and the wound looked severe. Immediately, Favill left to seek out the closest ambulance that may be found. Before he returned, however, the general was being placed upon a stretcher and was being carried to the rear. Zook came under the care of Surgeon Charles Wood, described by Favill as "one of our best doctors." who examined Zook's injury and told his companions that he believed it to be fatal and nothing could be done.[9]

A quick glance around revealed that there was no nearby shelter to house the general. They needed to move him away from the active battlefield as soon as possible. Favill recalled, "The enemy's shot frequently reaching the spot, we took the general on a stretcher, and carried him." The men had traveled but a short distance when they came to the G. Flemming Hoke tollhouse along the Baltimore Pike. There, they found the home already full of severely wounded men. To Favill, the "sight was most distressing; the howls of pain from the men in the hall and front room were so dreadful that we moved the general back into a small room cut off from the others, and here we spent the night." The men did what they could to make the general as comfortable as possible under the circumstances. Several times in the night, Favill and Broom left the room to look at the "ghastly scenes on the floors of the hall and parlor," as Favill noted, "As many men as could lay side by side completely covering the floors, which were streaming with blood, and the poor fellows seemed to give way completely to their misfortunes." More than twenty of the wounded in the tollhouse died during the night of July 2.[10]

General Zook remained calm despite the obvious severity of his injury. He ordered those "who carried him [to] put his blanket under him so that he would not bloody the bed." Quietly, he spoke to those around him and never to himself, seemingly suffering little from the pain. On the morning of July 3, his attendees moved the stricken general farther to the rear. On the way, the small band encountered crowds of soldiers, ambulances, trains, and disorganized infantry columns. They traveled nearly a mile when they turned and found themselves at an, what is now, unknown location. Several women occupying the residence tenderly cared for the dying general. The woman fed the tired band with some chicken soup and broth, of which the general took very little.[11]

Hours passed and the patient began to fail. Lieutenant Favill suggested that he see the chaplain of the 66th New York, James H. Dwight, always a favorite of Zook. The dying general declined, saying that it was "too late." Soon after, he instructed his comrades to look after his possessions and "then he calmly awaited the end," in Favill's words.[12]

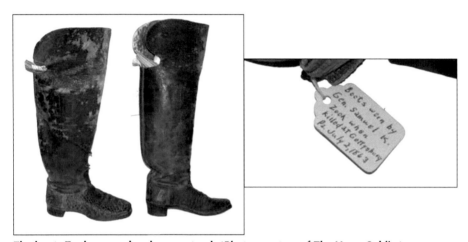

The boots Zook wore when he was struck (*Photo courtesy of The Horse Soldier*)

At times, the general began to show some hope for improvement. He spoke brightly and with "considerable animation." It gave the men around him such encouragement that they began to believe that, perhaps, the surgeon was mistaken in his grim diagnosis. It was so encouraging that the men began to attempt to get Zook to believe the same but the general shook his head, uttering that "there was no hope." Near five o'clock, the general began to slip away. He expired a few minutes later.

"Thus ended the career of a brilliant officer, an estimable gentleman, and a faithful friend," Favill wrote. "Killed at the head of his troops, on his native soil, defending the honor and integrity of the country he loved so well, is after all a glorious death to die, and so far as he is concerned, perhaps is the most fitting climax of a brilliant career… He was to all of us friendly in the extreme, just, exacting at times, but always ready to acknowledge and give us credit whenever we deserved it. His death interrupts all our plans for the future, and our interest in military affairs seems to have entirely evaporated. What a blank in our lives his death will cause. From the day I met him first on Staten Island, when I turned out the guard to please him, I have been with him and always close to him, and knew him more intimately than any other person in the army."[13]

COLONEL CROSS'S LAST MOMENTS

Another of Caldwell's key subordinates mortally wounded in the Wheatfield was the black-bandana wearing Col. Edward Cross. He had been taken to an unknown location, perhaps the William Patterson farm, where he received full medical attention from the surgeons around him. One of the only hints that we have as to the exact location is an account from Lt. Thomas Livermore, who stated that "it was a little dell, one through which a little stream ran, between the Taneytown road and Baltimore Road, and from a quarter to half a mile from my park going toward Gettysburg."[14]

Near midnight, according to Dr. Child of the 5th New Hampshire, "He was carried about one mile to a locality directly in the rear of the right wing of the army, near Culp's hill, into the midst of a wheat-field." Looking about, Child described that the crop had just been cut and bound, and "camp-fires crackled and glimmered, flashed and cast weird shadows around the group of friends and attendants." An artillery shell soon hurled across the sky, illuminating the entire plain as it burst overhead with a "stunning report." The grieving men gathered to witness the waning colonel's final moments including his brother, Maj. Robert Cross. He bent low by his brother's side while Assistant Surgeon Child silently watched the colonel slipping away.

"All faces were sad, all hearts were sorrowful," Child recounted. Colonel Cross then spoke a "kind word for all." He turned to his brother, still kneeling at his side, and gave his words of kindness. He asked Robert to send his "love to his sisters and brothers, and with tears and sighs urged his brother to care for the mother and to convey to her his tenderest regard and love." More artillery shells whizzed across the sky and a brief exchange of picket fire erupted a short distance from Cross's position. For a moment, some consideration was given to moving the colonel away from the potential danger but the decision was made to stay put. About 12:30 a.m., Cross began to murmur, "My brave men, my brave men" over and over. He lived but an hour longer, then fell silent before whispering his final words, "I think the boys will miss me."[15]

Meanwhile, Lieutenant Livermore had received word that Cross was mortally wounded. He desired to see the colonel as soon as possible. However, being in charge of the ambulance corps, Livermore had to refrain from that activity until he had completed his duties on the field. Finally, about midnight, Livermore was free to seek out the colonel. He halted his horse at the Peter Frey farm, dismounted, and began searching. "Here," he recalled, "under the shelter of some boulders lay a large number of our wounded and dead who had been brought from the field. They lay upon the ground covered with their blankets, and the living were nearly all silent, having fallen asleep from fatigue."

Livermore, like so many other concerned soldiers that night, picked through the dead and wounded on his way to find the colonel. Finally, in the dim light, he noted a Union officer lying on a makeshift bed. Unsure if it was Cross, Livermore asked a nearby officer if the man was indeed Colonel Cross. He affirmed that it was indeed Cross but he had died. Livermore slowly walked toward his beloved colonel's body. He "turned his blanket back from his face, and saw it was true that he was dead. The moonlight or starlight enabled me to see his features distinctly. They were placid and exceedingly lifelike, and it was hard to persuade myself that the flush of life had gone from them. His lofty forehead was smooth, his long, silky beard lay upon his breast disheveled, and looked more as he would if he slept than seemed possible."[16]

A passing soldier consolidated the visibly shaken Livermore, telling him that Cross had called his regiment to surround him in his final hour and had stated that "he did not regret death, except that he had hoped to see the rebellion suppressed; that he hoped they would be good soldiers and keep up the discipline and good conduct of the regiment."[17]

Livermore remained seated next to the dead colonel for some time. Eventually, he noticed a nearby lieutenant from the 2nd New Hampshire, likely mortally wounded, who apparently had been wounded near the Peach Orchard. Livermore recalled that "it was a mournful thing to think of his dying there, not only away from home, but away from those of his own regiment who might have cared for him," as he could not help comparing the two men. Livermore recalled that he was "oppressed" with regret that he had failed to come and see the colonel in his final moments before he expired.

Privately, he noted of his beloved Colonel Cross: "He was a very brave man, and clear-headed in a fight; he took the most excellent care of his men in a sanitary way, and was a good disciplinarian. He had his faults which injured him more than anyone else; such as jumping to conclusions, and criticizing and condemning men and measures without stint... If all the colonels in the army had been like him we should never have lost a battle. Other volunteer regiments, many of them, were composed of as good men as ours, but I do not think there were half a dozen in the army which were as good in every respect as ours, and we owed that to the colonel... Colonel Cross taught us—by rough measures, to be sure, sometimes— that implicit obedience to orders was one of the cardinal virtues in a soldier... He taught us to aim in battle, and above all things he ignored and made us ignore the idea of retreating. Besides this he clothed us and fed us well, taught us to build good quarters, and camped us on good ground, and in short did everything well to keep us healthy, well drilled, and always ready to meet the enemy."[18]

The Butcher's Bill

Another man lying dead on the field was the colonel of the 140th Pennsylvania, Richard P. Roberts. His ornate sword, which bore the inscription, "Presented to Captain R. P. Roberts by the citizens of Beaver," was missing, presumably taken by an unknown Rebel. Hundreds of other men and officers in Caldwell's Division were also now victims of the second day's fighting at Gettysburg.[19]

On the morning of the 4th of July, Maj. L.W. Bradley and a small party of soldiers from the 27th Connecticut ventured out into the fields and located the bodies of Lt. Willis Babcock and Capt. Henry Fuller of the 64th New York. They collected the remains and took them to the rear of the George Weikert farm, where they buried them. Bradley wrote on an envelope, "Lt. W. G. Babcock 64th Regt N.Y.V." and placed it on the body. The lieutenant's sword, memorandum book, and billfold were missing. Major Bradley recalled that, "At the head of Capt. F(uller's) grave I cut this mark 'T. F.' in the rock. We put up head boards to each grave, cut the name Lieut. W. G. Babcock, 64th N.Y. on the head board of Willis. We made the best coffin we could of boards, and rolled him in his blanket. On the top of his box coffin I placed a bent bayonet."[20]

The property owner later erected a small fence around the two graves. Throughout the battlefield, small planks and temporary graves dotted the landscape, but nothing like it was near the Wheatfield. After the battle, close to five hundred graves reportedly were spread across the area. The actual number, however, was probably fewer. It does not take away the importance the Wheatfield played during the Battle of Gettysburg.[21]

In the temporary field hospitals in and around Gettysburg, thousands of wounded men were receiving treatment. The often-gruesome scenes horrified onlookers unaccustomed to viewing battlefield injuries. The patients included Pvt. Robert L. Stewart, later the regimental historian of the 140th Pennsylvania. During the late afternoon, a shell fragment had temporarily paralyzed his leg. He was taken to the Second Corps field hospital near Meade's headquarters at the Widow Leister house. He later described the scene:

> Acres of ground were covered with wounded, dying and dead men. At times the stretcher carriers separated the dead from the living, but meanwhile others passed away in their places. Those who could care for themselves sat or lounged on the ground at the foot of a tree or beside a great rock, but the larger number were lying on their backs in long rows without pillow or shelter, for as yet the hospital supplies, somewhere in the rear, had not arrived. Between the rows of prostrate men there were narrow lanes to permit the attendants to pass. At intervals in the open spaces were long rows of tables around which faithful surgeons with sleeves rolled up to the shoulder had been at work since daybreak in two or three reliefs, each one working so long as his strength would hold out. In all serious cases chloroform was administered and thus much suffering was prevented; but, oh, the horror of the carving and the heaps of human legs and arms on the ground at the ends of the tables, and the pallid faces and the smothered moans of anguish, which could not be repressed. These and other sights and sounds that may not even be mentioned will remain while life lasts as the saddest reminders of those days of turmoil, suffering, and fraternal strife.[22]

Scores of stricken Confederates were intermingled with the wounded men of Caldwell's Division who still lay where they fell or crawled in the Wheatfield and environs. Wounded, but still conscious, Lt. W. E. James of the 8th South Carolina looked around in the twilight for any survivors from his Company F. He did not know that, of the 312 infantrymen engaged from his regiment, 172 were now casualties. After spotting a few of his men, James noticed Steven Bozeman "lying on the porch of a house with his arm broken." James walked over to the young man and comforted him the best he could. The time grew late, however, and he determined that nothing more could be done for his men that night.[23]

When he awoke the next morning and looked around, James found that more than half of his company lay around his location. He later wrote that "some of them (were) mortally wounded and all in need of attention." James immediately went to work to aid his fellow South Carolinians. When a nurse came to James, he suggested that the surgeon look at George Bozeman, who was still bleeding from a head wound. The nurse assured him that they were doing the best they could with what they had to work with, and he would be attended to as soon as possible. Not being satisfied, Lieutenant James located Dr. James F. Pearce and Dr. James Evans a short time later and made his appeal. Pearce noted, in response, that Bozeman had already been looked at but was "mortally wounded and must die today." Looking sorrowfully toward the young man, the physician noted, "We can't help him; we are trying to help those who may live." James turned from the surgeons and sought his friend to do the best he could for him.

The following day, George Bozeman (still alive somehow), along with James and others, was loaded upon wagons and taken southward to Williamsport, Maryland. The surgeons there, being less busy than the frantic pace at the field hospitals in Gettysburg, were summoned to examine Bozeman and verify his seemingly hopeless situation. One of them agreed to see if there was anything they could do for him. James recalled, "After several efforts with his forceps he drew from Bozeman's ear a grape shot weighing ten ounces which had entered the ear and lodged under the bones of his head." Bozeman eventually made a full recovery, giving a small glimmer of hope in those dreadful days.[24]

As the 9th Georgia had advanced toward the enemy, Captain Hillyer encountered a young soldier, apparently wounded, named John Stephens. His arms were dangling over a rail post. The captain quickly rushed toward his comrade and inquired, "What's the matter John?" Stephens did not mention that he was wounded. Instead, he matter-of-factly replied, "Captain, if you will help me over the fence, I will try to go on." When Stephens turned, Hillyer noted, "I got a view of his face and there, too, was the handwriting of a mortal stroke." The captain told him to lie down and he would have the litter corps carry him to the rear. That night, before he slept, Hillyer went to see what had been done for Stephens but, "I found a new made grave. He died just where he had when the fatal bullet struck him, and where his fine spirit had still impelled him to say, 'I will try to go on.'"

In the still night air of July 2, soldiers lay sprawled in all conceivable forms and fashions. The sight must have touched the most hard-hearted man. Captain Hillyer noted:

It was a moonlight night, and it was whilst this humane work [the litter corps had been in the field] was going on and during the existences of the truce I have mentioned, that one of our soldiers out between the lines, I think it was one of General McLaws' men, began to sing. He was probably a boy raised in some religious home in the South, where the good old hymns were the standard music. I have heard much that the world applauds in the way of high grade music, but considering the occasion and the audience, I have never heard music like that. Many wounded from a battle can walk away, and some are carried away by the litter-bearers. But in the still air and moonlight of that night, there were hundreds, perhaps thousands of desperately wounded men lying on the ground within easy hearing of the singer, whose fine voice rang out like a flute, and echoed up and down the valley and the little mountain in our front. Not only the wounded, but also five or ten thousand and maybe more of the men of both armies could hear and distinguish the words. There was a marked silence that could come only from attention. And I think the Federal line could hear him as well as ourselves. One of the hymns he sang was this familiar one.

> *'Come, ye disconsolate, wherever ye languish;*
> *Come to the mercy seat fervently kneel,*
> *Hither bring your wounded hearts, here tell your anguish,*
> *Earth hath no sorrow that Heaven cannot heal.'*

The last song he sang was then familiar, but now is an almost forgotten old ditty, 'When this cruel war is over.' At its close, I heard a clapping of hands and a cheer from the Yankee lines. Truly, 'One touch of nature makes all the world kin.'"[25]

CHAPTER 5

A Stiff Fight on July 3

"The muffled drum's sad roll has beat
The soldier's last tattoo;
No more on life's parade shall meet
That brave and fallen few.
On Fame's eternal camping-ground
Their silent tents are spread,
And Glory guards, with solemn round,
The bivouac of the dead."[1]

THE RIGHT WING OF THE FEDERAL ARMY—the Twelfth Corps and other elements—rested on Culp's Hill. After Confederates from Maj. Gen. Edward Johnson's division captured part of the breastworks on the night of July 2, they sought
to complete their task very early the next morning. About 3 a.m., the Rebels opened
with artillery fire. By dawn, musketry crackled from the opposing lines. Sleep was
impossible. According to Winthrop Sheldon of the 27th Connecticut, "The men
were roused from sleep by a furious cannonade from batteries posted... about half
a mile to the rear." Private Henry Meyer of the 148th Pennsylvania added, "The
battle opened with crash of musketry and thunder of cannon at our right."[2]

The ground began vibrating from the intense artillery fire. Lieutenant John
Noyes of the 28th Massachusetts related, "At 3½ A.M... the unwelcome sound of
cannon, and whizzing shells was our reveille." Orders soon came and the division
was directed forward, advancing to the cover of a slight ridge on Cemetery Hill
where they formed a new defensive line.[3]

For nearly an hour, "this thunder-toned reveille awoke the resting armies,"
Sheldon noted. On Culp's Hill, during the night, the Federal divisions that had
marched away from their breastworks the previous day to bolster the center and
left of the Federal line had attempted to return to their fortifications. Finding them
occupied, they made successive attacks along the lines. Troops as far away as the
Union left flank heard the fighting taking place on the right. A soldier lying in his
lines on Cemetery Hill "could hear the cheers of Geary's men, which came to us
on the morning air, mingled with the bullets which had missed the mark for which
they were intended... singing over our heads."[4]

Major General Winfield S. Hancock, meanwhile, began realigning his brigades, including Colonel Kelly's Irish Brigade. The Sons of Erin had returned to

137

their campsite of the previous night. On the morning of July 3, Hancock ordered Major Mulholland's 116th Pennsylvania to move forward to support the guns of Sterling's 2nd Connecticut Battery. Once in position, the men sat calmly "chewing hardtack" as they watched "great volumes of smoke arise from the timber, listening to the crash of the musketry, watching streams of wounded that poured out of the dark woods, seeing the reinforcements hurrying to the assaulted point, and joining." Company A, with Capt. John Evans now in command, of the 2nd Delaware was detached and ordered to move forward to establish a picket line. During the day, it was reported that 64 Rebel prisoners, mostly from North Carolina and Georgia, were sent to the rear.[5]

About 8 a.m., General Hancock ordered his soldiers, including those of Caldwell's Division, to construct breastworks in preparation for a possible enemy assault on the center. A soldier from Cross's Brigade recalled that Hancock rode up to the line and angrily asked Colonel McFarlane, "Where in the Hell is General Caldwell?" McFarlane matter-of-factly replied, "To the left of us." Hancock, known for his prolific use of profanity, turned and exclaimed, "Why in the Hell hasn't he got his men throwing up breastworks?" Not knowing how to answer the question, McFarlane deferred. An angry Hancock rode off to find Caldwell and demand an explanation. He located his subordinate whose excuse was a lack of tools, which simply did not allow his division to accomplish their task in a quick manner. That response did not sit well with the corps commander, so he sought a way for the task to be accomplished quickly. Within moments, he noticed a wooden fence off to the front of the division. Hancock ordered the men to use the rails in the construction of their works. A soldier recalled, "These fences disappeared as if by magic."

Still, Hancock was displeased with the slow progress of his men and, within a few minutes, he ordered the pioneers forward with "entrenching tool wagons dashing…, and shovels, picks and axes were thrown out while the wagons rushed along the line at a furious speed." Out came Sgt. Thomas Meyer of the 148th Pennsylvania along with several other pioneers and immediately set to work. "Men never worked harder or faster," Meyer claimed, "or with greater good will than the Second Corps boys did under a broiling July sun." The makeshift hasty works included rocks, logs, sticks, and battlefield debris taken from neighboring fences and other locations. After a few minutes, Thompson's Battery rumbled into position near the Irish Brigade. Meyer's pioneers borrowed some of their tools to use in constructing the works. Lieutenant Noyes recalled, "We brought rails and stones, piling them about two feet high, making the works as thick as possible… Soon two or three spades were passed along the line, and using the bayonet for a pick-axe the works were considerably strengthened." Major Mulholland of the 116th Pennsylvania disagreed slightly with Noyes' recollection. He stated, "The men gathered rocks and fence-rails and used them to erect a light breastwork. Had the necessary tools been distributed to the troops we could have entrenched this line and made it formidable, but we could not find a pick or shovel, and the works that we did attempt were very light, scarcely sufficient to stop a musket ball."[6]

General Hancock proceeded along Caldwell's line to Maj. James Coburn of the 27th Connecticut and Colonel Brooke. The men conversed for a few moments when Brooke, pointing to the small remnant of the 27th Connecticut, told of the strong conduct of the regiment the previous day. Hancock turned and addressed the infantrymen, "Stand well to your duty now, and in a few days you will carry with you and your homes all the honors of this, the greatest battle ever fought upon the continent."[7]

After the breastworks were finished, Caldwell's men prepared for the anticipated resumption of the battle along their front. Lieutenant Gilbert Frederick of the 57th New York recalled that his regiment had eaten a quick breakfast, then "accoutrements were put on, boxes refilled with cartridges, and all was ready for the fray." The rest of the division, meanwhile, listened while awaiting the fight to begin. Many others awaited word from Culp's Hill's fight. The anticipated proclamation of a victor in the engagement was too much for some men to bear as they continued to listen to the musketry. Finally, at nearly 11 o'clock, "the firing suddenly ceased," according to Major Mulholland, from that direction. Then, a cheer erupted from the hills. It traveled through the valley and up the banks of the adjacent hill to the ears of the men of Caldwell's Division. A soldier in the 116th Pennsylvania noted, "A minute later every man in the army knew we were again in possession of Culp's Hill."[8]

Earlier in the morning, on Seminary Ridge, General Lee had ordered Lt. Gen. Richard S. Ewell's Third Corps to make a demonstration at Culp's Hill in an effort to pull reinforcements from the Union center and left flank to the right flank of the army. However, Lee changed his mind and decided to postpone the assault until 11 a.m. Unfortunately for the Confederates, General Longstreet was not ready for the planned attack at 10 a.m., nor at 11, nor 12. As the hours passed, the soldiers along the Federal line in the center on Cemetery Ridge witnessed the massing of Rebel artillery along Seminary Ridge and environs. The enemy guns were ready to direct their fire toward the center of the Union lines, because Lee wanted to attack there.

Longstreet, in an interview well after the battle, reasoned with his decision to delay his attack, "I did not see General Lee that night. On the next morning he came to me, and, fearing that he was still in his disposition to attack, I tried to anticipate him by saying: 'General, I have had my scouts out all night, and I find that you still have an excellent opportunity to move around to the right of Meade's army, and maneuver him to attacking us.'" According to Longstreet, instead of Lee acknowledging the change of direction of the attack, the army commander simply said, "The enemy is there, and I am going to strike him." Longstreet felt his duty was to express his feelings. Being known as Lee's "Old Warhorse," there was nobody better suited to express his opinion to Lee. He famously stated, "General, I have been a soldier all my life. I have been with soldiers engaged in fights by couples, by squads, companies, regiments, divisions, and armies, and should know, as well as any one, what soldiers can do. It is my opinion that no fifteen thousand men ever arrayed for battle can take that position," and pointed toward

Cemetery Ridge. Lee was equally determined and, frankly, quite displeased with his subordinate when he ordered Longstreet to ready Pickett's Division to make the attack.[9]

The Confederate plan of attack for July 3 was "unchanged" from the previous day, per Lee's later report. He envisioned a lengthy cannonade followed by a multi-divisional infantry assault directed at the Union center, spearheaded by Maj. Gen. George Pickett's division of fifteen Virginia infantry brigades, while Trimble's and Pettigrew's divisions would assault from different angles. The fields where the three divisions would make their assault had been largely silent thus far this day other than a few sharp artillery reports directed toward the Bliss farm.

There, between Seminary and Cemetery ridges, the 12th Mississippi, from the brigade of Brig. Gen. Carnot Posey, had taken refuge. Their sharpshooters harassed the infantrymen on Cemetery Hill all morning. Eventually, the Federal artillery gave way to close-range musketry as elements of the 12th New Jersey and 1st Delaware (under Lt. William Brady) were sent forward to clear the buildings. The charge was successful but the 12th Mississippi turned and countercharged, recapturing the buildings. Afterward, the 14th Connecticut was dispatched to take the Bliss farm, which they did successfully. Brigadier General Alexander Hays of Hancock's Second Corps sent forward an order (carried by Sgt. Charles Hitchcock of the 111th New York) ordering the farm buildings to be burned. Hays, knowing the chances of a single soldier making it across the nearly 300 yards of open ground were slim, also sent Capt. James Postles of Col. Thomas Smyth's staff forward. In a dash, the two men were off and successfully delivered their messages. The Bliss farm buildings from then on were no longer a problem, having been set ablaze.

On his way back to the Union lines on Cemetery Ridge, Postles came under fire from Confederate sharpshooters scattered throughout the area. He zigged and zagged over the rough ground. An onlooker described the incident, "Miraculously, not one of the hundred bullets that whistled near him touched either rider or horse. On reaching our lines, though by no means out of range of the balls, he reined his horse round, waved his hat in the air, and made a graceful bow to the unseen marksmen, who, I really believe, were not sorry to see him escape unharmed." When Postles had completed his mission and returned alive, an admiring General Hancock, riding nearby, lifted his hat in "honor of the brave soldier."[10]

Shortly afterward, other Confederate artillery began to mass along Seminary Ridge. Some 140 to 160 guns directed their barrels toward the Union center and Cemetery Hill. Major Forster of the 148th Pennsylvania watched as the Confederates made "their intentions... apparent. Artillery is beginning to occupy every available spot along the crest... and every other point of advantage along their lines." The men of Pickett's Division massed in the trees along Seminary Ridge to the rear of the artillery and awaited the signal to advance. Their officers rode back and forth between intervals of trees to deliver orders to one another.

One of these officers was Longstreet's chief of artillery, Lt. Col. E. Porter Alexander. Nearly a half-hour before the cannonade commenced, he received a note from Longstreet, stating, "Colonel: If the artillery fire does not have the effect to drive off the enemy or greatly demoralize him, so as to make our effort pretty certain, I would prefer that you should not advise Pickett to make the charge. I shall rely a great deal upon your judgment to determine the matter and shall expect you to let Gen. Pickett know when the moment offers."[11]

Alexander gazed over the field and witnessed the strength of the Federal artillery on Cemetery Ridge, perhaps a mile away. However, he "had not doubted that we would carry it, in my confidence that Lee was ordering it." Nearby, Brig. Gen. Ambrose R. Wright also looked at the message that Longstreet had sent Alexander. The two exchanged their views of the upcoming assault. Alexander then penned Longstreet in reply: "General: I will only be able to judge of the effect of our fire on the enemy by his return fire, as his infantry is little exposed to view and the smoke will obscure the field. If, as I infer from your note, there is any alternative to this attack, it should be carefully considered before opening our fire, for it will take all the artillery ammunition we have left to test this one, and if result is unfavorable we will have none left for another effort. And even if this is entirely successful, it can only be so at a very bloody cost."

Longstreet soon replied, "Colonel: The intention is to advance the infantry if the artillery has the desired effect of driving the enemy's off, or having other effect such as to warrant us in making the attack. When that moment arrives advise Gen. Pickett and of course advance such artillery as you can use in aiding the attack."

General Wright, again reading the note given to Alexander, stood silently. Alexander asked him, "What do you think of it? Is it as hard to get there as it looks?" The tremendous pressure grew for the young artillerist to make a decision as Wright replied, "The trouble is not in going there. I went there with my brigade yesterday. There is a place where you can get a breath and re-form. The trouble is to stay there after you get there, for the whole Yankee army is there in a bunch." Alexander wrote Longstreet a final time before ordering his artillery to fire, "General: When our fire is at its best, I will advise Gen. Pickett to advance."[12]

James Longstreet (*Library of Congress* (*LC-DIG-ppmsca-38007*)

The two stationary armies baked in the mid-day sun, with some soldiers lying behind breastworks, some tending the artillery, some on horseback, and some sound asleep. The silence over the fields was, perhaps, the most suspenseful of all. Major General Carl Schurz of the Eleventh Corps recalled:

> From minute to minute, from half hour to half hour, and when it settled down into tranquility like the peaceful and languid repose of a warm midsummer morning in which one might expect to hear the ringing of the village church-bells, there was something ominous, something uncanny, in these strange, unexpected hours of profound silence so sharply contrasting with

the bloody horrors which had proceeded, and which were sure to follow them. Even the light-hearted soldiers, who would ordinarily never lose an opportunity for some outbreak of a hilarious mood, even in a short moment of respite in a fight, seemed to feel the oppression. Some sat silently on the ground munching their hard-tack, while others stretched themselves out seeking sleep, which they probably would have found more readily had the cannon been thundering at a distance. The officers stood together in little groups discussing the evident concern what this long-continued calm might mean. Could it be that Lee, whose artillery in long rows of batteries had silently been frowning at us all morning, had given up his intention to make another great attack? If not, why had he not begun it at an earlier hour, which unquestionably would have been more advantageous to him.[13]

On Cemetery Hill, the heat of the day and the prolonged silence cast doubt that anything of importance would take place. Sergeant Meyer and his pioneers of Caldwell's Division had been resting since building the breastworks earlier in the day. He had not eaten and pangs of hunger set in. He notified the men standing around him, "Boys, watch my outfit while I run down the Taneytown Road for something good to eat. I think I can make the trip before the thing begins again." With that, he was up and on a full run. After a mile, he came across a small farmhouse where a woman had just taken a batch of fresh cherry pies from the oven. He immediately made his purchase and hurried back on the run. He "covered the two miles in twenty minutes." He returned to his place in line puffing and sweating and shared his meal with the rest on top of the breastworks.[14]

A short distance away, Major Mulholland of the 116th Pennsylvania watched as "battery after battery appeared along the edge of the woods. Guns were unlimbered, placed in position, and the horses taken to the rear." Near him, Brig. Gen. John Gibbon, the commander of Hancock's Second Division, invited General Hancock over for lunch. About the same time, on Seminary Ridge, General Longstreet passed along an order to Col. James Walton, his artillery chief, "Colonel, let the batteries open. Order great care and precision in firing. When the batteries at the Peach Orchard cannot be used against the point we intend to attack, let them open on the enemies on the rocky hill." The order was taken to the signal gun of Merritt B. Miller's Third Company, Washington Artillery of New Orleans. The 116th Pennsylvania's Major Mulholland, witnessing Hancock's lunch, described what happened next: "The bread that was handed around—if it was eaten—was consumed without butter, for, as the orderly was passing the latter article to the gentlemen, a shell from Seminary Ridge cut him in two. Instantly the air was filled with bursting shells; the batteries that we had been watching for the last two hours going into position in our front did not open singly or spasmodically."[15]

After a slight mishap, a two-gun section of Miller's Battery fired with great effect. Apparently, in addition to the first round that cut the orderly in two, the second shot found its mark inside the William Patterson barn just south of the Federal lines. A fourteen-year-old servant of a New York officer had been taking care of his master in the farmstead when the cannonade began. The round broke through the barn and tore the arm off of the young boy.[16]

The earth shook with every terrible report. General Gibbon, an artillerist before the war, watched intently as "the whole air above and around us was filled with bursting and screaming projectiles, and the continuous thunder of the guns." A soldier in Caldwell's Division recalled, "The whole artillery of the enemy blazed forth round after round, and the shells are sent whizzing through the air... Then the Federal guns reply, sending whistling shells that burst and deal death upon every side, making such havoc that it amazes the coolest heads."[17]

According to Pvt. Henry Meyer of the 148th Pennsylvania, the Rebel artillery on Seminary Ridge "opened upon us... and with terrific roar belched forth a storm of shot and shell into our lines." To him, Seminary Ridge "appeared to be a volcano emitting smoke and flame." Lieutenant Gilbert Frederick of the 57th New York wrote, "Both Seminary and Cemetery Ridges seemed on fire with blaze and smoke; the air was full of hissing demons; the thunder benumbed the ears and shattered the nerves." Major Forster of the 148th Pennsylvania described the cacophony as a "mad roar of guns, the heavens above us seemed alive with screeching, shrieking missiles of destruction and death."[18]

After being taken to Seminary Ridge as a prisoner of war, the 57th New York's Pvt. Jacob Cole was being kept with many other captives from his division. He was resting when he heard the two opening Rebel artillery rounds in "quick succession." He recalled that "the air was full of shrieking shells and flying shot. The bursting shells sent their deadly fragments down in showers upon the rocky ridge, and over the plain behind the earth was thrown up in clouds of dust as the monstrous missiles buried themselves." Lying prone with time to think, a poem came to his mind. He recited it to himself as the heavy barrage of artillery continued:

> *A hundred guns; yes, fifty more,*
> *Rained down their shot and shell;*
> *As if from out its yawning door,*
> *Drove the red blast of hell.*
> *The hiss the crash, the shriek, the groan,*
> *The ceaseless iron hail;*
> *All this, for half the day, I won,*
> *It made the stoutest quail.*[19]

Much of the Confederate artillery was overshooting their intended targets but a few rounds did fall among the distant Union troops, at a range of about a mile. One struck the hasty works that Sergeant Meyer and his pioneers had just completed. Once the opening guns sounded, he and his men jumped behind the works for protection. A shell exploded nearby, sending "a dozen of us sprawling." Most of the men behind the works were safe, but several of those outside the defenses fell victims to the round. It fragmented on impact and sent a piece of shrapnel hurling toward Meyer's back. He yelled out when one of the men accompanying him asked, "Are you hurt?" Meyer replied, "I guess I am done for. Just look at my back." They glanced over the sergeant and assured him that he was all right, much to his relief.[20]

Winfield Hancock remained mounted despite the danger. Several Rebel artillery shells passed over his head and burst with great reports. One of his staff officers rode toward him to dissuade the him from remaining mounted. "General, the corps commander ought not to risk his life in that way," the aide scolded. Hancock famously replied, "There are times when a corps commander's life does not count." Fire grew in his eyes, because he knew that, at any second, the bulk of Lee's Confederate army would storm across the fields in front of his position.[21]

Hancock looked up and down his line of artillery and realized that some of the batteries were not firing. Instead, they remained idle and some of the gunners were lounging about or taking cover. Brigadier General Henry Hunt, chief of artillery for the Army of the Potomac, had neglected to inform Hancock that he had issued orders to have his batteries withhold their fire. When Hancock asked the nearby Capt. Patrick Hart why he was not firing his guns, he was told, "to reserve my fire when the enemy's artillery opened except that I should see a good opportunity of doing execution and to reserve all my effective ammunition to meet the great charge he expected." Hancock rode away, expecting Hart to open fire. When the artillery officer did not do so, Hancock again rode over "in a very mild manner" to Hart and demanded to know why his battery still had not opened. Hart repeated that he had received orders to reserve his fire, but Hancock wanted to hear none of it and ordered him to fire his guns. The captain, instead of immediately complying, said that the general should "give me a written order that I would open fire under protest."[22]

About that time, Freeman McGilvery, who commanded the artillery reserve batteries, rode toward the arguing pair. Hancock demanded of him, "Why in hell do you not fire with these batteries?" McGilvery told him that he was under orders to reserve his fire and spare his ammunition. Hancock demanded who the orders were from and McGilvery replied, "From the chief of artillery." Hancock retorted, "Gen. Hunt had no idea of anything like this when he gave his orders." But McGilvery, quick-wittedly responded that General Hunt "predicted just what was then occurring and that [his] orders were given to meet this very case." "My troops cannot stand this cannonade and will not stand it if it is not replied to," Hancock explained and again ordered him to open at once. Major McGilvery again declined. He later informed Hunt, "I could not see why the Second Corps could not stand the fire as well as the other corps, or as well as my gunners." Hancock stormed away after being ignored at least three times.[23]

McGilvery's stubborn obedience of Hunt's orders and abject failure to comply with the angry Second Corps commander did more than just conserve expensive, much-needed ammunition. A quick look at the typography of the fields surrounding the key artillery position on Cemetery Hill shows that McGilvery's reserve batteries were unlimbered in a low spot. Essentially, they were hidden from the Rebel batteries firing from Seminary Ridge nearly a mile away. When the enemy infantry eventually made their assault, the Union guns would be able to rain their effective fire from a location unknown to the Confederate observers.

Lee's artillery continued to pound away at the silent Union batteries on the southern part of the battle line. To the north, some of the Federal batteries did reply; Porter Alexander mistakenly identified the fire as coming from 18 guns in the cemetery. Unknown to him and the rest of the Confederate commanders, the smoke obscured their view of the Union position so much that they believed that they were knocking out the Federal guns when, in essence, they were over-shooting most of the time. This circumstance did not have the desired effect that Alexander wished on the Union batteries or the infantrymen huddled behind the breastworks. However, as the Rebel guns continued to overshoot, Meade's headquarters at the Leister house became a dangerous place. He soon moved his headquarters across the road but found the enemy fire coming close there as well. He eventually moved his headquarters to Power's Hill farther to the rear.[24]

The bombardment continued unabated for what, to some observers, seemed like hours. Adjutant Charles Ramsey of the 148th Pennsylvania recalled, "The horses and caissons in the rear suffered, and I have in mind now hearing horses cry like human beings." Major Mulholland of the 116th Pennsylvania gave one of the most descriptive accounts: "I have read many accounts of this artillery duel, but the most graphic description by the most able writers falls far short of the reality. No tongue or pen can find language strong enough to convey any idea of its awfulness. Streams of screaming projectiles poured through the hot air falling and bursting everywhere. Men and horses were torn limb from limb; caissons exploded one after another in rapid succession, blowing the gunners to pieces. No spot within our lines was free from this frightful iron rain. The infantry hugged close to the earth and sought every shelter that our light earthworks afforded. It was literally a storm of shot and shell that the oldest soldier there… had not yet witnessed. That awful rushing sound of the flying missiles which causes the firm-est hearts to quail was everywhere."[25]

Eventually, some of the Union artillery batteries along Cemetery Ridge finally began to reply after a wait of nearly twenty minutes. "The earth trembled…," a soldier later recollected. "The air seemed full of hissing, screaming iron missiles; shells bursting high in air emitting lurid flame, the fragments coming down with discordant hiss and scream. When a shell bursts in the air, it leaves a globular puff of smoke which retains its form for several moments; the air was filled with these balls of white smoke."[26]

The Confederate bombardment continued because of Lieutenant Colonel Alexander's inability to discern if his fire was having the desired effect. He in-formed General Pickett that he would not fire any longer than thirty minutes more and he would be ordered forward "at the very first favorable sign." He listened intently as the supposed eighteen guns continuously blazed away in counterbat-tery fire. Even more guns seemed to begin to open as Alexander described the Federal artillery line as a "blazing… volcano." He sent a terse note to Pickett a few minutes later, "General: If you are to advance at all, you must come at once or we will not be able to support you as we ought. But the enemy's fire has not slackened materially and there are still 18 guns firing from the cemetery." He had no way of knowing it, but a few enemy officers on East Cemetery Hill were in deep discussion in how to lure the Rebel infantry out of their cover prematurely.[27]

The Eleventh Corps' artillery chief, Maj. Thomas Osborn, was posted near General Howard when Henry Hunt came to inspect his lines. Nearly two hours had passed and they were beginning to wonder if the Confederate infantry attack would ever commence. General Meade had just excused himself from Howard and Osborn a few minutes prior to Hunt's appearance. Before leaving, Meade had expressed the hope that Lee would launch his assault because he was confident that his entire line would hold without breaking. Major Osborn, once he arrived, suggested that the artillery should cease fire, or slacken at least, to lure the enemy out of the woods as Lee would believe the cannonading had been successful. Hunt was all in. The plan would conserve ammunition and spare unnecessary casualties. Hunt did worry that the shaky Eleventh Corps might not be able to hold its ground if the Union artillery slackened. The matter was brought before Howard, who responded, "I support Major Osborn's idea of stopping the artillery fire, and my men will stay!"[28]

The ruse worked and, as the artillery fire began to slacken across the Federal front, Alexander hastily reported to Pickett, "For God's sake come quick. The 18 guns have gone. Come quick or my ammunition will not let me support you properly." This message was followed by two verbal communications with the same effect.[29]

GENERAL PICKETT was near Longstreet at the time. He found him "like a lion at bay." Pickett approached him, leaped from his horse, and saluted. For several minutes, Longstreet sat in his position staring at him. Finally, the awkward moment passed and Longstreet spoke about the day's fight: "Pickett, I am being crucified at the thought of the sacrifice of life which this attack will make. I have instructed Alexander to watch the effect of our fire upon the enemy, and when it begins to tell he must take the responsibility and give you your orders, for I can't."

George Pickett and James Longstreet painting
(*Library of Congress LC-DIG-pga-11166 by*
H.A. Ogden)

Within a few minutes, Alexander's message arrived. Pickett opened it and read it. He refolded the letter and gave it to Longstreet, who also read it. Pickett inquired, "General, shall I advance?" Longstreet looked at Pickett for a moment, then extended his hand toward Pickett. Pickett, in turn, clasped his hand in Longstreet's and Longstreet clasped his other over his. Then, without speaking a word, he "bowed his head upon his breast. "Then, General, I shall lead my division on," Pickett inquired. He mounted his horse and "rode gayly to his command."[30]

Pickett penned a quick note to his future wife, Sallie, "If Old Peter's nod means death then good-by and God bless you, little one." He made it but a few paces away from Longstreet when he was overcome with the sensation that he should have Longstreet mail it for him in the case that this was his last battle. Pickett rode back to his corps commander and asked if he would attend to the request. Pickett later wrote, "As he took your letter from me, my darling, I saw tears glistening on his cheeks and beard. The stern old war-horse, God bless him, was weeping for his men and, I know, praying too that this cup might pass from them."[31]

Longstreet then went to check on Alexander's artillery for himself. The two conversed briefly. Alexander reported that there were eight Napoleons missing that, according to plan, were to follow the infantry to the Emmitsburg Road. Alexander supposed that artillery officer Col. R. Lindsay Walker had placed them elsewhere on the field. He also learned that the artillery supply trains had been sent farther down the road, and he could not be sure if he would have enough ammunition to support the infantry assault. Longstreet replied, "Go & halt Pickett right where he is, & replenish your ammunition." Alexander said, "General, we can't do that. We nearly emptied the trains last night. Even if we had it, it would take an hour or two, & meanwhile the enemy would recover from the pressure he is now under. Our only chance is to follow it up now—to strike while the iron is hot." Longstreet reportedly said, "I don't want to make this attack. I believe it will fail. I do not see how it can succeed. I would not make it even now, but that Gen. Lee has ordered & expects it." Alexander thought the general was on the verge of stopping the charge, so he remained silent, but as the two officers stood in their places, the infantry line began to stir.[32]

While Longstreet conversed with Alexander, General Pickett was busy preparing his division for the anticipated attack. After informing General Armistead to prepare to advance, Pickett rode over to Brig. Gen. Richard Garnett and told him to move forward. When Garnett asked about any other orders, Pickett replied, "Dick, old fellow, I have no orders to give you, but I advise you to get across those fields as quick as you can, for in my opinion you are going to catch hell." He then issued orders for Kemper's Brigade to move forward. The chant, "Remember Old Virginia," rang along the line, and the men began to advance eastward toward the waiting Yankees on Cemetery Ridge.[33]

Pickett's command emerged from the tree line along Seminary Ridge and advanced into the farm fields in their front. The injured General Garnett, kicked by his horse a few days prior to the battle, remained mounted. His command spanned the front of Armistead's Brigade, which would advance behind Garnett. Kemper's Brigade formed to the right of Garnett. Wilcox and Lang of Anderson's division would support Pickett's right. To the north, Pettigrew's men would lead, with Maj. Gen. Isaac Trimble's division in support. They deployed just to the rear of the heavily contested, and still burning, Bliss farmhouse. The Confederate line, more than 14,000 men, was more than a mile long.

When the attackers began to move forward, the artillery fire ceased and an ominous lull fell over the battlefield. The men paused, then received the order to "right shoulder shift, arms." General Pickett rode along the line and drew his sword. "Up men and to your posts!" he shouted. "Don't forget today that you are from Old Virginia!" Likewise, General Armistead addressed his own troops, "Remember, men, what you are fighting for. Remember your homes and your firesides, your mothers and wives and sisters and your sweethearts."[34]

George Pickett (*Library of Congress LC-DIG-cwpbh-00682*)

Within moments, the entire Rebel assault line was in motion. On Little Round Top, Lt. Benjamin F. Rittenhouse, who took over Battery D, 5th U. S. Artillery after the death of Lt. Charles Hazlett the previous day, watched as the distant Confederates began to sweep forward. He soon ordered his guns to open. However, not all of them could be fired effectively because of the lack of space on Little Round Top. Therefore, Rittenhouse could only fire two guns at any time. The Union artillery on Cemetery Hill also soon opened on the Rebels.[35]

An aide-de-camp of Brig. Gen. John Gibbon, Lt. Frank Haskell, probably said it best when he described the oncoming Confederates: "Every eye could see the enemy's legions, an overwhelming resistless tide of an ocean of armed men sweeping upon us! Regiment after regiment, and brigade after brigade, move from the woods and rapidly take their places in the lines forming the assault. Pickett's proud division, with some additional troops, holds their right; Pettigrew's (Heth's) their left. The first line, at short interval, is followed by a second, and that a third succeeds; and columns between support the lines. More than half a mile their front extends; more than a thousand yards the dull gray masses deploy, man touching man, rank pressing rank, and line supporting line. Their red flags wave; their horsemen gallop up and down; the arms of eighteen thousand men; barrel and bayonet, gleam in the sun, a sloping forest of flashing steel."[36]

Lieutenant Noyes of the 28th Massachusetts watched as the Confederate battle line deployed and began to move forward, "Now was our time," he remembered, "Blech forth, O' ye guns, for in numbers they are our superior." On the left of the line (as viewed from Seminary Ridge), the regiments marched forward while the right flank, Pickett's men, moved at a left oblique so they could attack the Union center at the proper point and coordinate with Pettigrew and Trimble. Otherwise, they would have traveled directly toward Caldwell's Division on Cemetery Ridge. Major Mulholland recalled, "It is now our turn… solid shot and shell are sent on their errand of destruction in quick succession. We see them fall in countless numbers among the advancing troops."[37]

The Union artillery fire tore great gaps into the enemy lines as they advanced across the field. General Hunt's plan worked as some 80 guns rained death and destruction on the Confederates. Major Mulholland recalled that the artillery was "tearing great gaps in their (the Confederates) ranks and strewing the field with dead and wounded, notwithstanding the destructive fire, under which they were placed." The bold movement won the admiration of friend and foe alike. Lieutenant Frederick of the 57th New York recalled, "It was a beautiful sight to see these long lines of men with bayonets fixed and glistening. From right to left a wave-like motion ran along the moving columns as they tramped down the sloping hillside into the valley."[38]

The Confederate tide continued forward as the Federal artillery blasted huge holes into their lines. "The ground over which they have passed is (now) strewn with dead and wounded," a soldier recalled, "But on they come. The gaps in the ranks are closed as soon as made." They marched up to the Emmitsburg Road and began to move in an oblique manner toward the center even more so to fill the gap that had been created between Pickett's left flank and Trimble's right. As the Rebels came closer, many Federals began taunting them: "'Come on, Johnnie, we long to embrace you,' 'They must be hungry for lead,' 'As they drop on our bayonets we will help them to the rear,' 'See them skedaddle.'"[39]

Nearly as soon as the Confederates reached the Emmitsburg Road, the Federal infantry on Cemetery Ridge stood and opened a heavy musketry. A Rebel recalled, "They were at once enveloped in a dense cloud of smoke and dust. Arms, heads, blankets, guns and knapsacks were thrown and tossed into the clear air. Their track as they advanced was strewn with dead and wounded. A moan went up from the field, distinctly to be heard amid the storm of battle." Yet, in Caldwell's Division, there was no infantry fire. No yelling, no cursing, just calm and ease as they watched their comrades shoot into the oncoming waves.[40]

On the right of the Union position, General Hays's line engaged part of Trimble's Division. The 8th Ohio advanced as a skirmish line and refused it on the opposite side of the Emmitsburg Road and fired into Col. John Brockenbrough's Virginia brigade. They broke when they were nearly directly in line with the Bliss farm buildings while the others maintained their order and moved forward. They halted along the Emmitsburg Road and fired.[41]

A Great Display of Guns

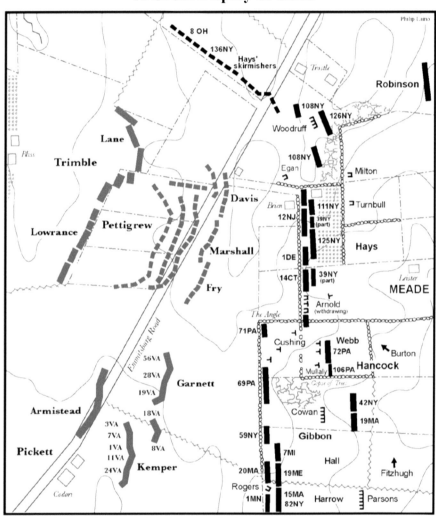

The Confederate advance on the afternoon of July 3.

South of Trimble's position, the men of Pickett's Division continued to press the attack as they crossed the Emmitsburg Road, past the Codori buildings, and pushed for the center. There, Gibbon's Division of the Second Corps met them with a heavy fire. Southerners fell left and right as they continued to move forward. In the melee, General Garnett, still mounted on his horse, directed his Virginia brigade. "Steady, men!" he cried out, "Close up! A little faster; not too fast! Save your strength." Major Charles S. Peyton of the 19th Virginia was nearby when he saw his beloved general, full of victory, fall from his horse, "He was shot from his horse while near the center of the brigade within about 25 paces of the stone wall."[42]

Onward they moved crossing over the field. Kemper rode back to visit his comrade and friend Armistead. "General," Kemper said, "I am going to storm those works, and I want you to support me." Armistead agreed to do so and, pointing forward, asked, "Look at my line; Did you ever see a more perfect line than that on dress parade?" "I never did," Kemper affirmed and rode onward. Shortly after that incident, Kemper was shot from his mount while his men rushed past him. After falling, he thought that he could almost point out the very man who had fired the shot that struck him. A squad of Federal soldiers rushed to the wounded Rebel general and attempted to capture him. The sharp cracks of a few Confederate rifles left the squad killed or wounded, saving Kemper from capture.

Meanwhile, after General Armistead ordered his men to "double-quick" the last quarter-mile, the North Carolina native thrust his sword through his hat. His balding head exposed, he ran forward at the enemy. By the time he reached the Federal line, his hat had slid down to the hilt. Armistead shouted after he crossed the Emmitsburg Road, "Follow me, boys; give them the cold steel." He and nearly two hundred men crossed the stone wall near the angle. Armistead placed his hand on a nearby cannon of Cushing's battery and ordered it to be turned. However, being outnumbered and outgunned, every man that crossed the wall was either killed, wounded, or taken prisoner. Armistead was perforated by Minié balls next to the artillery piece. He died a few days later at the George Spangler farm.[43]

Longstreet's grand assault had failed. Many of Pickett's beleaguered men began streaming westward back to Seminary Ridge. Pickett had advanced with Wilcox's and Lang's brigades in support on the right. All told, the 1,600 men marched forward straight at Caldwell's Division. One of Wilcox's Alabamans noted, "At a glance of the eye from the brow of the hill, where we formed, every private at once saw the madness of the attempt." Lieutenant Colonel Porter Alexander felt "great pity for the useless loss of life they were incurring, for there was nothing left for them to support."[44]

The 16th and 14th Vermont of Stannard's Brigade had swung around and fired into Lang's flank. Lang described the brief encounter: "The noise of artillery and small-arms was so deafening that it was impossible to make the voice heard above the din, and the men were by this time so badly scattered in the bushes and among the rocks (of Plum Run) that it was impossible to make any movement to meet or check the enemy's advance. To remain in this position, unsupported by either infantry or artillery, with infantry on both flanks and in front and artillery playing upon us with grape and canister, was certain annihilation."[45]

Major Mulholland remembered watching as some of the men pressed by Stannard's Brigade and continued forward. They came to within easy musket range of his line. He noted, "Every musket is tightly grasped and our men become impatient to begin their work, but the orders are to hold our fire and it took all the officers could do to keep the men from firing."

The Rebels advanced into a depression about 150 yards from the Federal line. Many of the Union officers ordered their men to "ready" when suddenly, "The air became filled as though by a great flock of white pigeons; it was the fluttering of hundreds and hundreds of white rags the tokens of surrender." The Confederates began to throw down their arms and move toward the Union line unarmed.[46]

J. Noonan of the 69th New York recalled that his command stood up when the Rebels came to within musket range. Suddenly, "a white flag appeared and the only part left to them was to gather in the prisoners." The 28th Massachusetts's Lt. John Noyes mentioned that, in front of his line, "the skirmishers have halted. They see the movement. Our expectant boys with capped guns in their hands, ready to fire, disappointed replace them against the works and rise to see the fun. Look at them, the gray bucks as they fall back in confusion… Many lie down. They are coming in, in large squads, (having thrown down their arms) into every part of our lines."[47]

Not far from the Irish Brigade's line of battle, the men of the 148th Pennsylvania watched intently as loud shouts began to arise from the ranks. Some of the Keystoners shouted at the Rebels, "Come in and surrender or we will fire on you." Still, the Confederates in this sector hesitated until a Union staff officer went forward to order them to "come in at once, or receive the fire of infantry and artillery." Hundreds of Rebels walked up the slope and over the breastworks to surrender to Caldwell's Division.[48]

Not all heeded this warning, however. Major Mulholland could not help but admire three Confederate hardheads that were "braver than their fellows." He watched as the masses of troops poured over the walls and these three men that "were seen running back over the fields with a stand of colors, and the men, in admiration of their heroism, refrained from molesting them."[49] Mulholland reported that nearly 5,000 men were captured as prisoners and 33 regimental flags. While these numbers were exaggerated, no doubt Caldwell's command captured a great many during their stand on Cemetery Ridge that day. Many of the prisoners exchanged food and other small articles from their knapsacks and haversacks with their captors before making the final trip to the rear.[50]

On Powers Hill, General Meade rode on as he awaited word from the front. Near him was Thomas Livermore, his son and aide Fred Meade, and Lt. Frank Haskell who remembered that Meade's "face [was] very white, the lines marked and earnest and full of care." Meade halted near Haskell and asked, "How is it going here?" "I believe, General, the army is repulsed," the lieutenant replied. "What?" Meade asked, "Is the assault entirely repulsed?" Haskell again answered, "It is, sir." Meade quickened to the crest of the hill and gazed over the battlefield

The Attack Fails

Broken elements of Lee's Army are thrown back amidst the Union Armies defenses. Wilcox and Lang make one final attack, but it too is repulsed.

to see scores of Confederate prisoners. Men were running to and fro carrying further orders as the remaining Rebels withdrew across the fields to Seminary Ridge. Meade exclaimed, "Thank God." He waved his hat and wheeled his horse as he exclaimed loudly, "Hurrah!"[51]

On Seminary Ridge, near the point of woods, General Lee remained mounted on his faithful horse, Traveller. He watched as men slumped back across the field. After some time, he rode over to an officer who was leaning on a pile of fence rails, worn out from the fight. Lee asked Lt. Randolph A. Shotwell of the 8th Virginia, "Are you wounded?" Shotwell responded, "No, General, not hurt I believe, but completely exhausted." Lee responded, "Ah, yes, it was too much for you. We were not strong enough. It was my fault, and I am very sorry, but we will try to repair it." Shotwell later believed it "was the saddest imaginable expression in [Lee's] voice and upon his features, yet with all a calm intrepidity marvelous to see."[52]

Lee rode on until he spotted Pickett. He rode up and instructed, "General Pickett, place your division in rear of this hill, and be ready to repel the advance of the enemy should they follow up their advantage." Pickett stood before Lee with his head dropped to his breast, "General Lee," he quietly said, "I have no division now, Armistead is down, Garnett is down, and Kemper is morally wounded." Lee sat stunned in the seat of Traveller. "Come," Lee said, "this has been my fight and upon my shoulders rests the blame. The men and officers of your command have written the name of Virginia as high today as it has ever been written before." The two men rode off in separate directions.[53]

"Bind up your wounds and take up your musket," Lee encouraged several soldiers that he soon encountered. He spotted a captain whipping a horse to get it in the position he wanted it to be in. "Don't whip him," "Marse Robert" called, "I've got just such another foolish horse myself, and whipping does no good."[54] Toward the southern part of the battlefield, Brig. Gen. Elon Farnsworth charged a Confederate line and was repulsed. Farnsworth lost his life, and the Rebels held their ground. With that, the heavy fighting in Gettysburg on July 3rd ended.

The Aftermath

As with any battlefield during the Civil War, as night began to fall so too came the time to bury the dead and tend to the wounded. In front of the Federal position, much of Lee's attacking force laid strewn across the fields. Across meadows, along streams, over fences, in the road, in wood lots, the death and destruction that all war brings, was prominent. In the 145th Pennsylvania, Capt. John Hilton recalled the scene in his front, "What a frightful cost! ...thousands of brave men lay dead upon the field, and thousands are groaning and dying from wounds received during the terrible conflict, leaving many widows and orphans to struggle through the world alone."[55]

One of the wounded from the Wheatfield fight, Jacob Cole, watched from the woods of Seminary Ridge as Pickett's men were repulsed. He claims that a band on Cemetery Hill began to play the *Star-Spangled Banner*, and it was then he "knew that Pickett's grand charge at Gettysburg had failed and that the Union troops had won the victory." He watched an onslaught of Confederate troops rush back from their advanced positions to their point of start. He described, "After the repulse of Pickett's charge the rebel soldiers scattered all over the field like a lot of sheep without a head." Cole continued to lay in this position for the night with his heart, undoubtedly, full of victory and pride.[56]

While the sun was setting on July 3, other men began to converse with their prisoners. Private Henry Meyer of the 148th Pennsylvania recalled, "One of the Confederate prisoners with both eyes shot out was led into our lines, crying bitterly. A Confederate officer related that the most pitiful spectacle he ever beheld was that presented by some officer in their division [Pickett's], sitting with his back to the fence along the Emmitsburg road, having his lower jaw shot clean away; sitting there with staring eye watching the men as they passed by to the charge."

Private Meyer would never forget those few days he spent in Gettysburg. In his account in the 148th Pennsylvania's regimental history, he mentioned the story of a Confederate officer watching from the Lutheran Seminary who noted, "When the smoke of battle lifted, Pickett's Division had melted away; a few scattered, disorganized remnants were left on the field and drifted back to their own line."[57]

"In front of the Second Corps the dead lay in great heaps," Maj. St. Clair Mulholland penned. "Dismounted guns, ruins of exploded caissons, dead and mutilated men and horses were piled up together in every direction." He looked over the fields that had so nobly been defended by members of his Second Corps and noted: "Out on the field where Longstreet's Corps had passed, thousands of wounded were lying. We had no means of reaching these poor fellows, and many of them lay there between lines until the morning of the 5th... The stench from the dead became intolerable, and we tried to escape it by digging up the ground and burying our faces in the fresh earth."[58]

Also walking among the dead and wounded was Lt. Thomas Livermore. After a hard night with the loss of his beloved Colonel Cross, he endeavored to help the wounded in any way that he could. He "saw men, horses, and material in some places piled up together, which is something seldom seen unless in pictures of battles, and the appearance of the field with these mounds of dead men, and horses, and very many bodies lying in every position singly, was terrible, especially as the night lent a somber hue to everything the eye rested on." Yet, Livermore walked on, continuing his duty to remove the wounded from the field and get them to their proper places in the hospitals. Men like him are what saved so many lives during these times of battle.

Livermore discovered a gravely wounded soldier in a "cow shed" who had been lying on his face. An artillery shot had carried away all the flesh of his "hams," exposing the bone. The soldier, however, did not complain about his wound. Shocked, Livermore leaned in close and asked him if he "desired to be moved." The wounded man said, in a calm manner, that "he did; that if he lay there he should surely die, but that if he got to a hospital he might live." Livermore began to do all that he could for his newfound friend who told him "that he was an artilleryman and that his position in the battery caused him to stand with his side toward the enemy." He spoke of how an artillery round, fired by the enemy, soared across the open sky, struck his body and passed through his legs. Livermore recalled that his friend "hated to be shot in the rear, and seemed to care more for that than for being so grievously hurt." Afterwards, Livermore called for some of his men to lift the artilleryman up and place him in an ambulance. All the while, as he watched his friend being carried away, he never heard a single complaint from him.[59]

CHAPTER 6

Pursuing Lee's Army

"Meanwhile, your sisters for the years
Which hold in trust your storied tombs,
Bring all they now can give you-tears,
And these memorial blooms."[1]

ON THE MORNING OF JULY 4, THE WEATHER was "dark and gloomy," according to Maj. St. Clair Mulholland of the 116th Pennsylvania. The opposing armies stared at each other for much of the day. A heavy downpour of rain swept across central Adams County. It washed much of the blood away from the battlefield, and pools of mud intermingled with the detritus of battle. One of John Caldwell's soldiers questioned, "Why does it always rain after a battle? Rain after Antietam, after Fredericksburg, Chancellorsville, and Gettysburg, as though the compassionate skies would weep for the fallen brave… in sweet mercy hasten to wash away from the soiled earth the crimson stains."[2]

Sergeant Thomas Meyer of the 148th Pennsylvania again led his pioneers about the field of Pickett's Charge. He described it as "a dreadful sight; the dead were already in a terrible state of putrefaction. Faces black and charcoal and bloated out of all human semblance; eyes, cheeks, forehead, and nose, all one general level of putrid swelling, twice the normal size with here and there great blisters of putrid water, some the size of a man's fist on face, neck and wrists; while the bodies were bloated to full capacity of the uniforms that enclosed them." Meyer observed how some of the dead left on the battlefield had been robbed. He looked at the lifeless forms that had their pockets cut open and their personal belongings scattered after having been "rifled" through. Disgust set in as he admitted that some of his own men were among the thieves but, "All regiments had them."

Work details continued to collect the dead and place them into long rows "laying one against another, heads all one way, Union and Confederate in separate rows." Meyer added, "These burial trenches were dug here, there, and everywhere over the field and contained three or four or fifty as the number of dead near required." As with so many of the men that had been robbed, few had any identification. Therefore, when they were buried, they were given a simple wooden plank, sometimes etched with "unknown," as their headstone. Just a soldier, with a mother, father, and life before the battle, yet, most likely, never to be known by anyone again.[3]

Another of Caldwell's soldiers that took notice of the dead was Pvt. Robert L. Stewart of the 140th Pennsylvania. He recalled, "Their unburied dead were left on the field and thousands of their wounded were left in our hands." Another officer noted, "The field of battle presented a curious sight. Parties were gathering up the arms abandoned by the enemy and sticking the bayonets in the ground, so that there were acres of muskets standing as thick as trees in a nursery."[4]

Private Henry Meyer also examined the fields over which the Rebels had charged. He carefully picked across the open ground as artillery pieces occasionally roared on Seminary Ridge, sending a few of the troops scattering. "The plain in our front was strewn with dead soldiers and dead horses," Meyer penned. "Hats, haversacks, canteens, accoutrements, shells, solid shot, and muskets, wrecked gun carriages, and all the debris of great battle were scattered in promiscuous confusion over the field and in the woods. The ground was torn up in deep furrows by the enemy's solid shot and shell. I noticed one point where three such furrows had crossed each other, one having been made by a ball coming from the northwest, one from the west, and one from the southwest, showing how the fire was concentrated on that part of the line."

Meyer walked around the battleground, sadly looking at all the carnage. The wounded horses dragging themselves about the field presented an image that would never leave his mind. Some of them tried "to nibble a tuft of grass not trampled into the ground." One of his comrades, Cpl. S. M. Spangler, was part of a detail assigned to "shoot the wounded horses in that part of the field." The thought sickened Meyer and he headed back to his regimental line.

Eventually, curiosity got the better of Meyer and he decided to inspect a nearby field hospital. He found his way to the rear of his regiment's position and walked about the farmland. Although this exact location is unknown, speculation points that it may have been the Patterson farm or the Michael Frey farm. Whatever the case, Meyer came across a small orchard that was "literally covered with the dead; they presented a shelter tent, lying there in the rain and mud." Nearby, he noted a small spring that the men frequently used while they had held their position. He recounted, "During the rain, surface water carried blood from the field into the spring, but water being scarce in the locality, the boys were obliged to fill their canteens with the tainted liquid."[5]

Meanwhile, Sergeant Thomas Meyer and his pioneer crew continued to walk the fields. He described the scene:

> The stench on the battlefield was something indescribable, it would come up as if in waves and when at its worst the breath would stop in the throat; the lungs could not take it in, and a sense of suffocation would be experienced. We would cover our faces tightly with our hands and turn the back toward the breeze and retch and gasp for breath.
>
>   The dead were found in all manner of positions, lying, sitting, isolated, in groups, in heaps. Many there were without a visible wound or mark to cause death. Down beyond the "Bloody Angle," there remained standing a few panels of post fence, only the lower rails remaining. Against this a smooth faced soldier boy was sitting, his elbow resting on the second rail, his head resting on his right hand, his head upright the face turned toward us. Thinking he was sick or wounded I went out to offer assistance, and found he was dead. We examined him and found he had been shot through the left breast, in the hand to

hand fighting at the "Bloody Angle" with Pickett's men the day before, then sat down just as we found him and died without a struggle. Being perfectly poised he did not even roll over. There was nothing about him by which he could be identified. His accoutrements were all still in place, his cartridge box nearly empty.[6]

A captain in the 116th Pennsylvania walked out to a pool of standing water in front of the regiment's battle line. He desperately needed a wash and decided to make good use of the pool. No sooner had he got to work when distant Confederate sharpshooters began to fire at him. A bullet nearly struck the officer which caused him to hastily move away. Other soldiers, witnessing the act, began to smile. The captain remarked, "Ah, well, if the Rebs send a ball through my shirt there will be more lives than mine lost!"[7]

On the morning of July 5, it became apparent that the entire Army of Northern Virginia had retreated from Gettysburg. One of Caldwell's soldiers recalled, "In the morning… we found the enemy had gone, and then what a scene!... What a cheer went up; a cheer that swelled into a roar and was taken up by the boys on Cemetery Hill, rolled along the rest of Round Top and then back again."[8]

About eleven o'clock in the morning, elements of the Union Second Corps was ordered forward to inspect the ground and probe the Confederate lines. Many soldiers, having been wounded during the conflict and taken as prisoners, were freed. One such liberated captive was Jacob Cole. He was taken to the Second Corps field hospital where his wounds were properly dressed. There, he witnessed the unspeakable horrors of a field hospital in operation. He observed, "I saw physicians cutting off an arm from some, legs from another, and piling them in heaps outside the hospital to be afterwards buried." Cole, and many others, would never forget what they saw within the walls of so many of the buildings that dotted the town and farmlands.[9]

After inspecting the vacated Confederate lines, the Second Corps formed on the Baltimore Pike and marched toward Maryland. As they crossed a small stream, they gazed with interest at the trees along the war-torn road. A soldier recalled that the woods had been "literally riddled with musket balls. Some of the limbs of the trees bore the marks of more than a score of missiles, and there was scarcely a tree in sight… of which was not chipped and gashed with minie balls or fragments of shells."[10]

Onward they continued until they reached Two Taverns. There, they paused for the next two days to rest and resupply. At 5 a.m. on July 7, they were again ordered to march. They reached Taneytown, Maryland, about 11 p.m. They had covered ten miles "on empty stomachs." To their relief, they found a train that had been waiting for them with supplies. Once their needs were met, they rested for the night. The following day, July 8, heavy rain showers pelted the men as they continued to march through the Maryland countryside. Toward evening, they reached outskirts of Frederick.[11]

On July 9, the Second Corps passed through Frederick. Here, the familiar town took on a much different appearance. The citizens had been informed of a great victory at Gettysburg and in the South near Vicksburg just days prior. Private Stewart of the 140th Pennsylvania recalled, "Here… we found flags flying, apparently from every house, and despite our seedy appearance and mud stained garments, the good people gave us, as we passed through, a most cordial welcome." Also witnessing the tribute to the Federal soldiers was Winthrop D. Sheldon of the 27th Connecticut. He wrote in his regimental history, "Now, Frederick City put on its most smiling face. Flags were flung to the breeze, and the people gave an enthusiastic welcome to the regiments as they passed through in pursuit of Lee's army."[12]

Sergeant Meyer of the 148th Pennsylvania was with his men during this leg of the march, walking in mud "to the belt." While passing through the town, the townspeople came out on the sidewalks and porches to watch the passing column. One gentleman and his family stood on the walkway leading from the road to their house. There was a discussion between the man and his wife while they watched the ranks march pass their house. It finally piqued the interest of one of their daughters enough that she yelled out, "Papa, don't soldiers care for rain or mud?" With no apparent response from her father, a younger sibling responded, "No; they just love to walk in the mud and water. But they do care when their shoes and clothes are all covered with mud. They would look nice if they were not so dirty." The wife shouted, "Evidently they have no remorse for having just fought and killed and wounded twenty thousand men! Oh, isn't war a dreadful thing?"[13]

Near the outskirts of the city, a Confederate spy that had been captured was seen "swinging from the limb of an oak tree." After some of the men questioned the townspeople, they received a response entailing of how the man was "arrested on suspicion, tried and convicted" of gathering information on the army. It was later determined that "in connection with the death sentence it was ordered that

Isaac Plumb's gravesite (*Personal collection of Frank Walker*)

his body should be hanged, as a warning to others who might pass that way, for three days" against the act of spying.[14]

On July 10, Caldwell's Division marched near the former Antietam battlefield, passing it starting about 1:30 p.m. Near Jones' Cross Roads, the van of the Second Corps caught up with Lee's rear guard and shelling ensued. The Union infantry threw up breastworks but no Confederate attack came. General Meade remained cautious. Caldwell's men camped six miles from Williamsport. On the 11th, the rest of the Second Corps finished the final leg of the march to Jones' Cross Roads. For two days, the men stayed in their respective positions, holding their breastworks. Finally, on the 13th, Meade decided to make an effort against the works and attempt to take them from the enemy. The Confederates were pinned on the bank of the Potomac River because it was too high to cross safely. Major Mulholland of the 116th Pennsylvania recalled, "The enemy were found strongly entrenched… their line forming a semi-circle with the ends resting on the river." Five out of seven of Meade's corps commanders opposed the proposed attack but the general decided to attempt it the following day. During the night, preparations were made and at daybreak on July 14, Caldwell's Division was ordered to take the lead on the reconnaissance mission.[15]

The men hurried across a small depression in the earth. A soldier recalled, "Advancing rapidly across the intervening space we expected every moment to receive the fire of the enemy." Soon, they spotted the Confederate breastworks and made a dash to seize them. To their relief, they found that they had been "almost deserted." They found that the previous evening the Confederates had crossed the Potomac River and "made good of their escape."[16]

CHAPTER 7

Conclusion and Epilogue

"Ye return, but our tears will fall as ye come,
For the mournful notes of the muffled drum
Are borne on the breeze over mountain and wave,
As it beats the dirge by your comrades' grave."[1]

THE GETTYSBURG CAMPAIGN WREAKED HAVOC amongst the troops in Caldwell's Division. In total, his battle strength was 3,320 men. By the time the Gettysburg Campaign had subsided, 1,275 men would be lying across the ground, in field hospitals, or buried on the field. Broken families would forever be scared and would never be repaired. It could easily be said that the Battle of Gettysburg was decided on July 2. The Confederate tide that streamed through the fields and wood-lots around the Rose farm and surrounding areas would have continued unabated until reaching Little Round Top. If the Confederates would have sustained the tide awaiting them there, there may have been a different victor in Gettysburg.[2]

Caldwell's Division swept the Wheatfield at a critical time. In the wake of their advance, a trail of tears and bloodshed could be followed directly leading to each brigade of the division. Powder-burned, begrimed faces shouted for victory on those July days. While by appearance they were almost like any other division in the Army of the Potomac; by zeal, attitude, and chance, they may have saved the Army of the Potomac.

After the battle, Maj. Gen. George Sykes of the Fifth Corps cast criticism on Caldwell. The accusations lead to a review of General Caldwell's command which was conducted by General Hancock. After a brief investigation, it was found that Caldwell had not led his division properly during the battle. With his reputation continually being stained, he was relieved from duty when the army was reorganized in 1864.[3] Caldwell later served on the honor guard for President Lincoln's funeral train. He practiced law until his death in Calais, Maine, in 1912. He is buried at St. Stephen Rural Cemetery in St. Stephen, New Brunswick, Canada.[4]

After Col. Edward Cross was killed, Col. Henry B. McKeen temporarily led the brigade. An 1853 graduate of Princeton, McKeen was a strong and intelligent young commander. By the fall of 1863, he had returned to command the 81st Pennsylvania and led the regiment at the Battle of Bristoe Station in October. He held that position until the Battle of the Spotsylvania in the spring of 1864 when he took over for the wounded Brig. Gen. Alexander Webb. During the Battle of

Cold Harbor on June 3, 1864, McKeen was shot while leading General Gibbon's troops. His wound was pronounced mortal and he died a short time later. He is buried at The Woodlands Cemetery in Philadelphia.[5]

Colonel Patrick Kelly resumed command of the Irish Brigade until officers of higher rank began to resume their actions within the brigade. During the Battle of Cold Harbor, he would again get his chance to lead the famed regiments when Col. Richard Byrnes was killed. During the Siege of Petersburg, Kelly was shot through the head while leading the brigade forward against the Confederate earthworks. His final resting place is located at the First Cavalry Cemetery in Woodside, New York.[6]

After the command of Zook's Brigade changed several times, Lt. Col. John Fraser found himself in charge. He would hold the post, but again found himself in command of the 140th Pennsylvania by the time of the Battle of Spotsylvania. There, he was wounded in the battle and released from the army a few months later. After the war, he became the chancellor of the University of Kansas, eventually becoming president of the Pennsylvania State University. He held the position until he was offered a position at Western University as a professor. In 1878, he contracted smallpox and died. He is buried at Green Ridge Cemetery in Kenosha County, Wisconsin.[7]

Colonel John R. Brooke remained in the army after the war. In 1866, he accepted a commission as lieutenant colonel of the 37th U. S. Infantry. He held the position for thirteen years until he received a promotion to colonel of the 13th U. S. Infantry. In 1888, he led the 7th U. S. Cavalry until the battle of Wounded Knee. Afterwards, he left the command in 1895. Two years later, he took command of the First Corps during the Spanish-American War. He eventually became the military governor and head of the U.S. government of Puerto Rico. Brooke served as the commander-in-chief of the Military Order of the Loyal Legion of the United States for two years (1905-1907) and was a member of the Military Order of Foreign Wars. He retired from the army on July 21, 1902. Brooke passed away at the age of 88 in 1926. He is buried in Arlington National Cemetery.[8]

Little is known of Colonel Edward Cross's family after the period of mourning. While not much is known of them, we know that most people who came into contact with the colonel felt a great deal of loss. His obituary stated:

> As a man, Colonel Cross was ardent, impetuous and unreserved in his acts and feelings. A true patriot, an earnest lover of his country, for which he gave his life... On all occasions, to canvass freely the policy and motives involved in the struggle, but his faith was not complete with words, for he subjected to the practical test of the battlefield, from whence it derived its purity.
>
> As an officer, he was a strict and unswerving disciplinarian, punishing with severity any shirking or neglect of duty, but ever prompt to recognize and reward actual merit. Brave to the utmost limit, his command was always at the front, where it performed prodigies of valor. He never asked his men to go, and they did well if they followed closely where he led.
>
> As a son and brother he was kind, attentive and observing. His parents and relatives were always the source of remembrance and solicitude; his practical kindness was frequent and abundant.[9]
>
> He is buried in Lancaster, New Hampshire.[10]

General Zook's remains were taken home to Norristown, Pennsylvania. There, hundreds gathered to watch the procession and to mourn the loss of a man, friend, and companion. He is buried not far from his corps commander, Winfield Scott Hancock, in Montgomery Cemetery.[11]

CAPTAIN DAVID ACHESON's body was recovered on July 13, 1863. Within days, his family had been notified and they began to make arrangements to bring their son back home to their loving arms. His brother, Sadie, wrote their father on July 12, "Not until Thursday did I see one word about the 140th, then in the Tribune I saw Col. Roberts' and Capt. Atkinson's death announced. Since then I've been in perfect agony to hear from home or the regt., hoping that it was not so, and that he was yet alive."[12]

David Acheson Rock (*Personal Collection of James Smith II*) David Acheson Grave (*Personal Collection of James Smith II*)

His grave was located with the help of the inscription left behind. James Blaine Wilson noted, "We were directed by J. B. Van Dyke, who had seen him buried, to the spot, near a large rock which was at the head of the grave. And on which the initial's D. A. had been rudely carved with a nail or some such article." His body was sent back to Washington County, Pennsylvania and currently resides in the Washington Cemetery today.[13]

Colonel Richard P. Roberts' body was located after the battle and shipped back to Beaver where the citizens gave him a proper burial. He currently rests in the Beaver Cemetery and Mausoleum. The legacy of his missing sword did not die, however. On May 6, 1864, at the Battle of the Wilderness, Company D of the 149th Pennsylvania had been scouring the area when James E. McIntyre "stooped down and pulled a sword from the scabbard of a dead Confederate officer." He recognized the inscription and the sword was eventually sent back to the colonel's family. Two conflicting accounts occur. The Pittsburgh *Gazette-Times* says that his wife never received the sword but received the scabbard. Another article stated that she had both.[14]

After the war, Josiah Favill settled down and started a successful transportation business in the Produce Exchange in New York City. He held this position until his death on April 23, 1913. He is buried in Green-Wood Cemetery in New York.[15]

HENRY MEYER was promoted to corporal on November 16, 1863. He continued to serve well until being wounded in the left hand at Po River on May 10, 1864. The hand was subsequently removed, leading to his medical discharge on September 12 of that same year. He lived until 1925 and is buried at Evangelical Cemetery in Rebersburg, Pennsylvania.[16]

Henry and Martha Meyer (*Personal Collection of Barbra Abbott*)

James J. Purman of the 140th Pennsylvania survived the war. He received the Medal of Honor on October 30, 1896, for his acts of heroism during the Battle of Gettysburg. James Pipes, who assisted in the attempted rescue of their comrade, also received the honor. Purman died on May 10, 1915. He is buried in Arlington National Cemetery.[17]

After the war, **CHARLES A. FULLER**, the former lieutenant in the 61st New York, studied law. The 1880 U. S. Census stated that he was from Chenango and was then a 38-year-old lawyer. He continued his practice until the early 1900's and passed away on October 27, 1916. Fuller rests in Sherburne Quarter Cemetery in Sherburne, New York.[18]

Major St. Clair Mulholland of the 116th Pennsylvania also survived the war. He was brevetted to brigadier general on March 13, 1865, and received the Medal of Honor on March 26, 1895, for his heroic acts on the Chancellorsville battlefield. He held great pride of this feat until his dying day on February 17, 1910. He is buried at the Old Cathedral Cemetery in Philadelphia.[19]

Private Jacob Cole of the 57th New York survived his wound and subsequent capture at Gettysburg. He eventually returned to his regiment and served faithfully until the end of the war. His health took a drastic turn downward in the early 1900s but he lingered until April 22, 1929. Cole is buried in Laurel Grove Cemetery in New Jersey.[20]

Charles Fuller Post-war (*Personal Collection of Frank Walker*)

Comrades in Capt. Henry V. Fuller's company of the 64th New York had marked his grave with a makeshift marker before the Army of the Potomac withdrew to pursue Lee toward Virginia. After the battle, friends shipped his remains back home to Cattaraugus, New York, where Fuller was re-interred in Little Valley Rural Cemetery.[21]

In all the war, very few troops displayed the fortitude and perseverance that the men of John Caldwell's Division did during those few July days at Gettysburg. It is with great respect that I bring you a letter written by Samuel Babcock, the father of the slain Lt. Willis "Willie" G. Babcock of the 64th New York, to his other children describing the death of their sibling. He wrote:

My Dear Children,

I wrote to Willoughby before leaving home for Gettysburgh intending it for you all and I do so now. I left home on Monday for the battlefield as I told you and came by way of Elmyra Harrisburg York to Gettysburg arriving there Wednesday eve, on the train I came was 13 cars filled with fathers and brothers looking as I was for killed and wounded, it seemed to me the largest train of mourners I was ever in and I could not keep back the tears, for my heart was sad O how sad. I thought of the last time poor Willie passed over the same road and of the sad parting I had with him at our depot when he left home for the last time and I thought of the letters you and I wrote him after the battle of Chancellorsville when he thought of leaving the army if he could do so with honor to himself and I must say I felt some misgivings over it and wished I had told him to do what he thought best under the circumstances. But that like many other things has passed and cannot be recalled. I thought at the time I did right, but my heart aches now while I think of it. But I must come to particulars. I found Codt Green and Eld Brigham on the ground. I at once made arrangements to have Willies's body disinterred and embalmed, but the crowd was grate and all wanting the same thing dun dead bodies were passing away from the battlefield by the hundreds and while I was waiting on Friday for the embalmer and his time a dispatch came to the express office to take no more bodys until further notice.

Doct. G. Eld. B. and I went over to his grave and they thought as he was buried in a quiet place well secured… I had better leave it until cold wether and then convey home. The man who owned the farm said he could lay with so much care by Maj. Bradley with a sad heart, but when I came to lay my weary self on the bed that night and think of leaving Willie on the battlefield I could not do it if I had to stay weeks I would not leave without him. In the morning I found at the express office that by Gettysburg a zinc coffin and then another one for the body to go inside and sealing up both after embalming they would take him. I lost no time in arranging all this and in company with the embalmer and his hands Dr. G and I proceeded to Willie's grave, he had been buried 14 days—found the body in tolerable good state of preservation. The ball struck him near the right collarbone Dr. G. things broke it and cut one or both greater veins and probably died in a few minutes. His face neck and hair was covered with blood and quite dark. We took him after the Doct. had got him embalmed and taken or cut his cloths from him rolled him in his army blanket put him in the coffin sealed both boxes tight and had him conveyed to the express office and Willie's body now while I write is on its way to the cemetery in Homer. While on the battle field and visiting the different Corps hospitals I saw several of the 64 and they all with one voice testified to his bravery good conduct and soldierly qualities. His chaplin in particular said he was the favorit of the Regt. And no one he thought more of.

I went all over the ground several times when the fight began and where Willie fell hoping to find some letter or scrap of his that I might recoginize as his but could find none.

I could hear nothing of his watch, sword, purse, or memorandum book but can but hope that the man who pined the envelop on his coat has them and will return them.

Willoughby, Willie has layed himself on the alter of his country. It was the bravery of him and others who saved the army from distruction and Penn. From pillage and turned the whole tide of things here with Gen. Meads army. A wounded soldier in the 64 told me the night before the battle Gen. M. issued an order to the officers alone and he inquired what it meant or what was up that they were called together and Willie told him it was that the country expected of every officer to do there duty and that very probably the fate of the country hung upon the coming battle. And now Willoughby I think you have dun your part of the fighting and I do hope you will take care of yourself in the future and as you can with honor to yourself will take leave of the battlefield and the army.

Things look now as if our hardest fighting had been dun, but I do feel as if our family had fully borne their part in this terrible war. I had no adequate idea of what our soldiers had to bare until I came down here. There are now at Gettysburgh and surrounding several thousand in other directions around town and the government has been carrying them away to Baltimore Harrisburg Pilidelphia Washington New York and other places two trains a day for the last two weeks. I went over the field of battle an arch of 7 miles considerably and the ground is the most admirable for fighting large rocks and ledges with heavy swells officering strong points quite often. It seems to me as if all the horses in the country had been killed, as they lay just as they were when killed scattered over all the vast battle ground. I counted 13 around one house and barn. Knapsack haversack blankets guns bayonets was every where to be seen and no one can visit the field without feeling that the fight was the most desperate on the continent. As I visited the hospital saw the wounded in every state from the dying to the conversant and see how cheerfully they all were I could but say our brave boys are heroes. O how much our army of the Potomac has endured. I can but feel bad when I think how much poor Willie has passed through in these terrible long and fatigueing marches but he is at rest now and I hope in Heven to join his mother and little Charlie who had gon before. May the lord sanctify this lesson to the good of us all. I paid $58.00 for his tow coffins and embalming his body and $26.00 express to Homer total $84. I should not have left him if it had cost twice that sum Doct. Greene is with here, we came here last eve and shall start this eve or tomorrow for home. Eld B. is still at Gettysburgh doing what he can for the boys.

I hope to find letter from Kil and Willoughby when I get home the papers say Port Hudson has surrendered and it rumored that Morris Island and Charleston has fallen which I hope may prove true. The riot in New York people feel here will work for the good of the country, it is generally thought it will kill Coperheadism or at least silence there claimers and show the strength of the government. Charles F. Pratt, Clark Stickney, John Owen and many other brave boys still on the battlefield. I saw the grave of Barksdale and many other Reb officers. I must close.

Your father,
Samuel Babcock[22]

Lieutenant Willis Babcock's body would arrive back in Homer City, New York. From there, it would be reinterred in Glenwood Cemetery.[23]

The Pennsylvania soil at Gettysburg soaked up the blood of thousands of men who wore the blue and gray. In Caldwell's Division, the figures were no different and pay as a tribute to the fallen as well as the ones that survived. While many of us still study the commands of the greatest generals ever to fight on a battlefield in General Lee, General Meade, and so on, we often forget that wars were won and lost within the ranks. Perhaps, Confederate Captain George Hillyer described it best. The Georgian wrote, "It is interesting to talk about the privates and line officers. We all admire the generals and our eyes kindle and beam, and our ears are full of enthusiasm as we pay deserved tributes to their fame. But it is to the private soldier and the line officers, many of them just as brave as the most famous general, to whom full justice has not been, and can never be done."[24]

Appendix

Losses in Caldwell's Division at Gettysburg

CROSS'S BRIGADE

Unit	Strength	Losses (k-w-c)	Percent Casualties
5th New Hampshire	179	80 (27-53-0)	44.7%
61st New York	104	62 (5-56-0)	59.5%
81st Pennsylvania	175	62 (5-49-8)	35.4%
148th Pennsylvania	392	125 (19-101-5)	31.9%
Total	853	330 (57-260-13)	38.7%

KELLY'S BRIGADE

Unit	Strength	Losses (k-w-c)	Percent Casualties
28th Massachusetts	224	100 (8-57-35)	44.6%
63rd New York	75	23 (5-10-8)	30.7%
69th New York	75	25 (5-14-6)	33.3%
88th New York	90	28 (7-17-4)	31.1%
116th Pennsylvania	66	22 (2-11-9)	33.3
Total	532	198 (27-109-62)	37.2%

ZOOK'S BRIGADE

Unit	Strength	Losses (k-w-c)	Percent Casualties
52nd New York	134	38 (2-16-10)	28.4%
57th New York	175	34 (4-28-2)	19.4%
66th New York	147	44 (5-29-10)	29.0
140th Pennsylvania	515	241 (37-144-60)	46.8%
Total	975	358 (49-227-82)	36.7%

BROOKE'S BRIGADE[1]

Unit	Strength	Losses (k-w-c)	Percent Casualties
27th Connecticut	75	37 (10-23-4)	49.3%
2nd Delaware	234	84 (11-61-12)	35.9%
64th New York	204	98 (15-64-19)	48%
53rd Pennsylvania	135	80 (7-67-6)	59.3%
145th Pennsylvania	202	90 (11-69-10)	44.6%
Total	851	389 (54-284-51)	45.7%

Notes

Chapter 1

1. Extract from Harry Wilson's account, *Pennsylvania at Gettysburg*, Vol. 1, 436

2. Larry Tagg, *Generals of Gettysburg*, 35-36; Caldwell's marriage certificate, 1857, National Archives file on John Caldwell

3. William Pickerill, *Indiana at Antietam*, 64; Tagg, *Generals of Gettysburg*, 35-56; *Official Records*, Volume 11, Part 2, 56

4. *OR* 11, pt. 2, 285

5. Ibid; Johnson, *Battles and Leaders of the Civil War*, Vol. 2, 558

6. *OR* 21, pt. 1, 48-61, 540-545

7. Caldwell's O.R., *The War of the Rebellion*, Series I, Volume XXI, 233

8. Ibid; U.S. War Department, *The War of the Rebellion*, (U.S. Government Printing Office, 1880-1901

9. Caldwell O.R., *The War of the Rebellion,* Series I, Volume XXI, 233-34

10. Ibid.; Goolrick, William K, and the Editors of Time-Life Books. *Rebels Resurgent*: 77-79

11. Caldwell O.R., *The War of the Rebellion,* Series 1, Volume XXI, 233-34

12. Caldwell O.R., *The War of the Rebellion,* Series 1, Volume XXV, 318

13. Ibid; Broady O.R., *The War of the Rebellion,* Series 1, Volume XXV, 318-319

14. Caldwell O.R., *The War of the Rebellion,* Series 1, Volume XXV, 318

15. Ibid

16. Dyer, Frederick, *Compendium of the Civil War* (Morningside Bookshop, 1978), 287

17. *New Hampshire in the Great Rebellion*, 263

18. Ibid; Slomba, *Stand Firm and Fire Low*, 1

19. Ibid; U.S. Census Records and Military Service; Pride and Travis, *My Brave Boys*, 6; National Archives

20. *New Hampshire in the Great Rebellion*, 264

21. Ibid, 265

22. Moore, *The Rebellion Record*, Vol 5, 93

23. Ibid; Robert Grandchamp, *Colonel Edward E. Cross, New Hampshire Fighting Fifth: A Civil War Biography* (University of New Hampshire Special Collections)

24. *New Hampshire in the Great Rebellion*, 265

25. Ibid; Colonel Edward E. Cross journal (University of New Hampshire)

26. *New Hampshire in the Great Rebellion*, 265; Cross Journal

27. Ibid, May 3

28. Tagg, *Generals at Gettysburg*, 34-35

29. National Archives RG-15, #227761

30. O'Grady, *Grand Army Review*, Vol. 1, No. 7 (Grand Army Publishing Company), 105

31. Murphy, T. L., *Faithful to us here: A Remembrance of Colonel Patrick Kelly*; National Archives RG 15 File # 227761

32. *Official Records*, Series 1, Vol 11, Kelly report, 88th New York

33. Kelly O.R., *War of the Rebellion*, Series 1, Volume XIX, 298

34. Ibid, Cross O.R., *The War of the Rebelion*, Series 1, Volume XXV, 318

35. Kelly O.R., *The War of the Rebellion*, Series 1, Volume XIX, 298-99

36. Patrick Kelly O.R., *The War of the Rebellion*, Series I-Volume XXI, 251

37. Ibid

38. Wilson, *Personal Recollections of the War of the Rebellion*, 357

39. Kelly O.R., *The War of the Rebellion*, Series I, Volume XXI, 252; Lazelle, *The War of the Rebellion*, 251-52

40. Warner, *Generals in Blue: Lives of the Union Commanders*, 576; *Final Report on the Battlefield of Gettysburg*, 407-09

41. Reid, James, *The Telegraph in American and Morse Memorial*, (Author, 1886), 118-119

42. Ibid; Annual Report Transmitted to the legislature; Weed, *New York in the War of the Rebellion*, 418

43. Favill, *The Diary of a Young Officer Serving with the Armies of the United States During the War of the Rebellion*, 130

44. Ibid, 419

45. Favill, *The Diary of a Young Officer*, 131

46. Ibid, 185

47. Ibid

48. Favill, *The Diary of a Young officer*, 185- 187

49. Favill, *The Diary of a Young Officer*, 187-88

50. Favill, 209- 10

51. Ibid, Zook, *The War of the Rebellion*, Series 1- Volume XX1, 255

52. Favill, *Diary of a Young Officer*. 211

53. Ibid, 211-217; Stewart, *History of the one Hundred and Fortieth Regiment Pennsylvania Volunteers*, 65

54. Stewart, *History of the One Hundred and Fortieth Regiment Pennsylvania Volunteers*, 65-70

55. Auge, *Lives of the Eminent Dead*, 419

56. Ibid, 420

57. General William French O.R., Camp at Fair Oaks, Va., June 3, 1862; *The War of the Rebellion*, V1-55, 1884, 782

58. Brooke O.R., *The War of the Rebellion*, Series I- Volume XIX, 299

59. *Ibid; Congressional Series of the United States Public Documents*, Volume 2572, (U.S. Government Printing Officer, 1889), 299

60. Ibid, 299-300; Brooke O.R, *The War of the Rebellion*, Series I- Vol. XXL, 261

61. Ibid; *The War of the Rebellion*, Vol 53," (Historical Times, 1888), 261

62. Brooke O.R

63. Brooke O.R., *The War of the Rebellion*, Series I- Volume XXV, Part I, 336

64. Ibid

65. Ibid

Chapter 2

1. Tremain, *Two Days of War*, 165

2. Library of Congress

3. Scott, *The War of the Rebellion*, Series I, Volume XXVII, 881-82

4. Goodrich, *The Life and Public Services of Winfield Scott Hancock*, 118-22

5. Corby, *Memoirs of Chaplain Life*, 174

6. Brigades based on various Official Reports from the Battle of Gettysburg.

7. Address of Major R. H. Forster, *Pennsylvania at Gettysburg*, 732; *United States Congressional Serial Set*, Issue 2773, (1891), 8

8. Ibid, 10

9. Sweeney, *History of Company K of the 140th Regiment Pennsylvania Volunteers*, 25

10. Livermore, *Days and Events, 1860-1866*, 216

11. Forster account, *Pennsylvania at Gettysburg, Volume 2*, 725; Livermore, 216

12. *Congressional Serial Set*, (U.S. Government Printing Office, 1865), 156; Dispatched June 6, 1863

13. Livermore, *Days and Events, 1860-1866*, 216- 219

14. Livermore's account in *Historical Sketches*, 22

15. Livermore, 219- 22

16. Muffly, Meyers account, *The Story of Our Regiment: A History of the 148th Pennsylvania Vols*, 455

17. David Acheson to Mother (G.N.M.P Library, VG-PA140, June 9, 1863)

18. Stewart, *History of the One Hundred and Fortieth Regiment Pennsylvania Volunteers*, 83

19. Ibid; Sweeny,25; Child, *A History of the Fifth Regiment, New Hampshire Volunteers, in the American Civil War, 1861-1865*, 202

20. Stewart, 84

21. Ibid; Child, 202

22. Child, 202

23. Stewart, *History of the One Hundred and Fortieth Regiment Pennsylvania Volunteers*, 84

24. Mulholland, *The Story of the 116th Regiment Pennsylvania Volunteers in the War of the Rebellion*, 114-15

25. Corby, William, *Memoirs of Chaplain Life*, (La Monte, O'Donnell, Printers, 1893), 171

26. Muffly, Meyers report, 456

27. Child, 202-03

28. Favill, Josiah, *The Diary of a Young Officer Serving with the Armies of the United States During the War of the Rebellion*, (R.R. Donnelley & Sons Company, 1909), 236-37; Child, 203

29. Letter of David Acheson, June 20, 1863 (G.N.M.P Library)

30. Stewart, 85; Sheldon, Winthrop, *The Twenty-Seventh*, (1866), 72

31. Fuller, *Personal Recollections of the War of 1861*, 60-61

32. Muffly, Meyers report, 457; Muffly, Hamilton's report, *The Story of Our Regiment*, 170

33. Mulholland, 115-16; 2nd Lieutenant John B Noyes papers, Gettysburg National Military Park Library

34. David Acheson letter to his mother, June 22, 1863, (G.N.M.P. Library)

35. Muffly, Meyer's account, 457

36. Muffly, Meyer's account, 458

37. Favill, 238

38. Ibid; Livermore, 236; General Hancock dispatches

39. Sheldon, 73; Stewart, 85-86; Child, 203; Fuller, 61
40. Favill, 239
41. Stewart, *History of the One Hundred and Fortieth Regiment Pennsylvania Volunteers*, 86; Favill, 239
42. Favill, 239
43. Favill, 239-40; Stewart, *History of the One Hundred and Fortieth Regiment Pennsylvania Volunteers*, 85
44. Child, 203; Stewart, 86; Sweeney, 26
45. Favill, 240; Fuller, 61
46. Muffly, Meyers account, *The Story of Our Regiment,* 458; Favill, 240
47. Favill, 240; Stewart, 86
48. Stewart, 86
49. Fuller, 61; Sweeney, 26
50. Fuller*, Personal Recollections of the War of 1861,* 61; Favill, *The Diary of a Young Officer Serving with the Armies of the United States During the War of the Rebellion,* 240
51. Sweeney, 26
52. Favill, *The Diary of a Young Officer Serving with the Armies of the United States During the War of the Rebellion,* 240
53. Muffly, Hamilton report, *The Story of Our Regiment,* 170; Mulholland, *The Story of the 116th Regiment Pennsylvania Volunteers in the War of the Rebellion,* 117
54. Mulholland, *The Story of the 116th Regiment Pennsylvania Volunteers in the War of the Rebellion,* 117
55. Livermore, *Days and Events, 1860-1866,* 236
56. Major Charles Hale account of Colonel Edward Cross, "With Colonel Cross in the Gettysburg Campaign," (G.N.M.P Library)
57. Stewart, *History of the One Hundred and Fortieth Regiment Pennsylvania Volunteers,* 87
58. Corby, William, *Memoirs of Chaplain Life,* (La Monte, O'Donnell, Printers, 1893), 173
59. Corby, *Memoirs of Chaplain Life,* 173-174
60. Acheson Letter to his mother, July 28, 1863 (G.N.M.P. Library)
61. Stewart, *History of the One Hundred and Fortieth Regiment Pennsylvania Volunteers,* 87
62. Favill, *The Diary of a Young Officer Serving with the Armies of the United States During the War of the Rebellion,* 241; Corby, *Memoirs of Chaplain Life,* 176
64. Favill, *The Diary of a Young Officer Serving with the Armies of the United States During the War of the Rebellion,* 242; Stewart, *History of the One Hundred and Fortieth Regiment Pennsylvania Volunteers,* 87; Muffly, Stevens account, *The Story of Our Regiment*, 197; Sickles, *Final Report on the Battlefield of Gettysburg..,* 419
65. Sickles, *Final Report on the Battlefield of Gettysburg,* 419; Corby, *Memoirs of Chaplain Life,* 176; Favill, *The Diary of a Young Officer Serving with the Armies of the United States During the War of the Rebellion,* 241
65. Favill, *The Diary of a Young Officer Serving with the Armies of the United States During the War of the Rebellion,* 241; Stewart, *History of the One Hundred and Fortieth Regiment Pennsylvania Volunteers,* 88
66. Muffly, Hamilton account, *The Story of Our Regiment,* 171
67. Hale, "With Colonel Cross in the Gettysburg Campaign" (G.N.M.P)
68. Martin Sigman account (G.N.M.P Library); Sickles, Frederick account, *Final Report on the Battlefield of Gettysburg,* 419

69. Muholland, *The Story of the 116ᵗʰ Regiment Pennsylvania Volunteers in the War of the Rebellion*, 118

70. Corby, *Memoirs of Chaplain Life*, 178

71. Fuller, *Personal Recollections of the War of 1861*, 61-62

72. Martin Sigman, *Account by Unidentified Soldier of the 64ᵗʰ New York Infantry*, (G.N.M.P Library)

73. Stewart, *History of the One Hundred and Fortieth Regiment Pennsylvania Volunteers*, 89

74. Sickles, Frederick's account, *Final Report on the Battlefield of Gettysburg*, 419

75. Forster account, *Pennsylvania at Gettysburg*, Volume 2, 740

76. Livermore, *Days and Events, 1860-1866*, 236

77. SHSP, (1877), 157

78. C. Tevis, *The History of the Fighting Fourteenth*, (1911), 81; Marye, *The First Gun at Gettysburg*, (1895), 30; *Biography written by Lt. Colonel Jesse Martinez*; Hard, *History of the Eighth Cavalry Regiment, Illinois Volunteers, During the Great Rebellion*, 256; *Annual Reunion of Pegram Battalion Association*, (1886), 15

79. Abbot, Willis, *Battle Fields and Camp Fires*, (Dodd, Meade & Company, 1890), 208

80. Bachelder Maps

81. Veil to McConaughy, (April, 7, 1864)

82. Smith, *Along the Lines of Devotion*, 138-55

83. Favill, *The Diary of a Young Officer Serving with the Armies of the United States During the War of the Rebellion*, 242; Stewart, *History of the One Hundred and Fortieth Regiment Pennsylvania Volunteers*, 89

84. Muffly, Ramsey account, *The Story of Our Regiment*, 346

85. Charles Hatch account, *Pennsylvania at Gettysburg*, Volume 1, 326; *War Papers Read Before the Commandery of the State of Wisconsin, Military Order of the Loyal Legion of the United States*, Volume 4, 404

86. Weld, *War Diary and Letters of Stephen Minot Weld, 1861-1865*, 229-30

87. Church, William, Hancock's account, *The Galaxy, Volume 22*, (W.C. and F.P. Church, 1876), 822

88. McFarland account, *Pennsylvania at Gettysburg*, Vol 2, 768

89. Church, Hancock's account, *The Galaxy*, Volume 22, 822; Walker, Morgan extract, *History of the Second Army Corps in the Army of the Potomac*, 265

90. Shallenberger account, *Pennsylvania at Gettysburg*, 687; Favill, *The Diary of a Young Officer Serving with the Armies of the United States During the War of the Rebellion*, 242; Muffly, Meyer account, *The Story of Our Regiment*, 459

91. Mulholland account, *Pennsylvania at Gettysburg*, Volume 2, 620; Muffly, D.W. Miller account, *The Story of Our Regiment*, 716

92. Muffly, Osman account, *The Story of Our Regiment*, 602

93. Schurz, Carl, *The Reminiscences of Carl Schurz*, 14

94. McFarland account, *Pennsylvania at Gettysburg*, Vol 2, 768

95. Fuller, *Personal Recollections of the War of 1861*, 62; Muffly, D.W. Miller account, *The Story of Our Regiment*, 716

96. Favill, *The Diary of a Young Officers Serving with the Armies of the United States During the War of the Rebellion*, 242

97. Fuller, *Personal Recollections of the War of 1861*, 62

98. Whipple, George, *Memories of George W. Whipple, Private Company "F," 64ᵗʰ N.Y.V., 1861-1865*, 19

99. Muffly, Osman account, *The Story of Our Regiment*, 602

100. Muffly, Meyer Account, *The Story of Our Regiment*, 459

101. Stewart, *History of the one Hundred and Fortieth Regiment Pennsylvania Volunteers*, 91-92

Chapter 3

1. extract taken from Muffly, Sophie Hall's account, *The Story of Our Regiment*, 42

2. Muholland's Account, *Pennsylvania at Gettysburg*, 621

3. Sigman account, *Account by Unidentified Soldier of the 64th New York Infantry* (G.N.M.P Library); Muffly, Miller Account, *The Story of Our Regiment*, 716

4. Muffly, Osman Account, *The Story of Our Regiment*, 602

5. Favill, *The Diary of a Young Officer Serving with the Armies of the United States During the War of the Rebellion*, 244; Hale, *With Colonel Cross in the Gettysburg Campaign*, (Gettysburg National Military Park Library)

6. Muffly, Meyer's Account, *The Story of our Regiment*, 460

7. Fuller, *Personal Recollections of the War of 1861*, 62

8. Shallenberger Account, *Pennsylvania at Gettysburg,* Volume 2," 688

9. Warren Map (Library of Congress)

10. Frederick account, Sickles, *Final Report on the Battlefield of Gettysburg*, 419

11. Hale*, With Colonel Cross in the Gettysburg Campaign*, (G.N.M.P Library)

12. Muholland account, *Pennsylvania at Gettysburg*, 625

13. Livermore, *Days and Events, 1860-1865*, 245; Corby, *Memoirs of Chaplain Life*, 180

14. Forster account, *Pennsylvania at Gettysburg*, 734; Noyes papers (G.N.M.P Library)

15. Stewart, *History of the One Hundred and Forieth Regiment Pennsylvania Volunteers*, 97-98

16. Noyes account, 28th Massachusetts (G.N.M.P Library); Muffly, Osman account, *The Story of Our Regiment*, 603

17. Tremain, Henry, *Two Days of War*, (Bonell, Silver and Bowers, 1905," 72; Berdan's O.R., *The War of the Rebellion,* Series 1- Vol. 53, 503

18. Pfanz, *Gettysburg- The Second Day*, 87; Ibid

19. Ibid

20. Stevens, *Berdan's United States Sharpshooters in the Army of the Potomac, 1861-1865*, 303

21. Tremain, *Two Days of War*, 48-54

22. Muholland address, *Pennsylvania at Gettysburg*, 626

23. Muffly, Hamilton account, *The Story of Our Regiment*, 172

24. Tremain, *Two Days of War*, 55-71; Shallenberger address, *Pennsylvania at Gettysburg*, Volume 2, 688

25. Hal Jespersen Civil War Maps www.cwmaps.com AI5

26. Youngblood, William, *Confederate Veteran*: in 'Personal Observations at Gettysburg, Volume 19', 286

27. Stewart, *History of the One Hundred and Fortieth Regiment Pennsylvania Volunteers*, 100; Mulholland address, *Pennsylvania at Gettysburg*, Volume 2, 626

28. Muffly, Henry Meyer account, *The Story of Our Regiment*, 536; Fuller, *Personal Recollections of the War of 1861*, 62

29. Sickles O.R; Mulholland address, *Pennsylvania at Gettysburg*, Volume 2, 627

30. Hale, *With Colonel Cross in the Gettysburg Campaign*, (G.N.M.P. Library)

31. Weygant, *History of the One Hundred and Twenty-fourth Regiment*, 175-185

32. Weygant, Charles, *History of the One Hundred and Twenty-fourth Regiement*, 181-184

33. Erasmus Gilbreath journal

34. Hillyer, George, *My Gettysburg Battle Experiences*, 10-13

35. *Confederate Union*, (August 11, 1863)

36. Hillyer, *My Gettysburg Battle Experiences*, 15

37. Toombs, *New Jersey Troops in the Gettysburg Campaign from June 5 to July 31, 1863*, 219; John P. Dune to John B. Bachelder, *The Bachelder Papers*, 1050-52

38. Daniel Gookin Journal, Lewis Leigh Collection, United States Army Military History Institute, Book 8 #39

39. *Maine at Gettysburg* (The Lakeside Press, 1898), 195

40. Alex McNeil Letters 2nd South Carolina Infantry, July 7, 1863 (G.N.M.P. Library); Kershaw to Bachelder, *The Bachelder Papers*, (April, 3, 1876), 474

41. Coxe, John, *The Battle of Gettysburg*, Confederate Veteran, 434

42. McNeil Letters 2nd South Carolina Infantry, july 7, 1863, (G.N.M.P. Library)

43. Frank Gaillard, 2nd South Carolina Infantry letter to his sister July 17th, 1863 (G.N.M.P. Library)

44. Anderson to Bachelder, *The Bachelder Papers*, Volume 1, (March 15, 1875), 449-50

45. ;Smith, *History of the Corn Exchange Regiment, 118th Pennsylvania Volunteers, from Their First Engagement at Antietam to Appomattox*, 244

46. Smith, *History of the Corn Exchange Regiment*, 244

47. Extracted from Smith, J.L., *History of the Corn Exchange Regiment*, 256

48. Kickert, *History of Kershaw's Brigade*, 241

49. Parker, *Henry Wilson's Regiment,"*335

50. John L. Smith to Hannah Smith, (July 9, 1863), Smith Papers HSP

51. *Maine at Gettysburg*, 150-161

52. King, *Camp-fire Sketches and Battle-field Echoes*, 223

53. *Pennsylvania at Gettysburg*, Volume 2, 638

54. Sweitzer's O.R., *The War of the Rebellion*, Series I- Volume XXIX, (U.S. Government Printing Office, 1889), 611

55. Hillyer Official report number 450, to Major H.D. McDaniel; Sweitzer's O.R., *The War of the Rebellion*, Series I- Volume XXXIX, 611; *Maine at Gettysburg*, 196-97

56. *Maine at Gettysburg*, 198

57. Shallenberger account, *Pennsylvania at Gettysburg*, 688

58. Muholland account, *Pennsylvania at Gettysburg*, 627; Hale, *With Colonel Cross in the Gettysburg Campaign*, (G.N.M.P. Library)

59. *Description of Father Corby at Gettysburg*, Author Unkown, Date Unknown, (Silbey Collection, Box B-12 G.N.M.P. Library)

60. Ibid; Mulholland account, *Pennsylvania at Gettysburg*, 628

61. Mulholland account, *Pennsylvania at Gettysburg*, 628

62. Source produced by multiple accounts from several regimental commanders and brigade commanders

63. Hale, *With Colonel Cross in the Gettysburg Campaign*, (G.N.M.P. Library)

64. Fuller, *Personal Recollections of the War of 1861*, 63; Hale, *With Colonel Cross in the Gettysburg Campaign* (G.N.M.P. Library); Lieutenant William P. Wilson to Bachelder, *The Bachelder Papers*, Vol 2," 1195

65. Busey and Martin, *Regimental Strenghts and Losses at Gettysburg*, (Longstreet House, Hightstown, N.J., 1986), 242; According to various Official Reports conducted by commanders of the regiments.

66. *Maine at Gettysburg*, 199

67. Based on Kershaw's Official report

68. Wilson to Bachelder, *The Bachelder Papers*, Volume 2, 1196; Muffly, Osman Account, *The Story of Our Regiment*, 603

69. Fuller, *Personal Recollections of the War of 1861*, 63

70. Hale, *With Colonel Cross in the Gettysburg Campaign*, (G.N.M.P. Library); Wilson to Bachelder, *The Bachelder Papers*, Volume 2, 1195; Fuller, *Personal Recollections of the War of 1861* 63; Muffly, Meyer account, *The Story of Our Regiment*, 537

71. Hale, *With Colonel Cross in the Gettysburg Campagain*, (G.N.M.P. Library)

72. Muffly, Private Henry Meyer's Account, *The Story of Our Regiment*, 537

73. According to various Official Reports from the *The War of the Rebellion*; Muffly, Henry Meyer's account, *The Story of Our Regiment*, 536; *The War of the Rebellion*, 382 (1889)

74. Hale, *With Colonel Cross in the Gettysburg Campaign*, (G.N.M.P. Library); K.O. Broady Official Report, *The War of the Rebellion,* Series I- Volume XXVII, 384; Forster report, *Pennsylvania at Gettysburg*, Volume 2, 736

75. Muffly, Lemuel Osman's Account, *The Story of Our Regiment*, 603

76. Hale, *With Colonel Cross in the Gettysburg Campaign*, (G.N.M.P. Library)

77. Child, *A History of the Fifth Regiment*, 207; Brooke Papers; Livermore, *Days and Events, 1860-1866*, 250

78. Pride and Travis*, Brave Boys*, 239; Livermore, *Days and Events, 1860-1866*, 250

79. Muffly, Private Meyer's Account, *The Story of Our Regiment*, 536-37

80. Muffly, Lemuel Osman account, *The Story of Our Regiment*, 603

81. Child, *A History of the Fifth Regiment*, 206; Fuller, *Personal Recollections of the War of 1861*, 63

82. Fuller, *Personal Recollections of the War of 1861*, 63-67

83. Muffly, Private Meyer account, *The Story of Our Regiment*, 537

84. Captain Henry Wilson account, *Pennsylvania at Gettysburg*, Volume 1, 417

85. Muffly, Osman's Account, *The Story of Our Regiment*, 603

86. Muffly, Meyer's Account, *The Story of Our Regiment*, 537

87. Tremain, *Two Days of War*, 81-83; Favill, *The Diary of a Young Officer Serving with the Armies of the United States During the War of the Rebellion*, 245

88. Tremain, *Two Days of War*, 84

89. Busey and Martin, *Regimental Strengths and Losses at Gettysburg*, 242; According to various accounts extracted from various Official Reports.

90. Purman to Bachelder, *The Bachelder Papers*, Volume 1, (November 3, 1871), 417

91. Stewart, *History of the One Hundred and Fortieth Regiment Pennsylvania Volunteers*, 102

92. Stewart, *History of the One Hundred and Fortieth Regiment Pennsylvania Volunteers*, 422; *St. Louisans Among Gettysburg Heroes*, Thomas B. Rodger's account, (G.N.M.P. Library)

93. Stewart, *History of the One Hundred and Fortieth Regiment Pennsylvania Volunteers*, 422; Favill, *The Diary of a Young Officer Serving with the Armies of the United States During the War of the Rebellion*, 246

94. Stewart, *History of the One Hundred and Fortieth Regiment Pennsylvania Volunteers*, 104-05

95. Major Peter Nelson Official Report, *The War of the Rebellion*, 399

96. Stewart, *History of the One Hundred and Fortieth Regiment Pennsylvania Volunteers*, 105

97. Shallenberger Account, *Pennsylvania at Gettysburg*, 688

98. Favill, *The Diary of a Young Officer Serving with the Armies of the United States During the War of the Rebellion*, 246

99. Sickles, Frederick's account, *Final Report on the Battlefield of Gettysburg*, 420; Favill, *The Diary of a Young Officer Serving with the Armies of the United States During the War of the Rebellion*, 246

100. Favill, *The Diary of a Young Officer Serving with the Armies of the United States During the War of the Rebellion*, 246

101. Purman account, *The Bachelder Papers*, Volume 1, 418

102. *The Washington Observer*, (May 30, 1898)

103. Shallenberger account, *Pennsylvania at Gettysburg*, 689; Stewart, *History of the One Hundred and Fortieth Regiment Pennsylvania Volunteers*, 104-05, 422; Unknown author of an extract found at the G.N.M.P. Library.

104. Shallenberger account, *Pennsylvania at Gettysburg*, 689; Stewart, *History of the One Hundred and Fortieth Regiment Pennsylvania Volunteers*, 104-05, 422; Unknown author of an extract found at the G.N.M.P. Library. It was written Aug. 21, 1910; Shallenberger papers, (28th, Aug, 1863); Bates, *Martial Deeds of Pennsylvania*, 508

105. Favill, *The Diary of a Young Officer Serving with the Armies of the United States During the War of the Rebellion*, 246

106. Powelson, *History of Company K of the 140th Regiment Pennsylvania Volunteers*, 29

107. Stewart, *History of the One Hundred and Fortieth Regiment Pennsylvania Volunteers*, 105; Cole, *Under Five Commanders: Or, A Boy's Experience with the Army of the Potomac*, 202-03

108. Based on various accounts given by the soldiers of Kershaw's Brigade; Lieutenant Colonel F. Gaillard 2nd South Carolina to Maria (July 17, 1863)

109. Stewart, *History of the One Hundred and Fortieth Regiment Pennsylvania Volunteers*, 104-05

110. Aiken, David W., *The Gettysburg Reunion*. What is Necessary and Proper for the South to Do. An Open Letter from Col. D. Wyatt Aiken to Gen J. B. Kershaw, (Charleston News and Courier, 21 June 1882, G.N.M.P. Library)

111. Aiken, *The Gettysburg Reunion* (21 June 1882, G.N.M.P Library)

112. Mulholland, *The Story of the 116th Regiment Pennsylvania Volunteers in the War of the Rebellion*, 125

113. Noyes, "Co. 'B' 28th MA INF (G.N.M.P. Library)

114. Busey and Martin, *Regimental Strengths and Losses at Gettysburg*, 242; Based on various accounts and official reports by the officers of their respective regiments.

115. J. Noonan, *The 69th New York History*, (Kenneth H Powers Collection (U.S.A.H.I); Papers of 2nd Lieutenant John B Noyes Co. 'B', 28th MA INF (G.N.M.P. Library)

116. Based on accounts by confederate officers from Kershaw's, Semmes, and Anderson's Brigades.

117. Mulholland's Account, *Pennsylvania at Gettysburg*, 629; James J. Purman's notes on a conversation taken place between he and Major Mulholland, *The Bachelder Papers*, Volume 1, 421

118. James J. Smith Official Report, *The War of the Rebellion*, Series I- Vol. XXVII, 389

119. Mulholland Account, *116th Pennsylvania at Gettysburg, July 17, 1863*, (Abraham Lincoln Foundation- Union League of Philadelphia, G.N.M.P. Library)

120. *New York at Gettysburg*, 479

121. Mulholland's Account, *Pennsylvania at Gettysburg*, 629

122. Letter of Peter Welsh, 28ᵗʰ Massachusetts Infantry to his Wife, (7-17-1863, Peter Welsh Papers, 1863 Folder, Manuscript Dept., The New York Historical Society); Mulholland, *The Story of the 116ᵗʰ Pennsylvania Volunteers in the War of the Rebellion*, 125

123. Mulholland's Account, *Pennsylvania at Gettysburg*, 629

124. Stewart, *History of the One Hundred and Fortieth Regiment Pennsylvania Volunteers*, 105-06

125. *The War of the Rebellion*, Volume 27, Part 2, 372; Alex McNeil Letter to his wife (July 7, 1863, G.N.M.P. Library)

126. Purman to Bachelder, *The Bachelder Papers*, Volume 1, 421; Mulholland Account, *Pennsylvania at Gettysburg*, 629

127. Hillyer, *My Gettysburg Battle Experiences*, 18

128. Mulholland, *The Story of the 116ᵗʰ Regiment Pennsylvania Volunteers in the War of the Rebellion*, 126; Mulholland account, *Pennsylvania at Gettysburg*, 630

129. Busey and Martin, *Regimental Strengths and Losses at Gettysburg*, 242; Based on Various accounts from various officers through the two brigades.

130. Mulholland, *The Story of the 116ᵗʰ Regiment Pennsylvania Volunteers in the War of the Rebellion*," 127

131. *Memories of George W. Whipple, Private Company "F," 64ᵗʰ N.Y.V., 1861-1865* (G.N.M.P. Library); Account of Martin Sigman, Co. C, 64ᵗʰ New York, *Account by Unidentified Soldier of the 64ᵗʰ New York Infantry* or *History of Cattaraugus County New York,* Written by Daniel G Bringham; *B.J. Warden's Gettysburg Experience*, Benson J. Warden Company F. 53ʳᵈ Pennsylvania Volunteer Infantry (Indiana State Library); Brookes Official Report

132. Captain John C. Hilton's Account, *Pennsylvania at Gettysburg*, Volume 2, 707

133. Hillyer, *My Gettysburg Battle Experiences*, 19-20

134. Clark, *The 27ᵗʰ Conn. At Gettysburg* (Connecticut Historical Society); Sigman, *Account by Unidentified Soldier of the 64ᵗʰ New York Infantry* (G.N.M.P. Library); Sheldon, *The Twenty-Seventh*, 77; Brooke's O.R.

135. Sigman, *Account by Unidentified Soldier of the 64ᵗʰ New York Infantry*, (G.N.M.P. Library)

136. Whipple, *Memories of George W. Whipple, Private Company "F," 64ᵗʰ N.Y.V.N 1861-1865*, (G.N.M.P. Library); Brooke to Bachelder *The Bachelder Papers*, Volume 2, 1234

137. Osborn, *The Battle of Gettysburg as I Remember It*

138. Brooke Official Report; A.E. Clark, *The 27ᵗʰ Conn. at Gettysburg* (Connecticut Historical Society); Brooke Official Report; Also based on various Confederate reports in *The Bachelder Papers*.

139. Griffin, *Warriors of the Wiregrass*, 276

140. Sheldon, *The Twenty-Seventh*, 77

141. Cochran, *Some Incidents on the March to Gettysburg*

142. Based on several battle reports done by the officers of the regiments.

143. Brooke's Official Report, *The War of the Rebellion,* Series I- Volume XXVII, 401

144. *The War of the Rebellion*, Sweitzer's Official Report, Series I- Volume XXVII, 611-12

145. Based on various accounts derived from the soldiers in Wofford's Brigade

146. John Alexander Barry Papers, July 8, 1863 (Southern Historical Society); Figg, *Where men only Dare to Go: or the story of a boy company, C.S.A,* 140-41; *Richmond Sentinel*, (July 27, 1863)

147. Bigelow, *The Peach Orchard: Gettysburg, July 2, 1863*, 55-56

148. *The Times 1860-1865*; Youngblood, William, *Confederate Veteran*, Volume 19, 287

149. *Confederate Veteran*, Volume 21, 434

150. Traditional Family Story acquired by them; Rutter Pension Records

151. Brooke O.R., *The War of the Rebellion,* Series I- Volume XXVII, 401

152. Hilton's Account, *Pennsylvania at Gettysburg*, Volume 2, 708; Brooke to Bachelder, *The Bachelder Papers*, Volume, 2 (March 18, 1886); Whipple, *Memories of George W. Whipple, Private Company "F," 64ᵗʰ N.Y.V., 1861-1865* (G.N.M.P Library)

153. Whipple, *Memories of George W. Whipple, Private Company "F," 64ᵗʰ N.Y.V., 1861-1865,* (G.N.M.P. Library)

154. Sigman, *Account by Unidentified Soldier of the 64ᵗʰ New York Infantry,* (G.N.M.P. Library); Whipple, *Memories of George W. Whipple, Private Company "F," 64ᵗʰ N.Y.V., 1861-1865,* (G.N.M.P. Library)

155. Whipple, *Memories of George W. Whipple, Private Company "F," 64ᵗʰ N.Y.V., 1861-1865,* (G.N.M.P. Library)

156. Sigman, *Account by Unidentified Soldier of the 64ᵗʰ New York Infantry,* (GN.M.P. Library)

157. Letter to Samuel Babcock from L.W. Bradley (July 5, 1863) (G.N.M.P. Library)

158. Sigman, *Account by Unidentified Soldier of the 64ᵗʰ New York Infantry,* (G.N.M.P. Library)

159. Powell, *The Fifth Army Corps (Army of the Potomac): A Record of Operations During the Civil War in the United States of America, 1861-1865,* 534-35

160. Fraser's Account, *The War of the Rebellion,* Vol. 1, 395

161. Frederick's Account, Sickles, *Final Report on the Battlefield of Gettysburg,* 420; Fraser's Account, *The War of the Rebellion,* Vol. 1," 395

162. Fraser's Account, *The War of the Rebellion,* Vol. 1, 395

163. Fredericks's Account, Daniel Sickles, *Final Report on the Battlefield of Gettysburg,* 420

164. Shallenberger's Account, *Pennsylvania at Gettysburg*, Volume 2, 688-89

165. Frederick's Account, *Final Report on the Battlefield of Gettysburg,* 420

166. Cole, *Under Five Commanders,* 203

167. Purman, *How I Won the Medal of Honor for Gallantry at the Battle of Gettysburg July 2, '63,* (Gettysburg Complier, August 23, 1911)

168. Commemorative Biographical Record of Washington County, Pennsylvania; Chicago; J.H. Beers and Company. (1893)

169. Livermore, *St. Louisans Among Gettysburg Heroes,* (G.N.M.P. Library)

170. Stewart, *History of the One Hundred and Fortieth Regiment Pennsylvania Volunteers,* 422-223

171. Powelson, *History of Company K of the 140ᵗʰ Regiment Pennsylvania Volunteers,* (1862-'65), 28-29

172. Chapman Official Report, *The War of the Rebellion,* Series I- Volume XXVII, 397

173. Stewart, *History of the Fortieth Regiment Pennsylvania Volunteers,* 108-09, 114

174. Unknown writer of a letter in the Timothy Brooks Collection, USAMHI

175. Mulholland's Account, *Pennsylvania at Gettysburg*, Volume 2, 630

176. Mulholland's Account, *Pennsylvania at Gettysburg*, Volume 2, 630-31

177. Papers of 2ⁿᵈ Lieutenant John B. Noyes Company, C 28ᵗʰ Mass Infantry (G.N.M.P. Library)

178. James Smith Official Report, *United States Congressional Seral Set, Issue 2771,* (1891), 389

179. Mulholland's Account, *Pennsylvania at Gettysburg*, Volume 2, 631

180. Mulholland, *The Story of the 116th Regiment Pennsylvania Volunteers in the War of the Rebellion*, 127-28

181. Richard Coffman, *A Vital Unit*,44

182. Fuller, *Personal Recollections of the War of 1861*, 64

183. Forrester Account, *Pennsylvania at Gettysburg*, Volume 2, 736-37

184. Caldwell's Official Report (Extract taken from Forrester's account, *Pennsylvania at Gettysburg*, Volume 2, 737

185. Forster, *Pennsylvania at Gettysburg*, Volume 2, 737; Busey and Marin, *Regimental Strengths and losses*, 35, 242

186. Forster, *Pennsylvania at Gettysburg*, Volume 2, 735-36; Muffly, Private Meyer's Account, *The Story of Our Regiment*, 538

187. Muffly, Private Meyer's Account, *The Story of Our Regiment*, 538

188. Muffly, Wadding Account, *The Story of Our Regiment*, 780

189. Muffly, Osman Account, *The Story of Our Regiment*, 604

190. Hale, *With Colonel Cross in the Gettysburg Campaign*, (G.N.M.P Library)

191. Jacob Lee Carter Diary, 2-32

192. Sweitzer's Official Report, *The War of the Rebellion*, Series I- Volume XXVII, 401

193. *Michigan at Gettysburg, July 1st, 2d, and 3rd, 1863, June 12th, 1889*, (Winn and Hammond, 1889), 85; Sweitzer's Official Report, *The War of the Rebellion*, Series I- Volume XXVII, 401

194. *Journal of James Houghton, 4th Michigan* (Bentley Historical Library, University of Michigan); *Michigan at Gettysburg*, 86

195. Sweitzer's Official Report, *The War of the Rebellion*, Series I- Volume XXVII, 401

196. *Michigan at Gettysburg*, 86

197. Parker, Francis, *The Story of the Thirty-Second Regiment Massachusetts Infantry*,170-71; West, Oscar, *On Little Round Top*, (The National Tribune, November 22, 1906)

198. Patterson's Account, *Pennsylvania at Gettysburg*, Volume 1, 381

199. *Journal of James Houghton, 4th Michigan*; Hendricks Account; *Michigan at Gettysburg*, 86; Henry Seage to John B. Bachelder, *The Bachelder Papers*, Volume 2, 1071-1072; Campbell, Robert, *Pioneer Memories of the War Days of 1861-1865*, 562-72

200. *Journal of James Houghton, 4th Michigan*, (Bentley Historical Library, University of Michigan)

201. Hendricks's report, (Detroit Free Press, July 8); *Journal of James Houghton, 4th Michigan*, (Bentley Historical Library, University of Michigan)

202. *Michigan at Gettysburg: Proceedings Incident to the Dedication of the Michigan Monuments upon the Battlefield of Gettysburg, June 12, 1889*, 85-86

203. Military Muster Rolls; Burbank Official Report; West Point Alumni Roll

204. *Congressional Series of United States Public Documents*, Volume 2771, (U.S. Government Printing Office, 1891), 645

205. Purman, *How I won the Medal of Honor for Gallantry at the Battle of Gettysburg July 2, '63*, (Gettysburg Compiler, August 23, 1911)

206. *The War of the Rebellion*, Report of Major Arthur Lee, (1889), 646-47

207. Letter of Terrance McCabe (September 25, 1863, Fort Lafayette, N.Y.H)

208. Letter of George Hamilton (Letters in the G.N.M.P. Library)

209. Ayres Official Report

210. Powell, *The Fifth Army Corps*, 535

211. According to battle maps produced by John B. Bachelder; Also based on Official Reports of the various batteries

212. Gibb's Official Report, *The War of the Rebellion*, Series I- Volume XXVII, 662

213. Powell, *The Fifth Army Corps*, 535-36

214. Ibid

215. Robins, *The Regular Troops at Gettysburg*, 1

216. Crawford's O.R., Hillyer, *My Gettysburg Battle Experiences*, 21; Smith, *History of the Corn Exchange Regiment, 118th Pennsylvania Volunteers, from Their First Engagement at Antietam to Appomattox*, 252

217. Based on multiple accounts given in official reports by Nevin, Crawford, and Mc-Candless

218. Hillyer, *My Gettysburg Battle Experiences*, 21-24

219. SHSP (1885), 203

220. Minnigh, H., *History of Company K. 1st (Inft,) Penn'a Reserves*; Jackson's Account, *Pennsylvania at Gettysburg*, Volume 1, 281

221. Parker, *Twenty-second Massachusetts*, 313

222. Samuel Crawford to Peter F. Rothermel, (March 9, 1871, Peter Rothermel Papers, Pennsylvania State Archives, Harrisburg, PA)

223. Jackson's Account, *Pennsylvania at Gettysburg, Volume 1*, 281; Woodward, *Our Campaigns*, 269

224. Fuller, *Personal Recollections of the War of 1861*, 64

225. Hillyer, *My Gettysburg Battle Experiences*, 24

226. Fuller, *Personal Recollections of the War of 1861*, 65

227. Jackson, *Pennsylvania at Gettysburg*, Volume 1, 281; Minnigh, *History of Company K. 1st (Inft,) Penn'a Reserves*

228. Hillyer, *My Gettysburg Battle Experiences*, 24

229. Report of the Committee, *Pennsylvania at Gettysburg*, Volume 1, 102-03

230. Longstreet, James, *Lee in Pennsylvania*; *The Annals of the War*, 425

231. Based on The Bachelder maps; Warren Map

232. *The Last Day at Gettysburg*, (The Independent, Volume 50, 1898), 31; Gibbon Official Report, *The War of the Rebellion*, Part I- Vol. XXVII, 127

233. According to military cooristompdents

Chapter 4

1. Poem located in *The Washington Observer* (May 30, 1898)

2. Crawford Official Report; Carter, *Four Brothers in Blue; or, Sunshine and Shadows of the War of the Rebellion; a Story of the Great Civil War from Bull Run to Appomattox*, 324-25

3. Forster, *Pennsylvania at Gettysburg*, Vol. 2, 737; Muffly, Hamilton's Account, *The Story of Our Regiment*, 171-73

4. Fuller, *Personal Recollections of the War of 1861*, 65-68

5. Purman, *How I won the Medal of Honor for Gallantry at the Battle of Gettysburg July 2, '63*, (Gettysburg Complier, August 23, 1911)

6. Ibid; Purman to Bachelder, *The Bachelder Papers*, Volume 1, 417

7. Purman, *How I Won the Medal of Honor for Gallantry at the Battle of Gettysburg July 2, '61*, (Gettysburg Complier, August 23, 1911)

8. Muffly, Meyer account, *The Story of Our Regiment*, 460-62

9. Favill, *Thee Diary of a Young Officer Serving with the Armies of the United Sates During the War of the Rebellion*, 247

10. Ibid; Article in the Adams Sentinel (July 15, 1863)

11. Linn, John B. *Journal of my Trip to the Battlefield of Gettysburg. July, 1863*, 64; Favill, *The Diary of a Young Officer Servicing with the Armies of the United States During the War of the Rebellion*, 247

12. Sterling, *The Book of Englewood*, 64; Favill, *The Diary of a Young Officer Serving with the Armies of the United States During the War of the Rebellion*, 248

13. Favill, *The Diary of a Young Officer Serving with the Armies of the United States During the War of the Rebellion*, 248

14. Livermore, *Days and events, 1860-1866*, 211-13

15. Child, *A History of the Fifth Regiment*, 211-12

16. Livermore, *Days and Events, 1860- 1866*, 254-55

17. Ibid; Hale, *With Colonel Cross in the Gettysburg Campaign*, (G.N.M.P. Library)

18. Livermore, *Days and Events, 1860-1866*, 256-58

19. *75 Years Ago*. Article of newspaper located under the 140th Pennsylvania's file; Stewart, *History of the One Hundred and Fortieth Regiment Pennsylvania Volunteers*, 440

20. Letter of Bradely, *Lieutenant Willis Babcock, 64th New York* (July 5, 1863, G.N.M.P. Library)

21. S.G. Elliott map

22. Stewart, *History of the One Hundred and Fortieth Regiment Pennsylvania Volunteers*, 121

23. Buesy and Martin, *Regimental Strengths and Losses at Gettysburg*, 280; *Some Experiences of the Battle of Gettysburg Written by General W. E. James for the John K. Melver Chapter*, (The Darlington News and Press, June 11, 1908, G.N.M.P. Library)

24. *Some Experiences of the Battel of Gettysburg Written by General W. E. James for the John K. Melver Chapter*

25. Hillyer, *My Gettysburg Battle Experiences*, 14, 25-26

Chapter 5

1. Extracted from the Bivouac of the Dead by Theodore O'Hare.

2. Sheldon, *The Twenty-Seventh*, 79; Muffly, Private Meyer's Account, *The Story of Our Regiment*, 539

3. Noyes, *Co. 'B', 28th Ma INF*, (G.N.M.P. Library)

4. Sheldon, *The Twenty-Seventh*, 79

5. Mulholland, *The Story of the 116th Regiment Pennsylvania Volunteers in the War of the Rebellion*, 129; Mulholland's account, *Pennsylvania at Gettysburg*, 633; Bailey O.R. *The War of the Rebellion*, Vol. 2 403

6. Forster, *Pennsylvania at Gettysburg*, 738; Noyes, *Co. 'B', 28th Ma INF*, (G.N.M.P. Library); Sheldon, *The Twenty-Seventh*, 79; Mulholland's account, *Pennsylvania at Gettysburg*, 632

7. Sheldon, *The Twenty-Seventh*, 80

8. Mulholland, *Pennsylvania at Gettysburg*, 633

9. Extract taken from Hoke, Jacob, *The Great Invasion of 1863*, 360-61

10. Fiske, *Mr. Dunn Browne's Experiences in the Army*, 210- 218

11. Forster, *Pennsylvania at Gettysburg*, 738; Alexander, *Military Memoirs of a Confederate*, 421

12. Alexander, *Military Memoirs of a Confederate*, 421-22

13. Schurz, *The Reminiscences of Carl Schurz*, 25-27

14. Muffly, Meyer's Account, *The Story of Our Regiment*, 464

15. Mulholland, *Pennsylvania at Gettysburg*, 633; Longstreet, *From Manassas to Appomattox*, 390

16. Coco, *A Vast Sea of Misery*, 65

17. Gibbon, *Personal Recollections of the Civil War*, 146-47; Hilton's Account, *Pennsylvania at Gettysburg*, Vol. 2, 708

18. Sickles, *Final Report on the Battlefield of Gettysburg*, 421; Muffly, Private Meyer's account, *The Story of Our Regiment*, 539; Forster, *Pennsylvania at Gettysburg*, Volume 2, 738

19. Cole, *Under Five Commanders*, 204-05

20. Muffly, Sergeant Meyer's Account, "The Story of Our Regiment," 464

21. Letter of T.L. Livermore, (March 30, 1914)

22. Patrick Hart's Letters, *The Bachelder Papers*, Volume 3, 1798

23. Hunt to Bachelder, *The Bachelder Papers*, Volume 1, 432-33

24. Alexander, *Military Memoirs of a Confederate*, 423; Meade's memoirs

25. Muffly, Ramsey account, *The Story of Our Regiment*, 346; Mulholland, *Pennsylvania at Gettysburg*, Vol. 2, 634

26. Muffly, Private Meyer's account, *The Story of Our Regiment*, 540

27. Alexander, *Military Memoirs of a Confederate*, 423

28. Osborn, *The Artillery at Gettysburg*, (Philadelphia Weekly Times, May 31, 1879); Third Day at Gettysburg, *Battles and Leaders*, Volume 3, 373-74

29. Alexander, *Military Memoirs of a Confederate*, 424

30. Pickett letters; Longstreet, *From Manassas to Appomattox*, 392; Alexander, *Military Memoirs of a Confederate*, 424

31. Pickett Letters; Longstreet, *From Manassas to Appomattox*, 392

32. Alexander, *Fighting for the Confederacy*, 261

33. *Confederate Veteran*, (Nashville: Privately Published, 1915), 175

34. *Confederate Veteran*, Volume 22, (S.A. Cunningham, 1914), 503

35. W. Lindsay Walker's letters; Randall's letters

36. Haskell, *The Battle of Gettysburg*, 57-58

37. Noyes, Co. 'B', *28th Ma INF*, (G.N.M.P. Library); Mulholland, *Pennsylvania at Gettysburg*, 634

38. Mulholland, *116th Pennsylvania at Gettysburg, July 17, 1863*, (G.N.M.P. Library); Sickles, Frederick's account, *Final Report on the Battlefield of Gettysburg*, 421

39. Mulholland, *Pennsylvania at Gettysburg*, Volume 2, 634; Frederick's Account, *Final Report on the Battlefield of Gettysburg*, 421

40. Abbot, *Battle Fields and Camp Fires*, (Dodd, Mead & Company, 1890), 250

41. Rhodes, *History of the Civil War*, 235-42

42. *Confederate Veteran*, Volume 23, (S.A. Cunningham, 1915), 391; Official report of Charles Peyton, *The War of the Rebellion*, Series I- Volume XXVII, Part II, 387

43. *Confederate Veteran*, Volume 22, 503-04

44. Alexander, *Fighting for the Confederacy*, 265; *The Alabama Historical Quarterly*, Volumes 38-39, (Alabama State Department of Archives and History., 1977)

45. Lang's O.R., *The War of the Rebellion*, Part I- Volume XXVII, Part 2, 632

46. Mulholland, *Pennsylvania at Gettysburg*, Volume 2, 635

47. Noyes, Co. 'B', *28th MA INF*, (G.N.M.P. Library); Noonan, *The 69th New York History*, (G.N.M.P. Library Extract)

48. Muffly, Sergeant Meyer's Account, *The Story of Our Regiment*, 465

49. Mulholland, *The Story of the 116th Regiment Pennsylvania Volunteers in the War of the Rebellion*, 131

50. Mulholland, *Pennsylvania at Gettysburg*, Volume 2, 635; Hatch's Account, *Pennsylvania at Gettysburg*, Volume 1, 335

51. Haskell, *The Battle of Gettysburg*, 69-70

52. Shotwell, *Papers*, Volume 2, 25

53. Brock, *Southern Historical Society Papers*, Volume 31-32," (Reb. J. William Jones, 1903), 234

54. Blackwood, William, *Blackwood's Edinburgh Magazine*, Volume 94, (1863), 382

55. Hilton's account, *Pennsylvania at Gettysburg*, Volume 2, 708

56. Cole, *Under Five Commanders*, 206

57. Muffly, Private Meyer's account, *The Story of Our Regiment*, 541

58. Mulholland's account, *Pennsylvania at Gettysburg*, Volume 2, 635

59. Livermore, *Days and Events*, 1860-1866, 266-67

Chapter 6

1. The poem "Ode" by Henry Timrod, 1866

2. Mulholland, *The Story of the 116th Regiment Pennsylvania Volunteers in the War of the Rebellion*, 131; Cole, *Under Five Commanders*, 209

3. Muffly, Sergeant Meyer's Account, *The Story of Our Regiment*, 465-66

4. Stewart, *History of the One hundred and Fortieth Regiment Pennsylvania Volunteers*, 127-28

5. Muffly, Private Meyer's account, *The Story of Our Regiment*, 541-43

6. Muffly, Sergaent Meyer's account, *The Story of Our Regiment*, 465-68

7. Mulholland, *The Story of the 116th Regiment Pennsylvania Volunteers in the War of the Rebellion*, 159

8. Mulholland's account, *Pennsylvania at Gettysburg*, Volume 2, 635

9. Stewart, *History of the One Hundred and Fortieth Regiment Pennsylvania Volunteers*, 145; Cole, *Under Five Commanders*, 210

10. Stewart, *History of the One Hundred and Fortieth Regiment Pennsylvania Volunteers*, 145

11. Mulholland, *The Story of the 116th Regiment Pennsylvania Volunteers in the War of the Rebellion*, 156; Hatch's account, *Pennsylvania at Gettysburg*, Volume 1, 326; Stewart, *History of the One Hundred and Fortieth Regiment Pennsylvania Volunteers*, 146

12. Sheldon, *The Twenty-Seventh*, 83; Stewart, *History of the One Hundred and Fortieth Regiment Pennsylvania Volunteers*, 145-46

13. Muffly, Sergeant Meyer's account, *The Story of Our Regiment*, 469

14. Stewart, *History of the One Hundred and Fortieth Regiment Pennsylvania Volunteers*, 146

15. Mulholland, *The Story of the 116th Regiment Pennsylvania Volunteers in the War of the Rebellion*, 156; Stewart, *History of the One Hundred and Fortieth Regiment Pennsylvania Volunteers*, 147

16. Stewart, *History of the One Hundred and Fortieth Regiment Pennsylvania Volunteers*, 147

Chapter 7

1. Extract taken from poem located in Sheldon, *The Twenty-Seventh Connecticut*, 86

2. Martin and Busey, *Regimental Strengths and Losses*, 241

3. Tagg, *The Generals of Gettysburg*, 35-37

4. *Ibid.,* 37; Main Census of 1910 along with death certificate; Find-a-grave.com

5. *General Catalogue of Princeton University* (Princeton University, 1908), 186; Rush, *Hours with My Lyre*, 108; Find-a-grave.com

6. Young, *The Battle of Gettysburg: A Comprehensive Narrative,* 391

7. *A Standard History of Kansas and Kansans,* Volume 3, 1232; Find-a-grave.com

8. Tagg, *The Generals of Gettysburg*, 42-44; find-a-grave.com; Brooke, John R., *Report of the Military Governor of Puerto Rico on Civil Affairs*

9. Child, *A History of the Fifth Regiment, New Hampshire Volunteers, in the American Civil War, 1861-1865*, 213-14

10. Find-a-grave.com

11. Find-a-grave.com

12. Letter from Sandie Acheson to his father. (July 12, 1863, G.N.M.P. Library)

13. Find-a-grave.com; Wilson's diary

14. Pittsburgh *Gazette-Times*, (July 27, 1910); Article extract in the G.N.M.P. Library

15. *Green-Wood Tribune*; Find-a-grave.com

16. Barbra Abbott. Meyer's G-G-Granddaughter through marriage.

17. Find-a-grave.com; Medal of Honor recipients list and Soldiers and Sailors Museum

18. 1880 Census; Find-a-grave.com

19. 1880-1890 Census; Find-a-grave.com

20. Find-a-grave.com

21. Find-a-grave.com

22. Babcock, Samuel. "Letter to Sons," (July 19, 1863)

23. Find-a-grave.com

24. Hillyer, *My Battle of Gettysburg Experience*, 13

Appendix

1. Based on regimental rolls on June 30, 1863, from official reports of the brigade officers after the battle of Gettysburg; information taken from several monuments on the Gettysburg battlefield; and from Busey & Martin, *Regimental Strengths and Losses at Gettysburg*, 242

Bibliography

Newspapers
Adams County (PA) Sentinel
Charleston (SC) News and Courier
Confederate Union (Milledgeville, Georgia)
Gettysburg Compiler
Green-Wood Tribune
Lutheran Observer
National Tribune
Pittsburgh Gazette-Times
Richmond Sentinel
Washington Observer

Letters, Journals, and Collections
Abraham Lincoln Foundation, Union League of Philadelphia
 St. Clair Mulholland Papers
Adams County (PA) Historical Society
 Jacob Carter Diary
Fort Lafayette, NY, Historical Society
 Terrance McCabe Letter
Gettysburg National Military Park Library and Archives
 David Acheson Letters
 Samuel Babcock Letters
 John Alexander Barry Papers
 S. G. Elliot Map
 Frank Gaillard Letters
 Charles Hale Papers
 George Hamilton Letter
 Thomas L. Livermore Letters
 Alex McNeil Letters
 John B. Noyes Papers
 Martin Sigman Letters
 Warren Map
 George Whipple Papers
Historical Society of Pennsylvania, Philadelphia
 John Smith Letters
Indiana State Library
 Benson Warden, "B. J. M. Warden's Gettysburg Experience"
National Archives, Washington, D. C.
 Erasmus Gilbreath Journal

Jesse Martinez Biography
George Pickett Letters
Southern Historical Society Papers
United States Census Records,1840-1890
William L. Walker Letters
New York Historical Society, New York City
Peter Welsh Letters
Pennsylvania State Library
Samuel Crawford Letter (Peter Rothermal Papers)
University of Michigan, Bentley Historical Library, Ann Arbor, MI
James Houghton Journal
University of New Hampshire, Durham, NH
Colonel Edward E. Cross's Journal
United States Army Heritage and Education Center, Carlisle, PA
Daniel Gookin Journal
J. Noonan, "The 69th New York History" (Kenneth H. Powers Collection)

Books and Articles

A Standard History of Kansas and Kansans, Vol. 3 (Lewis Publishing Company, 1919)
Abbot, Willis, *Battlefields and Campfires* (Dodd, Meade and Company, 1890)
Aiken, D. W., "The Gettysburg Reunion. What is Necessary and Proper for the South to do. An open Letter from Col. D. Wyatt Aiken to General J. B. Kershaw," (*Charleston News and Courier*, 21, June 1882)
Alexander, Edward P., *Military Memories of a Confederate* (C. Scribner's Sons, 1907)
Annual Reunion of Pegram Battalion Association (s. n., 1866)
Auge, Moses, *Lives of the Eminent Dead* (s. n., 1879)
Bachelder, John, *The Bachelder Papers*, Vols. 1-3 (Ladd & Sauers, eds., Morningside Books, 1995)
Bates, Samuel, *Martial Deeds of Pennsylvania* (T. H. Davis and Company, 1876)
Bigelow, John, *The Peach Orchard: Gettysburg July 2, 1863* (Kimball Store Company, 1910)
Blackwood, William, *Blackwood's Edinburgh Magazine* (Vol. 94, 1863)
Brooke, John, *Report of the Military Governor of Puerto Rico on Civil Affairs* (Government Printing Office, 1902)
Busey, John and David Martin, *Regimental Strengths and Losses at Gettysburg* (Longstreet House, 1986)
Campbell, Eric, "Caldwell Clears the Wheatfield," *Gettysburg Magazine,* #3 (July 1990)
Campbell, Robert, *Pioneer Memories of the War Days of 1861-1865* (Michigan Pioneers and Historical Society, 1906)
Carter, Robert, *Four Brothers in Blue: or, Sunshine and Shadows of the War of the Rebellion, a Story of the Great Civil War from Bull Run to Appomattox* (Washington Press of Gibson Bros., 1913)
Child, William, *A History of the Fifth Regiment New Hampshire Volunteers in the American Civil War, 1861-1865* (s. n., 1893)
Church, William, *The Galaxy*, Vol. 22 (W. C. and F. P. Church, 1876)
Clark, Almond E., *The 27th Conn. At Gettysburg* (Connecticut Historical Society, n. d.)
Cochran, A., "Some Incidents on the March to Gettysburg," in *Atlanta Journal* (August 31, 1901)
Coco, Gregory, *A Vast Sea of Misery* (Thomas Publications, 1996)

Cole, Jacob, *Under Five Commanders: or A Boy's Experience with the Army of the Potomac* (News Printing Company, 1906)

Congressional Series in the United Public Documents, Volume 2372 (U. S. Government Printing Office, 1889)

Corby, William, *Memoirs of Chaplain Life* (La Mote O'Donnell, Printers, 1893)

Coxe, John, "The Battle of Gettysburg," in *Confederate Veteran* (Volume 21, 1913)

Dickert, August, *History of Kershaw's Brigade* (E. H. Aull Company, 1899)

Dreese, Michael, *Never Desert the Old Flag!* (Thomas Publications, 2002)

———, *This Flag Never Goes Down* (Thomas Publications, 2004)

———, *Torn Families: Death and Kinship at the Battle of Gettysburg* (McFarland and Company, 2009)

Dyer, Frederick, *Compendium of the Civil War* (Morningside Bookshop, 1978)

Favill, Josiah, *The Diary of the Young Officer Serving with the Armies of the United States During the War of the Rebellion* (R. R. Donnelley and Sons, 1909)

Figg, Royall, *Where Men Only Dare to Go: or the Story of a Boy Company, C. S. A.* (White and Sepperson, 1885)

Fiske, Samuel, *Mr. Dunn Browne's Experiences in the Army* (Nichol and Noyes, 1866)

Fuller, Charles, *Personal Recollections of the War of 1861* (New Job Printing House, 1906)

Gibbon, John, *Personal Recollections of the Civil War* (G. P. Putnam's Sons, 1928)

Goodrich, Frederick, *The Life and Public Services of Winfield Scott* Hancock (Lee and Shepard, 1990)

Goolrick, William, and Editors of Time Life Books, *Rebels Resurgent: Fredericksburg to Chancellorsville* (Time-Life Books, 1985)

Gottfried, Bradley, *Brigades of Gettysburg* (Skyhorse Publishing, 2012)

Grandchamp, Robert, *Colonel Edward E. Cross, New Hampshire Fighting Fifth: A Civil War Biography* (University of New Hampshire Collections)

Hannah, Charles, *Gettysburg Medal of Honor Recipients* (Bonneville Books, 2010)

Hard, Abner, *History of the Eighth Cavalry Regiment, Illinois Volunteers, During the Great Rebellion* (s. n., 1868)

Hartwig, Scott, "John C. Caldwell's Division in the Wheatfield," in Gary Gallagher, ed., *The Second Day at Gettysburg* (Kent State University Press, 1993)

Haskell, Frank, *The Battle of Gettysburg* (Military Order of the Loyal Legion of the United States, 1908)

Hillyer, George and Gregory Coco, ed., *My Battle of Gettysburg Experiences* (Thomas Publications, 2005)

Hoke, Jacob, *The Great Invasion of 1863* (W. J. Shuey, 1887)

Johnson, Robert, *Battles and Leaders of the Civil War*, Vol. 2 (Century Company, 1887)

Jorgensen, Jay, *Gettysburg's Bloody Wheatfield* (White Mane Books, 2001)

King, W. C., *Campfire Sketches and Battle-field Echoes* (s. n., 1886)

Laino, Philip, *Gettysburg Campaign Atlas* (Gettysburg Publishing, 2014)

Linn, John, "Journal of my Trip to the Battlefield of Gettysburg, July 1863," in *Civil War Times Illustrated* (September-October 1990)

Livermore, Thomas, *Days and Events, 1860-1866* (Houghton Mifflin, 1920)

Loffman, Richard, "A Vital Unite," in *Civil War Times Illustrated* (June 1982)

Longstreet, James, *From Manassas to Appomattox* (J. B. Lippincott, 1895)

Longstreet, James, "Lee in Pennsylvania," in *The Annals of the War* (Morningside House, 1989)

Maine at Gettysburg (Maine Gettysburg Commission, 1898)

Michigan at Gettysburg, July 1st, 2nd, and 3rd, 1863 (Winn & Hammon, 1889)

Minnigh, H., *History of Company K. 1st (Inft.) Penn'a Reserves* (Home Print Publisher, 1891)

Moore, Frank, *The Rebellion Record,* Vol. 15 (G. P. Putnam, 1864)

Muffly, Joseph, *The Story of Our Regiment: A History of the 148th Pennsylvania Vols.* (Kenyon Printers, 1904)

Mulholland, St. Clair, *The Story of the 116th Regiment Pennsylvania Volunteers in the War of the Rebellion* (F. McManus Jr. and Company, 1903)

Murphy, T. L., *Faithful to us here...A Remembrance of Colonel Patrick Kelly"*

"New Hampshire in the Great Rebellion (Tracy Chase Company, 1870)

O'Grady, P., *Grand Army Review*, Vol. 1, Vo. 7 (Grand Army Publishing Company)

Official Records of the War of the Rebellion, Series 1 (U. S. Government Printing Office, 1887)

Osborn, S. A., "The Battle of Gettysburg as I remember it," in *Shenango Valley News* (April 1915)

Osborn, Thomas, "The Artillery at Gettysburg," in *Philadelphia Weekly Times* (May 31, 1879)

Parker, Francis, *The Story of the Thirty-Second Regiment Massachusetts Infantry* (C. W. Calkins and Company, 1880)

Parker, John L., *Henry Wilson's Regiment* (Regimental Association, Press of Rand Avery Company, 1887)

Pennsylvania at Gettysburg, in 3 volumes (W. S. Ray, State Printer, 1914)

Pfanz, Harry, *Gettysburg: The Second Day* (University of North Carolina Press, 2011)

Phisterer, Frederick, *New York in the War of the Rebellion 1861-1865* (Parsons and Company, 1890)

Pickerill, William, *Indiana at Antietam* (Aetna Press, 1911)

Powell, William, *The Fifth Army Corps: A Record of Operations During the Civil War in the United States of America, 1861-1865* (G. P. Putnam's Sons, 1895)

Purman, James, "How I won the Medal of Honor for Gallantry at the Battle of Gettysburg July 2, '63," in *Gettysburg Compiler*

Rhodes, James, *History of the Civil War* (s. n., 1917)

Robins, Richard, "The Regular Troops at Gettysburg," in *Philadelphia Weekly Times* (January 4, 1879)

Rush, Edwin, *Hours with My Lyre* (Globe Printing House, 1884)

Schurz, Carl, *The Reminiscences of Carl Schurz* (Doubleday, Page and Co., 1909)

Sears, Stephen, *Gettysburg* (Houghton Mifflin Company, 2004)

Sheldon, Winthrop, *The Twenty-Seventh* (s. n., 1866)

Shotwell, Randolph, *Papers*, Volume 2 (North Carolina Historical Commission, 1931)

Sickles, Daniel, *Final Report on the Battlefield of Gettysburg* (J. B. Lyons Company, 1902)

Slomba, Elizabeth, *Stand Firm and Fire Low* (U.P.N.E., 2003)

Smith, J. L., *History of the Corn Exchange Regiment, 118th Pennsylvania Volunteers: from their First Engagement at Antietam to Appomattox* (s. n., 1888)

Smith, James, *Along the Lines of Devotion* (Fonthill Media, 2017)

Smith, Robert, *An Account of the Services Rendered by the Second Regiment Delaware Volunteers in the War of the Rebellion* (Historical Society of Delaware, 1909)

Sterling, Adaline, *The Book of Englewood* (Mayor and Council of the City of Englewood, NH, 1922)

Stewart, Robert, *History of the One Hundred and Fortieth Regiment Pennsylvania Volunteers* (Franklin Bindery, 1912)

Stevens, Charles, *Berdan's United States Sharpshooters in the Army of the Potomac, 1861-1865* (Price-McGill Company, 1892)

Sweeney, Alexander, *History of Company K of the 140th Regiment Pennsylvania Volunteers* (Carnahan Print Company, 1906)

Tagg, Larry, *The Generals of Gettysburg: The Leaders of America's Greatest Battle* (Da Capo Press, 2008)

The Alabama Historical Quarterly, Volumes 38-39 (Alabama State Department of Archives and History, 1977)

Toombs, Samuel, *New Jersey Troops in the Gettysburg Campaign from June 5 to July 31, 1863* (Evening Mail Publishing House, 1888)

Travis, C., *The History of the Fighting Fourteenth* (s. n., 1911)

Travis, Mark and Pride, Mike, *My Brave Boys* (U.P.N.E., 2003)

Tremain, Henry, *Two Days of War: A Gettysburg Narrative and of the Excursions* (Bonnell, Silver, and Bowers, 1905)

Waite, Otis, *New Hampshire in the Great Rebellion: Containing Histories of the Several New Hampshire Regiments, and a Biographical Notices of many of the Prominent Actors in the Civil War of 1861-1865* (University of California Libraries, 1870)

Walker, Francis, *History of the Second Army Corps in the Army of the Potomac* (C. Scribner's and Sons, 1886)

War Papers Read Before the Commandery of the Loyal Legion of the United States (The Commandery, 1914)

Warner, Ezra Jr., *Generals in Blue: Lives of the Commanders* (Louisiana State University Press, 1964)

Warriors of the Wiregrass: Histories of Selected Georgia Regiments in the War of for Southern Independence (Sons of Confederate Veterans)

Weld, Stephen, *War Diary and Letters of Stephen Minot Weld, 1861-1865* (s. n., 1912)

Weygant, Charles, *History of the One Hundred and Twenty-Fourth Regiment* (Journal Printing House, 1877)

Wilson, James, *Personal Recollections of the War of the Rebellion* (Commandery, 1891)

Woodward, Evan, *Our Campaigns* (J. E. Potter, 1865)

Young, Jesse, *The Battle of Gettysburg: A Comprehensive Narrative* (Harper, 1913)

Youngblood, William, "Personal Observations at Gettysburg" in *Confederate Veteran,* June 1911